AN ALABAMA SONGBOOK

AN ALABAMA SONGBOOK

Ballads, Folksongs, and Spirituals

Collected by
BYRON ARNOLD

Edited with an Introduction by
ROBERT W. HALLI JR.

THE UNIVERSITY OF ALABAMA PRESS
Tuscaloosa

In Memoriam

Robert Nicolosi

et

Henry Jacobs

Contents

PART 2. FOLKSONGS

Introduction

Alabama is a state rich in folksong tradition, from the old English ballads sung along the Tennessee River to the delightful children's game songs of Mobile, from the work songs of the railroad gandy dancers of Gadsden to the deeply moving spirituals of the Black Belt around Livingston. Sung by blacks and whites, rich and poor, young and old, these songs are a living part of our cultural heritage.

Some of these songs are very old. The legend of little Sir Hugh, found in the ballad "It Rained, It Mist," dates back to the Middle Ages. An early version of "The Frog He Would A-Courting Ride" was registered to be printed in 1580. The rollicking "Lank Dank" dates to 1627, "Last Night I Dreamed of My True Love" to 1631, "Barbara Allen" to 1666, and many other songs to the seventeenth and eighteenth centuries. Some of these songs were born in the twentieth century. Near Guntersville, Uncle Bill Gross composed his cheerfully satiric Alabama ballads. "Little Mary Phagan" tells of the murder of a fourteen-year-old girl in 1913. But no matter how long it has existed, each song is made new whenever it is sung, because that is the essence of a folksong.

A folksong is a song preserved in the memory of the people and passed from singer to singer without reliance on printed words or tune. Of course, someone almost surely composed (but not necessarily wrote down) the "original" version of each song in this book. That original has gone through changes of addition, deletion, and alteration, both of text and tune, to become the song printed here. The names of most of the composers of the first versions are unknown and unknowable. There are exceptions, however, and I have given credit to all those authors and composers I could determine. For instance, we know that Lady Anne Lindsay composed "Auld Robin Gray" in 1751, that Henry Clay Work copyrighted "Kingdom Coming" (the original of our "The Year of Jubilo") during the American Civil War, and that "Carve Dat Possum" is attributed to Samuel Lucas, one of the first great black American showmen. But the singers from whom these songs were collected knew none of these things, and most were amazed when informed that their songs had appeared in print. The material from print had passed into an oral tradition and had become the property of the folk. Some scholars claim that a folksong begins to die when it is committed to paper, but printing is also a preservation, a transplanting of folk material to new soil. The songs printed in this book need not remain static but may well find new singers who will pass them back into a vigorous oral tradition. This sort of thing is done with endangered species of animals and birds; surely it can be done with something as precious and lovely as folksong.

No folksong repeats itself perfectly from one rendition to another, even when sung by the same person. Obvious changes from performance to performance occur in those children's game songs which use the names of participants, such as "The Little White Daisies," "Green Gravel," and "Here Comes Someone A-Roving." In spirituals, such as "All My Sins Been Taken Away," in banjo and fiddle tunes, such as "Cindy," and in those songs of forsaken love whose most famous exemplar is "Old Smoky," the number of stanzas and the order in which they appear vary greatly each time they are sung. Even the familiar ballads, such as "Barbara Allen" or "Stagalee," are never sung in quite the same way twice: a word will be changed here, a musical phrase altered there. Their capacity for and delight in change affirm the vitality of the folksongs in this book.

The singers represented here come from many different backgrounds. There are songs from white women living in some of the finest old plantation homes in Alabama and songs from black domestic servants and laborers. Some of the finest songs come from an illiterate white woman, Callie Craven of Gadsden, and an excellent spiritual comes from a black college professor, Linton Berrien of Alabama A&M. Our singers learned their songs from mothers and grandfathers, from mammies and teachers. Or they learned them from singers in traveling tent or medicine shows, from vaudeville performances, from professionals heard on phonograph recordings or over radio stations, or from sheet music. They are songs to be sung in the nursery, on the porch, at work, and at play. There are songs meant to be sung by groups: game songs such as "Miss Jennie O. Jones," work songs such as "Lining Track," spirituals such as "Tall Angel at the Bar." And there are songs to be sung by a single voice: the despairing ballad of "Johnson City" ("The Butcher Boy"), the haunting blues song "Another Man Done Gone," and "The Soldier's Fare," which details the singer's hard lot in military service. The collection reflects the lively variety of people, subjects, and moods found in Alabama.

It is important to remember that a folksong is a combination of words and music. It is neither a poem written out on a page nor a tune to be picked out on the piano. The folksong really exists only while it is being sung: the tune conveys the words, and the words lend point to the tune. Even the ballads, whose texts seem most complete and self-contained, rely on their tunes for interpretation. Callie Craven observed that sprightly professional renditions of "Barbara Allen" miss the point of the folksong: "I have heard [it] many times over the radio but they never get it right and I don't like it. It's a dwellin' song and must be sung slow and mournful, dwellin' on the long notes." And the overly melancholy mood of the words of "Lord Lovel" contrasts starkly with the ballad's gay and lilting tune. Because of this interdependence of text and tune, many singers, when asked by a collector to repeat a verse, cannot recall it without singing it. Here we include the tune for the first verse of each song, and also the tune for the chorus if it is different. Because singers normally vary their tunes slightly from stanza to stanza, however, you may have to be a bit creative in applying the basic tune to stanzas longer or shorter than the first. In doing so you will take on part of the artistry of the folksinger.

Byron Arnold noted that the songs in his collection "were sung quietly, naturally, never dramatically, and entirely without the mannerisms and clichés of the concert soloist. It was as if each song, as I heard it, was a creation by the singer for the satisfaction of an inner compulsion." The true folksinger enjoys the songs, and enjoys singing them. Mrs. Julia Greer Marechal of Mobile is a good example. When Byron Arnold met her in the summer of 1947, she was ninety years old, blind, and hardly able to walk. But she recorded thirty-three songs in a continuous three-hour session which Arnold confessed wore out both him and his recording technician. Marechal concluded the session by saying, "This has been so thrilling; I wish I knew more songs to record." And the true folksong audience is supportive, appreciative, and polite. Mildred Meadows admired her mother's singing and awaited her chance to perform:

> It was always my ultimate objective to sing also, and my first opportunity came when I was five years old. It happened that we were having "prayer meeting" at our church and the minister asked that someone lead a hymn. Glad of the opportunity to lead a song, I began with a little song I had learned, "Go Tell Aunt Tabby Her Old Gray Goose Is Dead." No one laughed, but joined in the singing instead. I think of that little incident each time I am asked to lead a song of any sort.

Folksingers are almost uniformly grateful for the collectors' efforts to preserve their songs. When Arnold thanked Isaiah Holmes for singing his deeply moving spirituals, Holmes replied: "I thank you in like manner back."

Women generally have been found to play a more important role than men in remembering and singing folksongs, and certainly that has been the case in Alabama. Although scores of singers have been recorded in the Arnold collection, about half the songs in this book come from six or seven singers. This is not as strange as it may seem. The strongest singers generally have the largest repertoires of songs. In choosing the songs for this collection, I have proceeded on the basis of variety and interest, seeking the largest number of different types of folksong and the best examples of those types. I have included all rare and local items in Arnold's collection, but, judging solely on the merits of the songs themselves, I have made no effort to represent as many different singers as possible.

After selection of material, questions of its arrangement become important. No editor has ever developed a perfectly satisfactory system for laying out a collection of folksongs. Indeed, there is nothing that folksong editors apologize for so much as their ordering of the material. Recognizing that all divisions are to some extent arbitrary, editors have also recognized that some divisions must be made. The initial division here was made on the basis of subject matter, and the religious songs were split off from the secular ones. Within the secular songs, the division was made on generic grounds, and ballads were separated from folksongs. This division harks back at least to the eighteenth century when English poet William Shenstone wrote: "It is become habitual to me, to call *that* a *Ballad,* which describes or implies some *Action;* on the other hand, I term that a *Song,* which contains only an expression of *Sentiment*" (cited in Brown III, 3). Thus the word *folksong* takes on two meanings. In its general sense, it refers to all songs maintained in an oral tradition, including ballads and spirituals. In its limiting sense, it refers to secular songs of emotion or sentiment, as opposed to secular songs of narration. The division of material into the categories of ballads, folksongs, and spirituals is not a clean one. "Winter's Night," made up of ballad stanzas, has yet replaced most of its narrative with lyric sentiment and could justifiably be called a folksong. "Rosalee," although its point is a subjective one, tells as coherent a story as many ballads. Because it offers religion as a refuge from sorrow, the sentimental ballad "Little Dove" has been included in religious publications, and could have been included in the last section. Donald Mead's version of "All My Sins Been Taken Away" contains two conventionally religious stanzas and three stanzas of parody of that spiritual. It is in the spirituals section mainly to appear with other versions of that song. His "Bible Tales," however, lacks any seriousness and hence appears in the folksong section, though its subjects are taken from the book of its title. In the large sections, the songs are grouped by type, and within type by singer. Finally, it is heartening that the worth of the songs has never depended on their particular positions in a collection.

THE BYRON ARNOLD COLLECTION OF
ALABAMA FOLKSONGS

In September 1938, Byron Arnold, a graduate of the Eastman School of Music, came to Tuscaloosa to join the music faculty of The University of Alabama. Less than two weeks after his arrival, he was taken to a Sunday "foot-washing" at a black church in Northport. He was deeply stirred by the chantlike singing and by the singers' religious fervor revealed in bodily movements to the rhythm and flow of the music. During that fall he was impressed with some old folk tunes hummed by a friend as she prepared dinner, and he encountered a student in his elementary school music class who said that her grandmother knew "Barbara Allen" and that the blacks on her father's plantation sang spirituals, but not like the versions in the class text. Such experiences convinced Arnold that Alabama was a state full of folksong, whose riches had not been explored systematically.

The first important collector of folksongs in Alabama had been Newman I. White, an instructor at Alabama Polytechnic Institute (now Auburn University). Between 1915 and 1917 he gathered African-American songs, some firsthand from informants, but most from white college students who had learned the songs from blacks. When he left Alabama in 1917, White had put together about half the collection that would become his edition, *American Negro Folk-Songs.* From 1934 to 1940, John A. Lomax intermittently collected songs in the state for the Library of Congress. He recorded many songs from black convicts and some game songs from schoolchildren, but his most important work was done among the blacks of the Livingston area. Ably assisted by local folklorist Ruby Pickens Tartt, Lomax recorded a great trove of folksong from Vera Hall, Dock Reed, and other black friends of Tartt. Several of these songs are featured on Library of Congress recordings and in the collections published by John A. Lomax and his son Alan. Also for the Library of Congress, Alan Lomax collected seven songs in Scottsboro in 1938, and Herbert Halpert recorded about twenty-five songs in the same area the next year. In the early 1940s, Mrs. Edward M. McGeehee collected some old English ballads and folksongs in and around Troy and did some comparative annotation of her collection. Never published, this material has been deposited with Arnold's in The University of Alabama Library. All of these were relatively narrow efforts, and Arnold was the first to seek a statewide collection of many different types of folksong. It should be noted that Arnold's work was followed shortly by that of Ray B. Browne, whose statewide collection made in the summers of 1951, 1952, and 1953 is represented in his book *The Alabama Folk Lyric*. Browne's work deliberately excludes both ballads and black folksongs.

In early spring 1945, Byron Arnold, assistant professor of music, applied for and received support from the Research Committee of The University of Alabama for field collection of folksongs. For six weeks during the late summer of 1945, Arnold toured the state and took down tunes and texts in music tablets of about ninety pages. He had no automobile and so was limited to those areas accessible by bus transportation. Despite some problems, the venture, as Arnold describes it, was a success:

> I nonetheless visited three distinct areas. In the northern part of the state, the Tennessee Valley area from Florence east to Huntsville yielded old English ballads principally. This valley was settled by pioneers of English and Scottish ancestry who came down the Tennessee River from Virgina and the Carolinas.
>
> Across the center of the state from Montgomery to Demopolis, the Black Belt (so called from the color of the soil) produced spirituals and many folksongs founded on old minstrel music. This is the area of former plantations. Many white persons whom I met in the Black Belt remembered the songs sung to them by their black mammies. Most proved to be fragments of minstrel songs or little lullabies which were made up by the singer or derived from known sources.
>
> In the southern part of the state around Mobile and the Bayou Country I was disappointed to find no folksongs of French origin, for Cajun French is still spoken in isolated sections. I did, however, find several old English ballads there, a good many Negro songs, and, from Pansy Richardson, a splendid collection of play party songs.

He covered over two thousand miles, collected 258 folksongs, and picked up numerous leads for further exploration. During the 1945–46 academic year, Arnold selected 153 of the songs for his book *Folksongs of Alabama*, which was submitted to The University of Alabama Press early in 1946, though it was not published until 1950.

His first summer in the field taught Arnold the need for a good recording instrument to validate the texts and tunes he was copying down. The Research Committee granted him extra funds for a machine, and one was ordered in late August 1945. During the 1945–46 school year, Arnold carried on an extensive correspondence with his singers. This quickly became so heavy that he required the services of a secretary, Alice

Duggan, whom he praises consistently for her efficiency. By April 1946, 268 letters had been added to the files. There are indications in Arnold's grant applications and reports that this correspondence, which evidently included gifts of "ballet" books and submission of newly remembered verses for songs sung earlier, grew steadily in volume throughout his involvement in this project. All of this material has been lost. On a brighter note, Arnold somehow got three double-faced recordings of Callie Craven singing some of her very best folksongs. This was particularly lucky because she became ill in the spring of 1946 and died two weeks before Arnold returned to Gadsden in midsummer.

Supported by an extension of his research grant, but still without his long-promised and long-delayed recording equipment, Arnold set out on "another intensive folk song collecting trip . . . during the second term of summer school 1946." It is described in his October 1946 report:

> 226 songs were obtained to add to the 258 previously collected, bringing the total to almost 500. Profiting by last year's experience and the fact that I could get around the state in a private car instead of by bus, I managed to make many more contacts in a like period of time. I also spent more time in rural areas this year. Two itineraries were planned. On the first trip I visited Bessemer, Birmingham, Gadsden, East Gadsden, Boaz, Albertville, Guntersville, Fort Payne, Scottsboro, Huntsville, Athens, Decatur, Wheeler Plantation, Lexington, Florence, Tuscumbia, and Sheffield. The second trip included Greensboro, Union Town, Lowndesboro, Montgomery, Tuskegee, Union Springs, Troy, Luverne, Andalusia, Atmore, Bay Minette, Mobile, Bayou LaBatre, Coden, Toulmanville, and Grove Hill. This is twice the number of communities visited in 1945.

The recording instrument still had not arrived by the summer of 1947, and Arnold set out once again under the auspices of the Research Committee, this time bearing with him a portable recording machine borrowed from T. Earl Johnson of the university's speech department, and accompanied by James Abernathy, the university's electronics technician, whom Professor Johnson specified as the sole acceptable operator of his machine. Partly because he had good sense and partly because Abernathy's salary was more than his budget could bear for an extended period, Arnold began by recording singers whose songs he had noted down in his two previous field trips, and new singers, such as Vera Hall and Dock Reed, who were known to have large repertoires. He made "about one hundred double ten-inch recordings of folk songs. Everywhere the greatest interest was shown and the best cooperation offered." During the second half of this period, Abernathy and the machine were left in Tuscaloosa, and Arnold made field trips "up and around Birmingham, over to Selma, Carlosville, Evergreen, Troy, and down to Elba, working in many rural areas in between. This new territory was found to be very rich and many songs were collected." For this work, Arnold was paid the equivalent of his salary for one term of summer school—$325. He traveled for six weeks, half the time with a technician, on a budget of $400. One day in Tuskegee he bought breakfast for $.35, dinner and supper each for $.85, and treated a guest to dinner for $.75.

During the 1947–48 academic year, the university received $10 for equity in the copyrights of two of the songs Arnold collected. As Kathrine B. James, secretary of the Research Committee, noted in 1948, "This is the only project that has ever repaid one cent." At this point, Arnold had become something of an Alabama celebrity and was called upon to lecture on folksongs throughout the state. County folksong societies were being created, and James clearly expected that *Folksongs of Alabama* would have a fabulous sale when it appeared. Arnold asked for money to fund one last field and recording trip in the second half of the summer of 1948, after which he would spend his time in preparing for the press the five to seven different volumes projected from his collection, which now included almost a thousand different songs. At this point, none of the songs collected between 1945 and 1948 had ever been published. But it was not to be.

Arnold resigned his position at The University of Alabama in the early summer of 1948 and took one at California State University in Los Angeles, where he began work on his Ph.D. in music at the University of Southern California. He took with him his magnificent Alabama folksong collection, but seems never to have worked on it again after leaving the state. Arnold died in 1971 and, in his will, left his folksong materials to The University of Alabama.

Shortly after the collection's return to Tuscaloosa in 1974 and 1975, Robert Nicolosi, associate professor of music, began organizing it with a view to revising and enlarging Arnold's 1950 volume. Assisted by Deborah Harhai, then a graduate student in music, Nicolosi completed cataloging the collection during the 1980–81 academic year. Like Arnold's, Nicolosi's work was supported by funds from the university's Research Grants Committee, as it was then named. Arnold, Nicolosi, and Harhai dealt expertly with the collection's tunes, but none of them had specific expertise in the study of folksong texts. Arnold seems to have proclaimed his deficiency in this area by his frequent pronouncement that *Folksongs of Alabama* was not "academic in intent." Nicolosi asked me to evaluate the texts, and I joined the project as a consultant. Working together, we realized that a completely new edition of material in the Arnold collection was needed, rather than a mere revision and enlargement of the 1950 volume. Shortly after I became coeditor of the proposed volume, Nicolosi became ill and was unable to continue work on the project. I became sole editor upon Nicolosi's death in 1982.

EDITORIAL MATTERS

The Byron Arnold Collection contains three types of records of the folksongs noted by Arnold: the printed texts and tunes for 153 of the songs in *Folksongs of Alabama;* the transcriptions of texts and tunes in the music notebooks; and the recordings of the singers singing the songs themselves. The last, obviously, is the most reliable record of an individual performance, and wherever possible I have derived text and tune from recordings. Where there were no recordings I have turned to the notebooks, and in the very few instances in which there was no record of a performance in either notebook or on recordings I have used the printed record. This explains why some songs, recovered by Arnold in 1945 and included in his 1950 volume, are now dated 1947 or 1948.

I have based my entries on the phonograph records. As several reviewers of *Folksongs of Alabama* noted, Arnold was a superb recorder, transcriber, and editor of folk tunes. His transcriptions are always faithful reproductions of the tunes on the recordings.

In several other respects, however, Arnold's expertise was not so sound as we would like today. Like most of his contemporaries in the field, he sought the "old" songs and thus ignored vast tracts of folksong in Alabama: for example, white and black gospel, white sacred harp singing, blues and honky-tonk songs. He also ignored the fact that singers learned songs from phonograph recordings, from the radio, or from itinerant professionals attached to medicine, tent, or vaudeville shows. Arnold clearly expected certain types of people to sing certain types of songs: for example, whites in the hilly northern regions would sing ballads, while blacks in central Alabama would sing spirituals. It is not strange that his collection matched his preconceptions, and it is surely true that such a collection would not be offered today as a complete record of Alabama folksong by any folklorist collecting material. No attempt has been made here, however, to supplement Arnold's collection from other sources. I know of no other large body of unpublished Alabama folksongs, and, even if such a collection were available, it would be of dubious merit to mingle songs whose motive and methods of collection were different. If Arnold's practices were narrow, and are now superseded by others, they were nonetheless consistent, and they offer us an interestingly homogeneous representation of the Alabama folksong experience in the 1940s. In Arnold's defense, I note that his literary orientation was no different from that of most collectors of his day, that his musical expertise far surpassed most of theirs, and that he understood better than most other collectors the importance of gaining information on his informants, of presenting songs as parts of individual repertoires, and of attempting to learn the singer's attitude toward the songs sung.

It is also true, unfortunately, that Arnold's dealings with the songs texts and, in some instances, their structures were not always so successful as his dealings with their music. For example, in transcribing the text of "Rosalee" from the music notebook, he copied the verses from the first and third pages, evidently missing the second page, the middle of the song. Despite the fact that he has the chorus of "Rosalee" clearly listed as such in the notebook, Arnold printed it as the last stanza. The unchorused fragment printed in *Folksongs of Alabama*, however, received the warmest of praise from one reviewer. Without recordings against which to check his transcriptions, Arnold made numerous errors in individual words. In *Folksongs of Alabama*, for instance, Callie Craven begins "Winter's Night":

As I rode out last winter's night,
A-drinkin' of sweet wine,
Come versin' with that pretty little girl
That stole this heart of mine.

Arnold has a footnote on the third line: "I asked Miss Callie what 'versin'' meant and she replied, 'Why, that's meeting your girl down in the garden of an evening and reciting love verses to each other.'" The recording made of Craven before her death clearly reveals her singing "conversing." In Arnold's defense, we should note that he had no recordings to assist him in the editing of this material, since it all comes from that collected in the summer of 1945. And singers are not always cheerful about repeating a song many times to make sure the fellow from the university gets the words down right.

On several occasions Arnold altered a song's text to make its sense clearer or to make it fit a tune a little better. My editorial practices, however, are more conservative. Incorrect choices of diction are left alone. For instance, J. K. Estes in her "True Lovers Part" has her young man plead "Oh dear father, duty me." "Duty" makes no sense in this context, and should almost certainly be "pity." But Estes clearly sings "duty" on her recording, and it remains, though the headnote points out the difficulty. In May Randlette Beck's version of "The Frog He Would A-Courting Ride," Uncle Rat gives the hand of his niece, Miss Mouse, to our hero: "Take her, take her, with all your heart." Other versions have the conventional "with all my heart," but Beck makes perfect sense in Uncle Rat's stressing that the groom must love his bride completely, and no change is made. On the other hand, singers sometimes make obvious mistakes in singing their songs; even here I have not altered the received record, but I have pointed out problems in the headnote. Julia Greer Marechal begins the refrain too early in the last stanza of "The Year of Jubilo," and I do not alter that, though I do include another singer's conclusion in the headnote. Versions of songs merely cited in headnotes are, apart from the lines cited, little different from the versions included at length. When several versions of a song are of interest, I include them under A, B, C, and so forth. If a version is not complete, the omitted stanzas can be assumed to be much like corresponding stanzas in longer versions included.

In matters of spelling and punctuation I have taken more freedom, recognizing that neither is necessarily conveyed definitively in an oral performance. Punctuation is employed either to assist the meaning of the text or to help pace it as a song. Misspellings that do not affect the sounds of words have been silently corrected. When a spelling other than the normal one has a distinct effect on pronunciation, I have left the variant alone. In "Run, Nigger, Run" we find the line "The patterol'll catch you." Obviously, the word should be "patrol," and just as obviously the effect of the refrain depends on that word having three syllables. A more serious problem arises with dialect. Arnold very frequently uses "d" for "th" at the beginnings of words, especially if the singer is black. And he has a tendency to drop the "g" from the concluding "ing" for both black and white singers. There are other dialect indications involving contractions, usually of "going." Most of these usages are not supported by the recordings of the singers made after 1945, and I have restored the words to their customary forms. In some cases, however, where the singer very clearly uses a dialect pronunciation or when a rhyme or a cadence depends on dialect in a song for which there is no voice recording, I have left the dialect alone.

The headnotes are designed to assist the reader in approaching the songs. Frequently they place a song in its historical, literary, musical, social, or scriptural context. I mention the author, or a particularly influential singer, of a given song where either is known. I have tried to explain obscure terms, clarify difficulties of structure, and point out things remarkable to our text. Where the reader would seem to need no assistance, or where I have none to offer, there is no headnote. The title is that provided by the singer or, if no title was given, the first line of the song. More familiar titles of the pieces, if different from those used by the informants, are printed in parentheses, along with appropriate Child and Laws numbers for the ballads. I have tried to determine and indicate the marital status of female singers, and for married women I have followed incorrect social procedure and allied Mrs. with a given name, when it was known. The one major exception here is Vera Hall, who is always known as Miss, though she was married several times. For several informants even sex could not be determined, let alone marital status. To eliminate distractions to the reader approaching the individual songs, I have not followed the practice of many editors of including references to other published versions of the songs in the headnotes, but have placed this essential information in Appendix B. Many of the volumes there listed contain especially full bibliographic and discographic references, and the reader seeking full knowledge of a particular song is urged to consult them.

Byron Arnold arranged his collection by singer and provided biographical information for each of his major informants. He noted that this was not a common ordering principle and defended it on the basis of his interest in the individual singer. There is much sense to this, but it will not work with the present edition, because whatever biographical information Arnold possessed for singers recorded after 1945—and there is indication that it was a great deal—has been lost. As mentioned earlier, within the three large divisions of this book the material is arranged by type of song and then by singer. Arnold's procedure would have worked best had it been possible to include all the songs in each singer's repertoire. That is clearly impossible now, since the collection contains almost a thousand folksong versions, and it was not carried out even in Arnold's 1950 *Folksongs of Alabama*. The informant biographies originally printed by Arnold retain their interest, and they are included in Appendix A here. The entire Byron Arnold Collection, with indexes to singers, songs, phonograph recordings, and manuscript notebooks, is now located in the Hoole Special Collections Library of The University of Alabama.

ACKNOWLEDGMENTS

First of all, I am indebted to the singers who are represented here for singing their songs and to Byron Arnold for collecting them. Next, I am grateful to Robert Nicolosi for cataloging the Arnold collection and for the little work that we were able to do together. Dr. Nicolosi was a greatly talented and a gently humane individual, and all his friends were grievously affected by his death at age thirty-nine. I thank especially Deborah Harhai, who was his assistant and became mine. Ms. Harhai presided as musical authority over this collection and prepared the tunes for publication. For financial support for the project in all its stages, I thank the Research Grants Committee of The University of Alabama. Its monetary assistance enabled Arnold to collect these songs, Nicolosi to catalog the collection, and me to edit the songs for this volume and have the music prepared for publication. For cheerful forbearance I thank the staffs of the Circulation and Inter-Library Loan Departments of the Amelia Gayle Gorgas Library of The University of Alabama. For direct assistance and for providing me with workspace where there was not much space available, I thank Joyce Lamont and her staff in the Special Collections Department of the Gorgas Library. I appreciate the time and effort spent by my friends and colleagues who read drafts of this book, made many helpful suggestions, and saved me from at least one awful howler: John Burke, Henry Jacobs, Brenda McCallum, and Elizabeth Meese. I gratefully acknowledge the director and staff at The University of Alabama Press and copy editor Jonathan Lawrence, all of whom provided absolutely essential expertise, encouragement, patience, prodding, and good sense. I thank Judy Halli, who served as editor, proofreader, and general encourager through many early drafts. For patience with their often absent daddy, I thank my daughter Anne, who loved to sing with me dozens of verses of "Feed the Animals," and her younger brother Joe, who did not. Lastly, I thank Allen Jones, for all the reasons she knows.

PART 1
BALLADS

Ballads are folksongs that tell stories. Scholars believe, probably correctly, that the earliest versions of ballads were the longest and the most detailed. As ballads were passed from singer to singer in oral tradition, portions of the story with which the new singer was not familiar, or which he or she did not consider important, were either forgotten or omitted intentionally. Thus ballads have a tendency to grow shorter over time, keeping those stanzas and scenes that are most striking and moving. Descriptions and transitions are often dropped as singers concentrate on events and emotion. The stories are always told with more attention to action than to motivation. Generally avoiding sordid details, singers concentrate on the tragic aspects of the crimes they report.

In the late nineteenth century, Harvard professor Francis James Child compiled *The English and Scottish Popular Ballads*. This monumental collection is important because it was one of the first academic works to treat folksong seriously. Child printed extensive headnotes to each of the ballads he included, and he printed as many versions of each ballad as he could find. For ease of reference, he numbered the ballads as he proceeded, and the numbers he gave those songs have become attached to them permanently. There are nine versions here of ballads found in Child's collection, and they bear his numbers. Of course, a folksinger does not sing "Barbara Allen" because it is a Child ballad, but because it is a good song-story. Generally, folksingers make few distinctions among their songs, calling both the oldest English ballads as well as recent wanderers from the music hall "old-time love songs." In fact, if many folksingers are asked for a "ballad" they will produce not an oral performance but a copybook, a "ballet-book" in which the texts of all kinds of songs have been written down. Professor Malcolm Laws has classified by subject a number of ballads found in America, and the identifying letter and number he has assigned them have been included for the twenty-one ballads in this collection which he has treated. Each letter designates a type of song, and the number simply indicates the song's position in Laws's category. Letters A through I indicate "Native American Balladry," songs composed or dominant in North America. F, for instance, heads the "Murder Ballads," of which "Little Mary Phagan" is number 20. Laws also treats "American Ballads from British Broadsides," songs originally printed and sold on single sheets, broadsides, in the British Isles but which have now established a strong hold in American oral tradition. J and following letters designate these. "Oh Johnny" is the thirty-third song in category O, "Ballads of Faithful Lovers."

Our ballads begin with love's triumphs over impending death, social considerations, family opposition, or the hardships and anxieties of war. Then come love's tragedies, marked by violent death except for the ballad that is perhaps the most tragic of all, "Barbara Allen." In our third group, love ends in disappointment, through the death or fickleness of the beloved, the impossibility of marriage, or successful family opposition. There are two sections of sentimental or pathetic songs, the first dealing with children, the second with adults. These are less distinctly narrative and sometimes seem to be little more than monologues designed to tear our heartstrings. But they are traditionally grouped with ballads, do sometimes tell stories, and have had tremendous popularity in the United States. Four criminal ballads are then grouped together, highlighted by "Stagalee." The division closes out with humorous pieces, including "The Frog He Would A-Courting Ride," the ballad most frequently found in America. In "The Clerks of Parch's Cove" and "The Wedding of Bean Rock Hollow" we have two rollicking Alabama ballads of which any state would be proud.

Chapter 1
Love's Triumphs

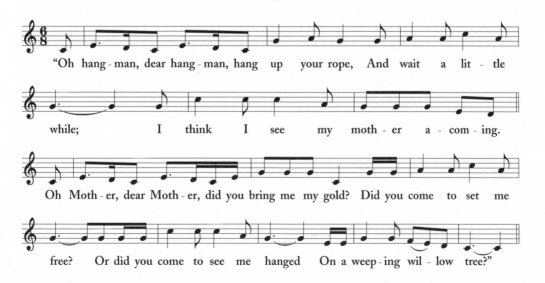

The Miller's Daughter
(Child 95, The Maid Freed from the Gallows)

In American tradition, this very popular ballad is generally called "The Hangman," and its condemned prisoner is just as likely to be male and his rescuer female as the reverse. The song is popular at least partly because it is easily remembered, even by little children, and it is inherently dramatic, perfectly suited for singing games and juvenile theatrical performances. Although there is little textual variation among recovered versions of the ballad, Mrs. Hester's is singular in that she sings three-line "Hangman" stanzas. All other versions have a fourth line in that stanza, usually something like "She's walked many a mile." But Mrs. Hester's treatment makes narrative and musical sense. She evidently considered the song a lullabye and, following the sixth stanza, she told Arnold: "Additional verses may be added here, substituting 'brother' or 'sister' or any other relative until you run out of breath. But you always end up with the truelove bringing the gold before the baby goes to sleep." The prisoner's calling the executioner "dear hangman" is found in many other versions of the ballad.

Sung by Mrs. Myrtle Love Hester, Florence, 8 June 1947.

"Oh Daugh-ter, dear Daugh-ter, I did not bring your gold, I did not come to set you free, But I came to see you hanged On a weep-ing wil - low tree."

4 "Oh hangman, dear hangman, hang up your rope,
And wait a little while,
I think I see my father a-coming.

5 "Oh Father, dear Father, did you bring my gold?
Did you come to set me free?
Or did you come to see me hanged
On a weeping willow tree?"

6 "My Daughter, dear Daughter, I did not bring your gold,
And I did not come to set you free.
But I came to see you hang
Upon a weeping willow tree."

7 "Then hangman, dear hangman, hang up your rope,
And wait a little while,
I think I see my sweetheart a-coming.

8 "Oh lover, dear lover, did you bring me my gold?
Did you come to set me free?
Or did you come to see me hang
On a weeping willow tree?"

9 "My darling, my darling, I brought your gold,
And I came to set you free.
But I did not come to see you hang
On a weeping willow tree."

Pretty Mohea

(Laws H 8, The Little Mohea)

Scholars of folksong have long debated this ballad's origin. Some contend it is derived from British broadsides, while others believe the broadsides were stimulated by this traditional song. Some believe the "Indian lass" is a member of the Miami tribe and the man English, because he must sail to get to his homeland. Others believe the girl is a South Sea Islander, an inhabitant of Maui in the Hawaiian Islands, and the man either an Englishman or, much more likely, an American. This last seems the strongest possibility, and it is supported by the fact that "Pretty Mohea" was sung as a sea shanty by the Pacific whalers. Singers of folksong do not worry about such scholarly matters. They have been taken by the ballad's rather exotic narrative and have spread it across America. The song was popular with early "hillbilly" radio and recording artists such as Buell Kazee, who earned a flat fee of under one hundred dollars for his recording, which sold about fifteen thousand copies. Mrs. Hester, who said that the song was also known as "The Cocoanut Grove," could not remember the second line of her last stanza.

Sung by Mrs. Myrtle Love Hester, Florence, 6 August 1945.

As I went out a-walk-ing for pleas-ure one day, In sweet rec-re-a-tion to while the time 'way, While sweet-ly a-mus-ing my-self on the grass, There who should I spy but a shy In-dian lass.

   2 She set down beside me, taken hold of my hand,
      And says, "You're a stranger and in a strange land.
      If you'd only consent, Sir, to come live with me
      And go no more roving far over the sea.

   3 "If you'll only consent to come live with me,
      I'll teach you the language of the pretty Mohea."
      "No, no, my dear maiden, that never could be,
      For I have a sweetheart and I know she loves me."

4 But when I had landed on my own native shore,
And my friends and relations gathered 'round me once more,
I looked all around me, but none could I see
That was fit to compare with the pretty Mohea.

5 And the girl I had trusted proved untrue to me
. . . .
I'll turn my course backward; from this land I'll flee.
I'll go spend my days with the pretty Mohea.

Katie Dear

(Laws M 4, The Drowsy Sleeper)

Descended from British broadsides and recorded frequently before World War II, this song is more widely distributed in the United States than "The Silver Dagger" (see p. 27), from which Mrs. Hester's version, like many others, borrows its weapon. Her version, however, lacks the familiar opening stanza in which the young man awakens "the drowsy sleeper" and calls her to the window so he can ask her the questions here. Much is also omitted between Hester's fourth and fifth stanzas. In some versions the girl says she will die of grief, in others (borrowing again from "The Silver Dagger") the two lovers commit suicide, and in a third group the girl decides to forsake her parents and flee with her lover. Hester's last stanza clearly links her version with this more cheerful sort, though it is impossible to determine whether Katie or Willie speaks those hopeful lines.

Sung by Mrs. Myrtle Love Hester, Florence, 7 August 1945.

"Oh Ka-tie dear, go ask your moth-er, Ask her if you my bride may be, And if she de-nies you, love, come and tell me, Then that'-ll be the last I'll trou-ble thee."

2 "Oh Willie dear, that would be useless.
  She's in her room taking her rest
  And by her side lies a silver dagger
  To plunge into my true love's breast."

3 "Oh Katie dear, go ask your father,
  Ask him if you my bride may be;
  And if he denies you, love, come and tell me,
  And that'll be the last I'll trouble thee."

4 "Oh Willie dear, that would be folly.
  He's in his room taking his rest
  And by his side lies a golden dagger
  To plunge into my true love's breast."

5 "Then don't you see that cloud a-rising
  To shield us from the rising sun;
  Oh, won't you be glad, my own true lover,
  When you and I become as one?"

Last Night I Dreamed of My True Love

(Laws M 13, Locks and Bolts)

This ballad's history can be traced back at least to a 1631 British broadside titled "The Constant Wife." "Locks and Bolts" has flourished in American oral tradition, though the basic premise of its story has usually been lost. In the original versions, the young woman is very rich and her beloved suitor very poor. To prevent their marriage, her family sends her away in secret to live as a prisoner in an uncle's house. Here she is found and rescued by her true love. Mrs. Hill's is one of the longest and finest versions of this ballad ever recovered in the United States.

The confused last line of Mrs. Hill's fifth stanza is probably the result of mishearing a line about the locks and bolts such as: "I broke 'em all asinder" (or "asunder"). Almost all American versions are confused at the point of Hill's seventh stanza. Tradition supports a stanza composed of the last two lines of Hill's sixth stanza and the fragmentary seventh. Sometimes a stanza is composed of the statement and repetition of the first two lines of the sixth stanza; or those lines are sometimes dropped—the first appears in Mrs. Hill's eighth stanza.

Sung by Mrs. Lena Hill, Lexington, 10 June 1947.

Last night I dreamed of my true love; All in my arms I had her. Her
yel-low hair, like chains of gold, Came a-stream-ing o'er my pil-low.

2 When I woke and found it was a dream,
   I was forced to stay without her.
   Next morning I rose, put on my clothes,
   Determed to find my lady.

3 I rode o'er hills and valleys through,
   Determed to find my lady.
   I rode up to her uncle's gate;
   I asked him about my lady.

4 He answered me so soft and low,
   "I have no such in keeping."
   She answered me my voice below,
   She answered me from the window,

5 Saying, "I'd not be here, I would not be here,
   But locks and bolts doth hinder."
   "I'll break them locks, I'll bend them bolts,
   I'll knock them into sinder."

6 I drew my sword in my right hand,
   And in that room I enter;
   Her uncle and another man
   Came stepping in together,

7 Saying, "Go out of here, go out of here,
   Or in your blood you'll wallow."

8 I drew my sword in my right hand,
   My lady in the other.
   "I'm in this room with my true love,
   And I'll die before I'll leave her."

9 We'll join our hands in wedlock bands,
   We'll live in peace and pleasure,
   We'll join our hands in wedlock bands,
   We'll live and die together.

Jack the Sailor

(Laws N 7, Jack Monroe)

After learning the identity of her love, Mary's wealthy father has him sent overseas to war. Mary follows in disguise, finds him, and (evidently) marries him. Although it carries no impact in Mrs. Hill's version, the father's calling his daughter "Mrs. Strater" (more frequently "Mrs. Frazier") is normally sarcastic, because he applies to her the surname of her love. Women who dress as men to accompany or seek out their lovers in battle appear with some regularity in Anglo-American balladry (see "Oh Johnny," p. 11). It is pleasant to find that Jack's "deadly mortal wound" is not fatal. The fourth line of each stanza is repeated, prefaced by "Oh."

Sung by Mrs. Lena Hill, Lexington, 10 June 1947.

2 She had sweethearts a-plenty,
   To court her day and night,
   But on Jack the sailor
   She placed her heart's delight.

3 Her father called his daughter one day,
   And quickly she went in.
   "Good morning, Mrs. Strater,
   I've learned your sweetheart's name."

4 She said, "Father, here is my body,
   And it you may confine.
   There's none but Jack the sailor
   That will ever suit my mind."

5   Her father flew in a passion,
    And quickly he did go
    To bargain with the captain
    To bear Jack far away.

6   Now Jack has gone a-sailing
    All o'er the deep bright sea,
    And there he'll spend his days
    In the war of Germany.

7   Now Mary sits at leisure
    With money at her command.
    She took a sneaking notion
    She would view some distant land.

8   She went into a tailor shop,
    Men's clothing she put on,
    Then bargained with some captain
    To bear her far away.

9   He said, "Before you go on board, Sir,
    Your name I would like to know."
    She smiled upon him and said,
    "You may call me Jack Monroe."

10   He said, "Your waist it is too slender,
    Your fingers are too small,
    Your face it is too delicate,
    To face a cannonball."

11   She said, "I know my waist is slender,
    My fingers they are small,
    But to get to see my true love
    I would face a cannonball."

12   She sailed east, she sailed west,
    Till she came to the war of Germany,
    And none but Jack the sailor
    Could run the raging sea.

13   She went up on the battlefield;
    She viewed them round and around.
    At length she found her true love
    With a deadly mortal wound.

14 She picked him up all in her arms;
    She carried him round and around.
    At length she found a physician
    That would heal his deadly wound.

15 Now Jack is well and married,
    And she is bringing him home.
    Now Jack is well and married,
    And she is bringing him home.

Oh Johnny

(Laws O 33, The Girl Volunteer)

This is a better version of "Oh Johnny" than most of those that achieved widespread popularity during the folk revival of the fifties and sixties. Although its story is similar in several points to that of "Jack the Sailor" (see p. 9), there are also significant differences between the songs, and it is most unlikely that both ballads derive from the same broadside source. The chorus is sung to the same tune as the stanzas.

Sung by Miss Callie Craven, Gadsden, 26 August 1945.

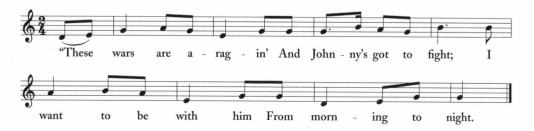

"These wars are a-rag-in' And John-ny's got to fight; I
want to be with him From morn-ing to night.

Chorus
"Oh Johnny, my jewel,
It seems as you're unkind;
It seems as I've loved you
From all other mankind.

2 "It seems as I've loved you,
   Which grieves my heart so.
   Oh, may I go with you?"
   "Oh no, my love, no.

3 “Tomorrow is Sunday
   And Monday is the day
   My captain commands me
   And I must away.”

Chorus

4 “You'll be standing on picket
   Some cold snowy day;
   Your red rosy cheeks
   Will soon fade away.

5 “Your red rosy cheeks,
   Which grieves my heart so.
   Oh, may I go with you?”
   “Oh no, my love, no.”

Chorus

6 “Oh Daughter, dear Daughter,
   You'd better stay at home,
   You had better stay with your mother
   Till Johnny comes home.”

7 “Oh Mother, dear Mother,
   You need not talk to me.
   I'll follow young Johnny
   Across the flowing sea.

Chorus

8 “I'll cut off my hair;
   Men's clothing I'll put on.
   I'll pass as your messmate
   As we march along.

9 “We'll cross over Jordan.
   Your troubles I will bless.
   Oh, may I go with you?”
   “Oh yes, my love, yes.”

10 “Farewell to all sweethearts,
   Farewell to all beaus,
   I'll follow young Johnny
   Wherever he goes.”

A Fair Damsel

(Laws N 42, Pretty Fair Maid)

This is one of the most popular of a large number of "returning lover" ballads. It appears on broadsides dating back to the early nineteenth century, was a favorite of early recording artists, and remains current in oral tradition on both sides of the Atlantic. No version makes clear why the damsel fails to recognize her lover immediately, but without that failure there would be no song. After testing her constancy, the soldier shows his damsel a token. Mrs. Griffin's treatment of this in the fifth stanza is somewhat obscure, probably the mishearing of a line such as "He pulled out the ring that was broken between them." This confirms the soldier's identity, and the lovers are happily reunited. Griffin's version is unusual because its first and fourth stanzas contain six lines.

Sung by Mrs. Mary A. Griffin, Lexington, 10 June 1947.

2 "Go way from here, you rebel soldier,
   My poor heart's in misery.
   My own true love is across the ocean,
   No man but him can marry me."

3 "Now suppose your own true love is drownded,
Or suppose he's in some battle slain,
Or suppose he's stole some girl and married,
His face you never shall see again."

4 "If he's drownded I hope he's happy,
If he's slain I wish him well,
And if he's stole some girl and married,
I once loved him, I love him still;
And if he's stole some girl and married,
I'll love the girl that married him."

5 He ran his hands all in his pocket,
His fingers seeming neat and small,
He took out a rule that was written between them,
And at his feet she humbly did fall.

6 He picked her up all in his sorrow,
The kisses he give was one, two, three.
"This is your poor little rebel soldier,
Returned back home to marry thee."

Chapter 2
Love's Tragedies

~

Billy Came Over the Main White Ocean
(Child 4, Lady Isabel and the Elf-Knight)

Among the most widespread of traditional songs is this ballad about a young woman who disposes of a villain as he would have disposed of her. In the United States, however, the mysterious, supernatural elf-knight of British and European variants has been rationalized into a greedy human suitor. Mrs. Hill's sixth and seventh stanzas are particularly interesting because they contain the heroine's request, unique in America, that the man turn away to ponder the moral consequences of murder. His doing so, of course, provides her the opportunity to kill him in self-defense. Most frequently, she asks him to avert his eyes from her nakedness, as in Mrs. Ezell's version, which is otherwise less complete and interesting than the A text. Like a number of American singers, Hill may have considered allusion to a naked woman in poor taste. In many versions, when the heroine returns home her parrot threatens to tell all it knows of her rendezvous and is silenced only by the promise of a fine new cage. All that is left here of this scene is the somewhat confusing last stanza and a misplaced reference to the heroine herself as "pert bird" in the fifth stanza.

As sung by Hill, the third, fourth, and fifth stanzas are defective. Mirroring the preceding, the third stanza should probably include the second stanza's second line, and perhaps the first line of the fifth stanza should really be the third line of the fourth stanza, with "They rode" dropped from "the length of a long summer day, day, day." Following the record of other American texts, we can locate what seem to be the results of mishearings in Hill's rendition. "Damsel" in the fourth and tenth stanzas should probably be "dapple," and "false-haired" should be "false-hearted." But "false-haired" certainly carries intriguing implications. Other American versions also open with a stanza in the first person.

A

Sung by Mrs. Lena Hill, Lexington, 10 June 1947.

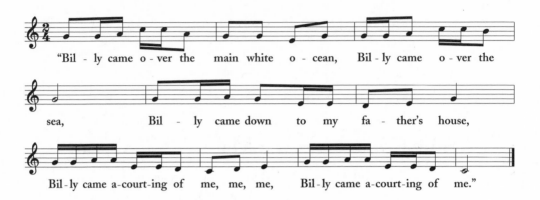

"Bil - ly came o - ver the main white o - cean, Bil - ly came o - ver the sea, Bil - ly came down to my fa - ther's house, Bil - ly came a-court-ing of me, me, me, Bil - ly came a-court-ing of me."

2 "Go and choose you a part of your mother's gold
And a part of father's fees,
And to some fair country we will go,
And it's married we will be, be, be,
And it's married we will be."

3 She went and took a part of her mother's gold,
And down to her father's stable,
And there they took a choice of thirty and three, three, three,
The choice of thirty and three.

4 She mounted upon a milk white horse
And Billy on a damsel gray;
They rode the length of a long summer day, day, day,
The length of a long summer day.

5 They rode up to a seashore.
"Light you down, you little pert bird,
So light you down," said he,
"For the six kings' daughters I've drowned in here,
And the seventh you shall be, be, be,
And the seventh you shall be."

6 "Turn your face all around and about
And view the green leaves on the tree,
And see what a scandal it will be
To drown me in the sea, sea, sea,
To drown me in the sea."

7 He turned his face all around and about
To view the green leaves on the tree;
She took him by his slender waist
And plunged him in the sea, sea, sea,
And plunged him in the sea.

8 "Reach forth, reach forth your lily-white hands
And take me out of the sea;
I'll fill all the promises I've made to you
And it's married we will be, be, be,
And it's married we will be."

9 "Lie there, lie there, you false-haired man,
You as well as to lie there as me,
For the six kings' daughters you have drowned in the sea,
And the seventh I won't be, be, be,
And the seventh I won't be."

10 She mounted upon a milk white horse,
A-leading of a damsel gray;
She rode up to her father's house
Just about three hours 'fore day, day, day,
Just about three hours 'fore day.

11 "Hush up, hush up, you little pert bird,
Don't you tell no tales on me,
For I left poor Billy a-lying beneath the waves
A-looking after me, me, me,
A-looking after me."

B

Sung by Mrs. Grace Hicks Ezell, Birmingham, 26 June 1947.

5 "Take off, take off these very fine clothes,
And hand them all to me.
They are too costly and too fine
To rot in the foam of the sea, sea, sea,
To rot in the foam of the sea."

6 "Turn your head around and around
And look upon the willow tree.
While I remove my wedding gown.
I will no man for to see, see, see,
I will no man for to see."

Love Henry

(Child 68, Young Hunting)

The speaker attempts to persuade Love Henry to dismount from his horse and spend the night with her. Although he initially denies her request and says he prefers another woman, he eventually gives in and, during the night, the jealous speaker kills him. Before he dies, in some versions, he claims that his statement about the other woman was just a teasing untruth, and that might help explain the woman's change of attitude in Mrs. Hill's fourth stanza. Deciding finally not to believe him, however, she disposes of the body and attempts to bribe her parrot, which has evidently witnessed the murder and its sequel, to remain silent. Although the oldest British versions of "Young Hunting" tell a long and detailed story, most American variants, like Hill's, have become shorter and rather confused. Still, there remains an intriguing power to the ballad's portrayal of character and action.

Sung by Mrs. Lena Hill, Lexington, 1 August 1945.

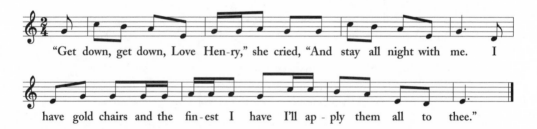

"Get down, get down, Love Hen-ry," she cried, "And stay all night with me. I have gold chairs and the fin-est I have I'll ap-ply them all to thee."

2 "I can't get down nor I shan't get down,
   Nor stay all night with you.
   Some pretty girl in Cornersville,
   I love true better than thee."

3 He laid his head on a pillow of down,
   The kisses she gave him three;
   With the penny knife that she held in her hand
   She murdered mortal he.

4 "Get well, get well, Love Henry," she cried,
   "Get well, get well," said she.
   "Oh, don't you see my own heart's blood
   A-flowing down so free."

5 She took him by his long yellow hair
  And also by his feet;
  She plunged him in well water
  Where it runs both cold and deep.

6 "Lie there, lie there, Love Henry," she cried,
  "Till the flesh rots off your bones.
  Some pretty little girl in Cornersville
  Will mourn for your return.

7 "Hush up, hush up parrot," she cried,
  "Don't tell no news on me;
  All these costly beads around my neck,
  I'll apply them all to thee.

8 "Fly down, fly down, pretty parrot," she cried,
  "And light on my right knee;
  The doors of your cage shall be decked with gold,
  And hung on a willow tree."

The Brown Girl
(Child 73, Lord Thomas and Fair Annet)

This tale of thwarted love, double murder, and suicide has been extremely popular for over three hundred years. Its tragedy springs from the familiar conflict of heart and purse: Lord Thomas loves a blond (fair Ellen) but weds a brunette (the brown girl) because she is wealthier. Depending on one's allegiance to heart or purse, the actions and words of the jilted fair Ellen are either brave and admirable or arrogant and deplorable. In either case, they are dangerous, and her mother's prophecy of Ellen's death in Mrs. Lambert's sixth stanza is both accurate and unique among American versions of the song. Another unusual feature here is Lord Thomas's request in the fourteenth stanza to have the fatal sword and penknife buried with him. Similar stanzas appear in "The Two Brothers" and other ballads, but in this song the more conventional request is that of Mrs. Lambert's fifteenth stanza. Thomas's actions upon the head of his new bride may be in poor taste, but they are also in almost all other American versions of the song.

Sung by Mrs. Corie Lambert, Mobile, 3 September 1945.

"It's a rid-dle, it's a rid-dle, oh my dear Moth-er, To make us both as one. Say shall I mar-ry fair El-len, Or bring the brown girl home, Or bring the brown girl home?"

2 "The brown girl has a house and land,
   Fair Ellen she has none.
   I'll ask it all to you as a blessing
   To bring the brown girl home,
   To bring the brown girl home."

3 He rode till he reached fair Ellen's door,
   A knot pulled down the ring,
   And none were so ready as fair Ellen herself
   For to rise and let him come in,
   For to rise and let him come in.

4 "Oh, what is the matter, Lord Thomas," said she,
   "Oh, what is the matter with thee?"
   "I've come to ask you to my wedding."
   "Oh, that is bad news for me,
   Oh, that is bad news for me."

5 "It's a riddle, it's a riddle, oh my dear Mother,
   To make us both as one.
   Say shall I go to Lord Thomas's wedding
   Or tarry at home alone,
   Or tarry at home alone?"

6 "Oh tarry, oh tarry, oh my dear Daughter,
   Oh tarry at home alone,
   For if you go to Lord Thomas's wedding,
   It's killed you're sure to be,
   It's killed you're sure to be."

7   She dressed herself in scarlet red,
    The rest were dressed in green,
    And as she rode along the street,
    She was taken for to be some queen,
    She was taken for to be some queen.

8   She rode till she reached Lord Thomas's door,
    The knot pulled down the ring,
    And none was so ready as Lord Thomas himself,
    For to rise and let her come in,
    For to rise and let her come in.

9   He took her by her lily-white hand
    And led her through the hall,
    And sat her down at the end of the table,
    Among the merry men all,
    Among the merry men all.

10 "If this is your bride, Lord Thomas," says she,
    "I am sure she is very brown,
    When you could have married as fair a lady
    As ever the sun shined on,
    As ever the sun shined on."

11 The brown girl had a little penknife,
    The point was keen and sharp.
    Between the long ribs and the short
    She pierced fair Ellen's heart,
    She pierced fair Ellen's heart.

12 "Oh what is the matter?" Lord Thomas said,
    "Oh what is the matter with thee?
    To see my own true love's heart blood
    Come trickling down by me,
    Come trickling down by me."

13 He took the brown girl by the hand
    And led her through the hall,
    Drew out his sword, cut off her head,
    And kicked it against the wall,
    And kicked it against the wall.

14 "Oh Father, oh Father, go dig my grave,
    Go dig it long and deep,
    And bury the sharp sword at my side,
    The penknife at my feet,
    The penknife at my feet.

15 "Oh Brother, oh Brother, go make my coffin,
And make it long and wide,
And bury fair Ellen in my arms,
And the brown girl by my side,
And the brown girl by my side."

16 He placed the sharp sword on the floor,
His back upon it lay,
He pierced the penknife in his breast,
"Here comes three lovers all at once.
Lord, send our souls to rest."

Barbara Allen
(Child 84)

This song, praised by Samuel Pepys in his diary in 1666, is the single most frequently found Child ballad, both throughout the United States and in Alabama. The story line of American versions shows great uniformity, because "Barbara Allen" was often printed on broadsides and in songsters, and was a staple of radio shows and of the "hillbilly" recording industry. In the late 1920s, for instance, Bradley Kincaid sang it almost weekly on WLS-Chicago's *National Barn Dance*, included it in his first published songbook, and turned it into a best-selling record marketed through the Sears Roebuck catalog. Individual versions, however, still diverge interestingly from one another in the details of the common story chosen for presentation or for special emphasis. This is certainly true of the versions from Mrs. Lambert and Miss Neely. Lambert has two stanzas before Barbara arrives at Sweet William's bedside; Neely has four. Their meeting is played out alone in two stanzas in Neely's song; it takes up four stanzas in Lambert's and evidently occurs in the midst of a crowd. Lambert's additions are unique to the ballad's tradition, and they amplify the deathbed scene without the repetition that is frequently used to make that scene longer. In her compression of this scene, Neely does not mention the slight that occurs in Lambert's version, but then she has already noted that Barbara has discouraged Willie's romantic advances for seven years. Although both the death bell and the small birds condemn Barbara's hardheartedness in Neely's version, such condemnation is absent from Lambert's, despite the fact that Barbara "came downstairs a-smilin'" and "all the ladies" "were ashamed" for her. The songs' conclusions are similar, though only in Lambert's version does Barbara kiss the corpse. The "long (soft) and narrow" bed requested by Barbara is, of course, her coffin.

A

Sung by Mrs. Corie Lambert, Mobile, 3 September 1945.

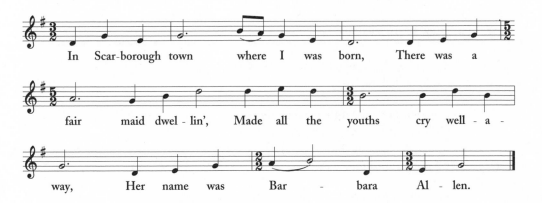

In Scar-borough town where I was born, There was a fair maid dwel-lin', Made all the youths cry well-a-way, Her name was Bar-bara Al-len.

2 He sent his servant to the town,
   Where Barbara was a-dwelling:
   "My master's sick and he sent for you,
   And for your sake he's dying."

3 Slowly, slowly, she rose up,
   And slowly she went to him,
   And all the ladies standing around
   Were ashamed for Barbara Allen.

4 "Don't you remember the other day,
   When you were in town a-drinkin',
   You drank and toasted the ladies all around,
   And slighted Barbara Allen."

5 "Yes I remember the other day
   When I was in town a-drinkin'.
   I drank and toasted the ladies all around,
   But slighted Barbara Allen."

6 He turned his pale face to the wall
   And turned his back upon her.
   "Adieu, adieu to the ladies all around.
   Be kind to Barbara Allen."

7 And as she turned to leave the room,
   She came downstairs a-smilin',
   And all the people standing around
   Gave way to Barbara Allen.

8   As she was walking through the town
    She heard his death bell ringing,
    And she looked to the east, she looked to the west,
    And saw his cold corpse coming.

9   "Lay down, lay down his corpse," she said,
    "That I may kiss upon him."
    The more she kissed, the more she wept,
    And bursted out a-cryin'.

10 "Oh Mother, oh Mother, make my bed,
    Go make it long and narrow;
    Sweet William died for me today,
    I'll die for him tomorrow."

11 Sweet William was buried in one churchyard,
    And Barbara in another;
    A rosebud sprang out of William's grave,
    Out of Barbara's sprang a green brier.

12 They grew and grew to the high church top,
    And there they grew no higher.
    They wrapped and tied in a true love's knot
    With the rose wrapped round the brier.

B

Sung by Miss Lola Neely, Section, 12 July 1947.

1   In London town where I once did dwell,
    There's where I got my learning,
    I fell in love with a pretty young girl,
    And her name was Barbara Allen.

2   I courted her for seven long years;
    She said she would not have me.
    Then straight way home as I could go,
    And liken to a died.

3   I wrote her a letter on my dying bed,
    I wrote it slow and moving.
    "Go take this letter to my old true love
    And tell her I was dying."

4 She took it in her lily-white hand,
   She read it slow and moving.
   "Go take this letter back to him,
   And tell him I'm a-coming."

5 As she passed by his dying bed,
   She saw his pale face quivering.
   "No better, no better I'll never be
   Until I get Barbara Allen."

6 As she passed by his dying bed,
   "You're sick and almost dying.
   No better, no better you'll ever be,
   For you can't get Barbara Allen."

7 As she went down the long stone steps,
   She heard the death bell toning,
   And every bell appeared to say,
   "Hard-hearted Barbara Allen."

8 As she went down the long piney walk,
   She heard some small birds singing,
   And every bird appeared to say,
   "Hard-hearted Barbara Allen."

9 She looked to the east, she looked to the west,
   She saw the pale corpse coming.
   "Go bring the pale corpse to me,
   And let me gaze upon him.

10 "Oh Mama, Mama, go make my bed;
   Make it soft and narrow.
   Sweet Willie died for me today,
   I'll die for him tomorrow."

11 They buried sweet Willie in the old church yard;
   They buried Miss Barbara beside him,
   And out of his grave there sprang a red rose,
   And out of hers a brier.

12 They grew to the top of the old church tower;
   They could not grow any higher;
   They hooked, they tied in a lovers' knot,
   The red rose and the brier.

Rosella

(Laws F 1, The Jealous Lover)

Although this ballad may be derived originally from a British broadside, it is clearly American. It has flourished in oral tradition and become one of this country's most popular folksongs. It was also quite popular among "hillbilly" recording artists in the 1920s and 1930s. This version is shorter than many recovered texts, but no version adequately explains the man's motive for murdering the woman usually called Florella. This omission suggests that the motive may have been "unspeakable": sexual jealousy or pregnancy out of wedlock. Mrs. Trotter tells us that "the jealous man was not Rosella's true lover. Her true lover wrote this ballad." This song is the subject of Thomas Hart Benton's famous painting, *The Jealous Lover of Lone Green Valley*.

Sung by Mrs. Pearl Trotter, Troy, 22 July 1946.

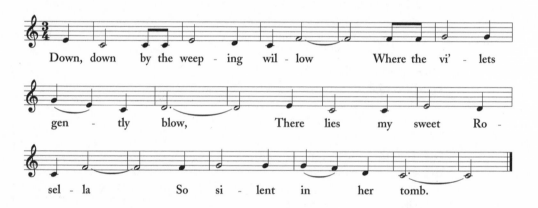

2 One night as the moon shone brightly,
   As bright as it ever did shine,
   She sat in her lonely cabin;
   Her jealous lover came by.

3 "My love, let's go and wander,
   My love, let's go and roam;
   My love, let's go and wander,
   My love, let's go and roam."

4 "The night seems dark and dreary,
   Too dark for me to roam;
   Unless someone was near me,
   I'd rather be at home."

5 He looked at her a moment;
  The fire flashed in his eyes.
  He said, "My sweet Rosella,
  This moment you must die."

6 Down, down she knelt beside him,
  And begged him to spare her life,
  But deep into her bosom
  He pressed that deadly knife.

True Lovers Part

(Laws G 21, The Silver Dagger)

Although the opening lines and various literary touches of this American ballad suggest its composition for the broadside press, no such printed version of "The Silver Dagger" has ever been located. The song is quite frequently found in southern and western states, less frequently in the Midwest, and hardly at all in the Northeast. It often shares images, or whole stanzas, with "The Drowsy Sleeper," though not with our Alabama version (p. 6). In Mrs. Estes's fourth stanza, it would seem that "duty" might be a mishearing for "pity."

Sung by Mrs. J. K. Estes, Fort Payne, 12 June 1947.

Come in fair maids and pay at-ten-tion To these few words I'm a-bout to write. They're just as true as ev-er was men-tioned Con-cern-ing a fair and love-ly bride.

2 I courted her to be my darling;
  I loved her as I loved my life;
  I often vowed and thought I'd make her
  My lawful and my wedded wife.

3 But when my parents came to learn this
   They strove to part us night and day,
   Saying, "Son, oh Son, oh Son, don't have her
   For she's a poor girl, I've heard them say."

4 Upon my bended knees I pleaded,
   Saying "Oh, dear Father, duty me.
   I beg, I beg to not be denied her
   For what would this world be without her to me?"

5 And when this maiden came to learn this,
   She soon resolved what she would do.
   She wandered far and left the city,
   No more the pleasant grove to view.

6 She wandered to a flowing river
   And there for death she did prepare,
   Saying, "Here I lay my youthful body
   For I must sink in deep despair."

7 She then drew forth her silver dagger
   And strove it through her snow white breast.
   At first she reeled and then she staggered,
   Saying, "Oh my love, I'm going to rest."

8 Me being close by and hearing her mourning,
   Knowing her familiar voice,
   I ran, I ran like one distracted,
   Saying, "Oh my love, I'm afraid you're lost."

9 I then picked up the bleeding body;
   I rolled it over in my arms.
   "Is there no friends or foes can save her,
   Or must she die with all her charms?"

10 Her coal black eyes like stars she opened,
   Said, "Oh my love, you've come too late.
   Prepare to meet me in Mount Zion
   Where all our joys will be complete."

11 I then picked up the bloody dagger
   And strove it through my own dear heart.
   Oh let this be a woeful warning
   To all who do true lovers part.

Johnson City

(Laws P 24, The Butcher Boy)

This ballad of a girl who commits suicide after being forsaken by her young man, usually a butcher boy, is widely current in the southern United States and has been often recorded, most notably by Buell Kazee. Its narrative technique is particularly interesting. The girl speaks the first four stanzas and, by committing to paper her despairing thoughts and burial instructions, is able to resume speaking in the last two stanzas, following a third-person narration of the finding of her dead body in the fifth stanza. It has not been determined whether this song is of British or American origin.

Sung by Mr. Robert Wallace, Tuscaloosa, 18 June 1948.

"In John-son City where I did dwell, There lived a boy I loved so well. He court-ed me my life a - way, And then with me he would not stay.

2 "There lived another girl in that same town,
   She took my love and set him down,
   He tells to her what he once told me,
   She has more silver and gold, you see.

3 "Her silver will melt, her gold will fly,
   And she will be as poor as I,
   And he will leave her all alone
   To sit and weep by a sad hearth stone.

4 "Oh Mother dear, go make my bed,
   Where I can lay my weary head,
   And bring a chair and I'll sit down,
   With a pen and ink I'll write it down."

5 Her father come home, the door he broke,
   He found her hanging by a rope.
   He took his knife and cut her down,
   And on her breast these words he found.

6 "Oh Mother dear, you cannot see,
   What sorrow this has brought to me;
   First I was to be this young man's wife,
   But on this rope I'll end my life.

7 "Go dig my grave both wide and deep,
   And put the stones at my head and feet,
   And on my breast place a white turtledove,
   To show the world I died of love."

Chapter 3
Love's Disappointments

Lord Lovel

(Child 75)

The oral tradition of "Lord Lovel" has been strongly influenced by the appearance of the song in numerous songbooks and broadsides. Because of this, its many American versions do not vary greatly. "Lord Lovel" is a classic argument for considering the ballad as song rather than as poem, because it combines a sad and sentimental story with a lilting and rollicking tune. Whether this works to its advantage or disadvantage must be left to the opinion of each listener, but it is certainly the element of the ballad that has caused versions similar to this to be considered a comic song and that has stimulated the many parodies written of it.

There are some interesting supernatural elements in "Lord Lovel." An ominous premonition seems contained in the "languishing thoughts" of the third stanza, and a lover's kissing the corpse of his beloved ensures his immediate death. In the union of the rose and brier, which concludes the ballad, we see the traditional symbolism of love transcending death. The beginning of the seventh stanza is a ballad convention and means simply that Lord Lovel died on the day following Lady Nancy Bell's death. "Kirk" in the eighth stanza is the Scottish word for "church." Among recorded American singers, only Miss Pillans uses that term, which jars with the ballad's setting of "London town."

Sung by Miss Laura Pillans, Mobile, 3 September 1945.

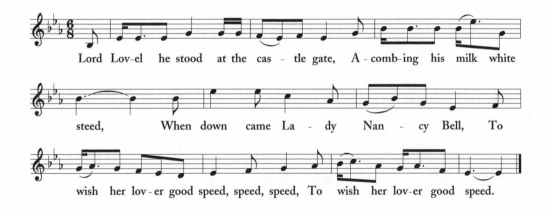

Lord Lov-el he stood at the cas - tle gate, A - comb-ing his milk white steed, When down came La - dy Nan - cy Bell, To wish her lov - er good speed, speed, speed, To wish her lov-er good speed.

2 "Oh where are you going, Lord Lovel?" she said,
"Oh where are you going?" said she.
"I'm going, my fair Lady Nancy Bell,
Far countries for to see, see, see,
Far countries for to see."

3 He traveled and traveled, a year and a day,
Or it might be two or three,
When languishing thoughts came into his head,
Lady Nancy for to see, see, see,
Lady Nancy for to see.

4 He traveled and traveled, as fast as he could,
Till he came to London town,
And there he encountered a funeral train,
With the mourners all weeping around, 'round, 'round,
With the mourners all weeping around.

5 "Oh, who is it dead, good people?" he said,
"Oh, who is it dead?" said he.
"'Tis the Lord's only daughter," the people replied,
"And they called her the Lady Nancy, 'cy, 'cy,
And they called her the Lady Nancy."

6 He bade them to open the coffin straightway,
And then he knelt right down,
And there he kissed the clay cold corpse,
While the tears they came trickling down, down, down,
While the tears they came trickling down.

7 Lady Nancy she died as it might be today,
Lord Lovel he died on the morrow,
Lady Nancy she died of pure, pure grief,
Lord Lovel he died of sorrow, 'orrow, 'orrow,
Lord Lovel he died of sorrow.

8 Lord Lovel was buried in St. Martin's Kirk,
Lady Nancy was laid in the choir,
And out of her bosom there grew a red rose,
And out of his bosom a brier, 'rier, 'rier,
And out of his bosom a brier.

9 And they grew and they grew till they reached the church top,
And then couldn't grow any higher,
And there they entwined in a true lovers' knot,
Which all true lovers admire, 'rire, 'rire,
Which all true lovers admire.

Sailor Shantey

(Laws K 12, The Sailor Boy I)

This ballad was published as a broadside in England during the nineteenth century, included in a number of twentieth-century American songbooks, and recorded by popular artists such as Vernon Dalhart and the Carter Family. Most traditional versions tell a story very similar to that of Mrs. Crooks. It is unclear whether the fair lady's handling of the boat in the fifth stanza springs from a desire to regain the shore or to kill herself. Both courses of action appear in other versions. The funeral directions in the last stanza are much the same as those that conclude "Johnson City" (p. 29).

Sung by Mrs. Gertrude Ladnier Crooks, Point Clear, 7 July 1947.

"Ear-ly, ear - ly all in the spring My love sailed out to save his King. The rag-ing sea and the wind blew high, When part-ed me from a sail-or boy.

2 "Oh Father, Father, build me a boat.
   Out on the ocean I mean to float
   To hail each friend's ship as they pass by,
   And I'll inquire of my sailor boy."

3 She had not sailed but a league or two
   When she was met by a ship's full crew.
   "Oh Captain, Captain, tell me true,
   Does my Sweet Willie sail among your crew?"

4 "Indeed, fair lady, he is not here.
   He's lost on an island, I do fear;
   As a long green island as I passed by,
   At last I saw your Willie die."

5 She wrung her hands and she tore her hair;
   She looked like a lady in great despair.
   She dashed her small boat amid the rocks,
   Saying, "How can I live when my love is lost?

6 "Go dress all sailors up in black,
   And on tomorrow I'll do the same.
   From the cabin boy to the mainmast high,
   I mourn for the loss of my sailor boy.

7 "Go dig my grave both wide and deep,
   Place a marble stone at my head and feet,
   And upon my breast a turtledove
   To show to the world that I died for love."

Fair Lady Bright

(Laws M 3)

Although this song of a lover's unhappy return from military service probably had an English origin, it is now much better known in the United States than in the British Isles. It seems that "never" in the third line of Miss Craven's first stanza should be either "love she" or "love I." No American text makes completely clear the meaning of the second half of the third stanza. Is it possible, because both are called "bright," that the sight of the soldiers' glittering arms reminds the lover of his lady's beauty?

Sung by Miss Callie Craven, Gadsden, in late 1945 or early 1946.

Once I court-ed a fair la-dy bright And on her placed my
whole heart's de-light. I court-ed her for love and
nev-er did ob-tain, Sure that she has no rea-son to com-plain.

2 I went to see my love, it was once or twice a day,
   To see whether I could forget my love or nay;
   But when I got there, she made me this reply,
   "I love the man that loves me and for him I'll die."

3 To the war I resolved then to go
To see whether I could forget my love or no;
But when I got there the army shined so bright,
The deepest of my thoughts was my whole heart's delight.

4 Three long years in the service of my land,
The end of three years I returned home again;
My eyes so full of tears, my heart so full of woe,
To her father's house I resolved then to go.

5 Her father saw me coming and he wrang his hands and cried,
"My daughter dearly loved you and for your sake has died."
"Oh where is my love and how does she do?
If this be her grave, how I wish mine here too."

6 There I stood like a lamb to be slain,
Tears falling down like showers of rain.
Come all ye fair lovers, come pity poor me,
Come pity my misfortune and sad misery.

Winter's Night

This ballad is made up of stanzas frequently found in other songs. The third and fourth stanzas appear in "The Lass of Roch Royal" (Child 76), in many other songs, and separately as a little song by themselves. The second stanza appears as the last stanza of Robert Burns's "A Red, Red Rose" but is most likely derived from Burns's source rather than from his poem itself. The fifth and sixth stanzas are shared with "The Lonesome Dove" (see p. 125). Perhaps because of this conglomeration, it is difficult to determine who is speaking at several points in Miss Craven's version. The male narrator clearly speaks in the first, second, third, and seventh stanzas; the woman speaks in the fourth stanza. But the fifth and sixth stanzas must be divided arbitrarily between the speakers, and the eighth stanza seems appropriate to either.

Sung by Miss Callie Craven, Gadsden, 27 July 1945.

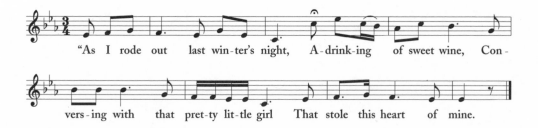

2 "So fare you well my own true love,
   So fare you well for a while.
   I'll go away and here you stay,
   If I go ten thousand miles.

3 "Oh, who will shoe your feet, my love,
   And who will glove your hands,
   And who will kiss your red rosy cheeks,
   While I'm gone to the foreign lands?"

4 "My father will shoe my feet, my love,
   My mother will glove my hands,
   And you may kiss my red rosy cheeks,
   When you come from the foreign lands."

5 Oh, don't you see that lonesome dove,
   A-flying from vine to vine,
   A-mourning for the loss of a mate,
   And why not me for mine?

6 Yes, love, I see that lonesome dove,
   A-flying from vine to vine,
   A-mourning for the loss of a mate,
   Just like I am for mine.

7 "If I am taken sick, my love,
   Whilst I'm so far from home,
   I hope that God will ease my pain,
   And listen to my mourn."

8 I wish to God I'd-a never been born,
   Or I'd-a died when I was young.
   I never would have mourned for the loss of a mate,
   Nor loved no other one.

The Rich Irish Lady

(Laws P 9, closely related to Child 295, The Brown Girl)

In "The Brown Girl" (Child 295), the title character is scorned by a young man who jilts her for a fairer lover. When he later falls in love with the brown girl and becomes "lovesick," she achieves her revenge by refusing to have anything to do with him, and he dies. This ballad is clearly related both to Child 84, "Barbara Allen" (see p. 22), and to Child 73, "Lord Thomas and Fair Annet," of which Mrs. Lambert's "The Brown Girl" (p. 19) is a variant. In America, a number of broadside ballads, usually titled "The Rich Irish Lady," reverse this pattern by having the woman scorn the man, and later die for lack of his cure. Mrs. Estes's ballad is in this tradition. In British versions of "The Brown Girl," as in all versions of "Barbara Allen," it is taken for granted that lovesickness can be cured if the ill one's love is returned by the beloved. "The Rich Irish Lady," however, rationalizes this concept in an interesting fashion by making the scorned young man a physician. Estes's sixth stanza, for instance, makes it clear that Sally has summoned the man to her sickbed because he is a doctor, not because he once loved her. In fact, she never says that his love would make her better, and he refuses to use his medical skill to cure her. So much for the power of love and the Hippocratic oath.

Sung by Mrs. J. K. Estes, Fort Payne, 12 June 1947.

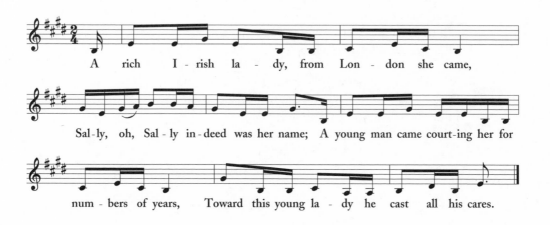

A rich I-rish la-dy, from Lon-don she came, Sal-ly, oh, Sal-ly in-deed was her name; A young man came court-ing her for num-bers of years, Toward this young la-dy he cast all his cares.

2 Her riches being great and her honor being high,
   Toward this young man she scarcely cast her eye.
   "I scorn for to hate you or any other man;
   As far as to love you I know I never can.

3 "I scorn for to hate you or any of your discourse,
  But I know I'll never marry you unless I am forced."
  "Oh Sally, oh Sally, oh Sally," says he,
  "I'm sorry that my love and your love cannot agree."

4 Five and twenty weeks came on and quickly passed.
  He heard of this young lady's downfall at last.
  She sent for this young man all like as to die;
  All tangled in love and she knew not for why.

5 He went stepping down all by her bedside;
  Said "Where is the pain, in your head or in your side?"
  "Oh no, my dear young doctor, you've hardly guessed the part;
  The pain lights a-piercing, it lights a-near my heart."

6 "Am I the young doctor that you have summoned here,
  Or am I the young man that once loved you dear?"
  "You are the young doctor to kill or to cure;
  Without your assistance I'll die, I am sure."

7 "Oh Sally, oh Sally, oh Sally," said he,
  Don't you remember the time you slighted me?
  I courted you with honor, you slighted me with scorn,
  And now I reward you of times past and gone."

8 "Of times past and gone, Sir, I hope you will forgive,
  Spare me, oh spare me, a while yet to live."
  "I'll never forgive you as long as I have breath;
  I'll dance on your grave when you lie cold and dead."

9 She's taken from her fingers, gold diamond rings three,
  Said, "Take these and wear them while dancing on me.
  I'll freely forgive you, so plainly as you see,
  I'm ruined, I'm ruined by following thee."

∽

Robin Gray

The Scottish ballad of "Auld Robin Gray" was written by Lady Anne Lindsay in 1771, when she was twenty-one years old. Lady Anne said she wished to create "some little history of virtuous distress in humble life." The song was a favorite of Sir Walter Scott, who cited it in his novel *The Pirate* and prepared an edition of the ballad, its sequels, and the story of its composition. Although sometimes recovered from oral tradition in Scotland, "Old Robin Gray" is very rare in America. Mrs. McClure said this was the favorite song of her mother, from whom she learned it.

Sung by Mrs. Venetia Danner McClure, Mobile, 8 July 1947.

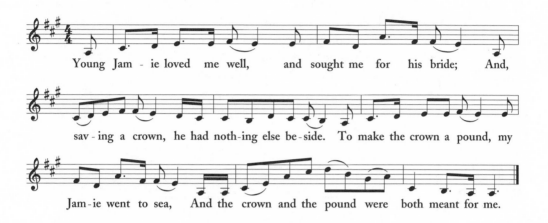

2 He had not gone long, a week and only two,
   When my father brake his arm and our cow was stole away;
   My mother she fell sick, and Jamie had to sea,
   And old Robin Gray came a-courting me.

3 My father urged me so. Though my mother did not speak,
   She looked into my face till I thought my heart would break.
   So I gave him my hand, though my heart was out to sea,
   And old Robin Gray is a good man to me.

4 I had not been a wife a week but only four,
   When sitting so sadly at my own cottage door,
   I saw my Jamie's ghost, for I could not think it he,
   Till he said, "I've come back, love, to marry thee."

5 O sad did we greet and muckle did we say.
   We took but a kiss, then we took ourselves away.
   I wish I were dead, but I'm not like to die,
   And why do I live to say "Woe is me."

6 I go like a ghost; I care no more to spin.
   I dare not think of Jamie, for that would be a sin.
   I do my best a good wife to be,
   For old Robin Gray, he's a good man to me.

Logan O. Bucken

Not frequently found in American tradition, the Scottish song "O Logie O' Buchan" was probably written by the Jacobite George Halket of Aberdeen in the mid–eighteenth century. Mrs. Crick has some difficulty with the song's dialect. In the earliest printed versions, the first and third lines of the chorus are these: "Then think na lang, lassie, though I gang awa' / The summer is coming, cold winter's awa'." To delve is to dig, as a gardener; a creepet is a low stool, here before a spinning wheel; and the broken six-pence serves as a lovers' token and means of identification.

Sung by Mrs. C. N. Crick, Sheffield, 10 June 1947.

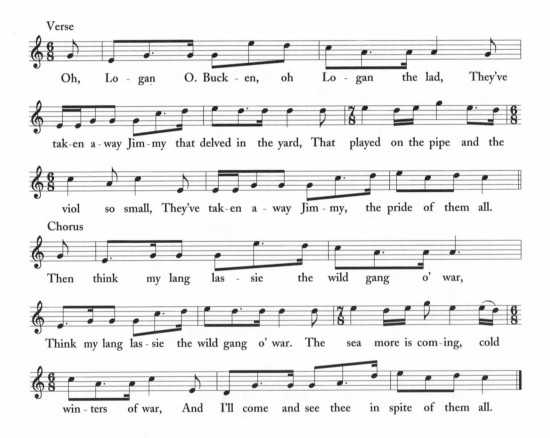

Verse

Oh, Lo-gan O. Buck-en, oh Lo-gan the lad, They've

tak-en a-way Jim-my that delved in the yard, That played on the pipe and the

viol so small, They've tak-en a-way Jim-my, the pride of them all.

Chorus

Then think my lang las-sie the wild gang o' war,

Think my lang las-sie the wild gang o' war. The sea more is com-ing, cold

win-ters of war, And I'll come and see thee in spite of them all.

2 My mother looks sulky, my daddy looks sour,
  And frown upon Jimmy because he is poor.
  I love them as well as a daughter could do,
  But ne'er half so well, my Jimmy, as you.

Chorus

3   I sit at my creepet and work at my wheel,
     And think of the laddie that loves me so weel;
     He had but a sixpence, he brake it in twa,
     He give me the halfet, and he gang the war.

Chorus

Joe Bowers

(Laws B 14)

This is one of the best-known songs about the California gold rush of the mid–nineteenth century. Although its authorship is disputed, "Joe Bowers" almost certainly comes to us from the professional minstrel stage. The song quickly entered oral tradition, however, and was sung enthusiastically by folks who had both a hard life and a sense of humor. The last two lines of Ms. MacDonald's fourth stanza are obscure, but they may mean that Joe did indeed strike gold ("the shiner"), a success often mentioned in other versions of the ballad. Many singers have fun with the second stanza's punning combination of "asked" (pronounced "axed") and "whack," but only this version extends that play to a third word by changing the girl's name to "Hack" from the usual "Black." "Joe Bowers" may have stimulated the composition of "Sweet Betsy from Pike," the best-known ballad of the westward migration. The humor in the ballads is very similar, and "Sweet Betsy" heads west with "her lover Ike." It does not stretch credibility to assume that Ike's last name might well have been Bowers.

Sung by Ms. Fannie MacDonald, Troy, 23 July 1947.

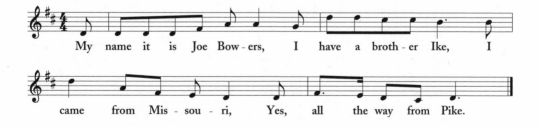

2 I fell in love with a girl out there,
And her name was Sally Hack.
I asked her if she'd marry me,
And she said it was a whack.

3 Said she to me, "Joe Bowers,
Before you hitch for life,
You'd better get a little house,
To keep a little wife."

4 I went to California;
Put in my biggest licks,
And came down on the shiner
Just like a thousand bricks.

5 I worked both late and early,
Through rain and ice and snow.
I was working for my Sally dear;
It was all the same by Joe.

6 At last I got a letter;
It was from brother Ike.
It came from Missouri,
All the way from Pike.

7 It said that Sally was false to me
And all her love had fled.
Sally had married a butcher,
And the butcher's hair was red.

8 More than that the letter said,
'Twas enough to make one swear,
And Sally had a baby,
And the baby had red hair.

Jack and Joe

Written for the vaudeville stage by William B. Gray in 1894, this song achieved wide popularity as recorded by Georgia "hillbilly" singer Riley Puckett. It quickly moved into tradition and has long been a favorite of many Alabama folksingers, whose versions differ little one from another. It is also known as "Give My Love to Nell."

Sung by Mrs. Etoel Prim, Black, 13 August 1946.

Three years a-go when Jack and Joe Set sail a-cross the foam, They vowed a for-tune each must make Be-fore re-turn-ing home.

In one year Jack gained his wealth And sailed for home one day. When those boys shook hands to part Poor Joe could on-ly say:

"Give my love to Nel-lie, Jack, And kiss her once for me. The dear-est girl in all the world, I know you'll say 'tis she.

Greet her kind-ly, Jack old boy, And tell her I am well." The part-ing words were "Don't for-get To give my love to Nell."

2 Three years had passed when Joe at last
Gained wealth enough for life.
He sailed across the foam one day
To make sweet Nell his wife,
But soon he learned that Jack and Nell
One year ago had wed.
He now regrets and sighs and frets
That he had ever said:

Chorus

3 They chanced to meet upon the street.
   Said Joe: "You selfish elf,
   The next girl that I learn to love
   I'll kiss her for myself.
   But all is fair in love they say,
   And since you've gone and wed,
   I'll not be angry with you, Jack."
   And once again he said:

Chorus

That Little Black Mustache

Copyrighted by John Foster and R. A. King in 1926, this music hall ballad has found considerable favor in Alabama and varies very little from singer to singer. Fragments remembered by three informants fit together neatly to form a coherent whole. In other versions, the second line of the fifth stanza appears as "She was worth her weight in gold."

A

Sung by Miss Callie Craven, Gadsden, 11 August 1945.

Oh, once I had a charm - ing beau, I
His pock - ets they were filled with gold, Al -

loved him dear as life; I sure - ly thought the
though he cut a dash With his dia - mond ring, a

time would come When I would be his wife.
watch and a chain, And his dar - ling black mus - tache.

Oh, that lit-tle black mus-tache, that lit-tle black mus-tache,
Ev-ery time I think of it, my heart beats quick as a flash. Oh, that
lit-tle black mus-tache, that lit-tle black mus-tache, But you must know that I've
lost my beau with his lit-tle black mus-tache.

B

Sung by Mrs. Myrtle Love Hester, Florence, 6 August 1945.

3 He came to see me last Sunday night
   And stayed till almost three;
   He said he never loved a girl
   As well as he loved me.

4 He said we would live in the finest style
   For he had plenty of cash,
   And then he placed upon my lips
   That charming black mustache.

   Chorus

5 There came along a sour old maid
   Who wore her wrath in gold;
   She wore false teeth, she wore false hair;
   She was forty-five years old.

C

Sung by Mrs. George Williams, East Gadsden, 1945.

6   So cruelly he deserted me
    Just for that old maid's cash,
    And that's the way I lost my beau
    With his little black mustache.

    Chorus

7   And now they live across the way
    In some grand mansion old.
    She married him for his black mustache;
    He married her for her gold.

8   Come all young ladies, take warning of me,
    And never be so rash,
    But leave alone those stylish lads
    With a little black mustache.

    Chorus

Chapter 4
Pathos/Children

～

It Rained, It Mist

(Child 155, Sir Hugh, or The Jew's Daughter)

In its early forms, this ballad presented the folk legend, first recorded in the thirteenth century, of little Sir Hugh of Lincoln, who was supposedly ritually tortured and crucified by Jews. In various supernatural ways, his dead body testified against his murderers, who were executed. The most famous literary rendition of this superstitious bigotry is Geoffrey Chaucer's "The Prioress' Tale." The anti-Semitism and miracles, essential to the original story, have dropped out of modern versions of the ballad, though the napkin placed on the victim's face may recall ritual murder. The attraction of the story for modern singers seems to lie in the malevolence of the beautiful lady's enticement, the brutality of the murder, and the rather extended pathos of the boy's death. Mrs. Young, who sang only the first four and the ninth stanzas here for Arnold, insisted that he get permission from her sister, from whom she had learned the song, before he printed it. From that sister, Mrs. Edith Procter of Morehead, Kentucky, Arnold received not only permission to print but also the fifth through eighth stanzas. Despite her insistence on the children's being allowed to play only "on the playing ground," Young does not make clear that the boy's ball must have been thrown from that "playing ground" into the lady's garden, or perhaps into her house through a window.

Sung by Mrs. Nell Young, Huntsville, 8 August 1945.

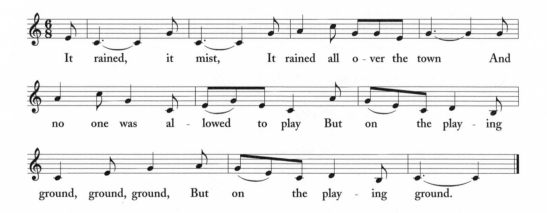

2 First too high and then too low
   All over St. John's town
   Where no one was allowed to play
   But on the playing ground, ground, ground,
   But on the playing ground.

3 Out stepped a lady
   All fairly dressed in green.
   "Come in, come in, my little one;
   You shall have your ball again, 'gain, 'gain,
   You shall have your ball again."

4 "I will come in, I won't come in,
   I will not enter your door,
   I've often heard little ones come in
   And never come out anymore, more, more,
   And never come out anymore."

5 First she showed him a red rosy apple,
   And then she showed him a chain,
   Then she showed him a gold diamond ring
   To 'vite the little one in, in, in,
   To 'vite the little one in.

6 She took him by the lily-white hand,
   She led him through the hall,
   She led him to the far back room
   Where no one could hear his call, call, call,
   Where no one could hear his call.

7 She placed a napkin over his face,
   She pinned it with a pin,
   And then she taken a little penknife
   And jobbin' his little heart in, in, in,
   And jobbin' his little heart in.

8 "Oh spare my life, oh spare my life,
   Oh spare my life," said he.
   "If you will only spare my life
   Some gold I'll give to thee, thee, thee,
   Some gold I'll give to thee.

9 "Place a prayerbook at my head,
   A candle at my feet,
   And if my playmates ask for me,

Just tell them that Willie is dead, dead, dead,
Just tell them that Willie is dead."

Three Babes

(Child 79, The Wife of Usher's Well)

"Three Babes" is now much more frequently found in the oral tradition of the American South than in that of the land of its origin. In its oldest British versions, the song tells of the reaction of "the wife of Usher's well" to the deaths at sea of her "three stout and stalwart sons." She places a curse on the sea that can only be lifted by the youths' return. The boys come back as ghosts and act very much like the babes of Mrs. Hill's version. In the ballad's movement from Britain to America, the young men become "babes" (of either sex) and most of the pagan elements are Christianized. At Christmas, the ghosts come home in response to a prayer, rather than to a curse, and they have to return to the paradise of "our Savior." Like most ballad ghosts, these are not luminous bits of ectoplasm but substantial flesh and blood. That they are dead is revealed by things other than their appearance: they refuse to eat mortal food and must depart at daybreak. Another conventional superstition—that excessive grief disturbs the dead—appears in a version sung by Mrs. Pearl Trotter (Troy, 22 July 1946). After bidding farewell to their mother, the babes ask her not to weep for them because "The tears you shed, sweet mother dear, / Will wet our winding sheet." Hill's rather awkward last two lines seem to mean that the babes will never again return to this world. Like "Lord Lovel" with its rose and brier motif, "Three Babes" achieves much of its emotional impact by presenting a grieving and deep love that endures even beyond death. In 1928, Buell Kazee made an excellent, very popular, and highly influential recording of the song.

Sung by Mrs. Lena Hill, Lexington, 10 June 1947.

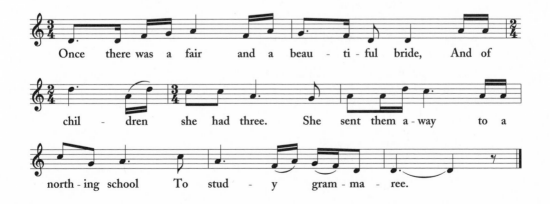

Once there was a fair and a beau - ti - ful bride, And of
chil - dren she had three. She sent them a - way to a
north - ing school To stud - y gram - ma - ree.

2 They had not been gone but a very short time,
Just three months to a day,
When sickness came all over that land,
And it took her babes away.

3 "There was a King in the heavens above,
Who choosed to wear a crown,
And I wish he would send home to me my babes,
Tonight or in the morning soon."

4 The Christmas times was a-drawing nigh,
And the nights both long and cold,
When those little babes come running home,
All into their mama's room.

5 She fixed the table in the backward room,
And over it spread a snow white cloth,
And over it set each bread and wine,
Where yonder her babes might eat.

6 "Come eat, come eat, ye three little babes,
Come and eat your bread and drink your wine."
"No, Mama dear, we cannot eat your bread,
Nor neither can we drink your wine."

7 She fixed the bed in the backward room,
And over it spread a snow white sheet,
And over it run a golden cover,
Where yonder her babes might sleep.

8 "Wake up, wake up," said the older one,
"For the fowls are crowing for day,
And yonder stands our Savior dear,
To Him we must retire.

9 "Farewell to Mommy and Poppy too,
Farewell to the kitty and the queen.
But as far as to be in the wickedsome world,
I never expect to be."

When the Parley Dew Is Faded

Some children really know how to rub it in. "Parley," of course, should be "pearly." The chorus is sung to the same tune as the verse.

Sung by Mrs. Lena Hill, Lexington, 24 August 1945.

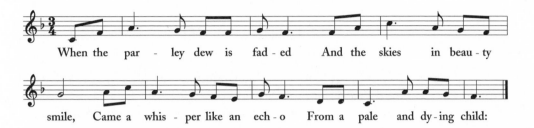

When the par - ley dew is fad - ed And the skies in beau - ty

smile, Came a whis - per like an ech - o From a pale and dy - ing child:

2 "Mother, in that golden region,
  With its parley gate so bright,
  Is there room among the angels
  For the spirit of your child?

  Chorus
  "Tell me truly, darling mother,
  Is there room in heaven for me;
  Shall I gain that land of spirit
  And a shining angel be?

3 "Mother, raise me just a moment.
  You forgive me when you told me
  I was always in your way,
  When I saw you was angry,

4 "You was sorry in a moment,
  I could see it on your brow;
  But you will not mind it, Mother,
  You need not recall it now.

  Chorus

5 "When my baby sister calls me
  And you hear my voice no more,
  When she plays among the roses
  By our little cottage door,

6 "Never chide her when you angry;
　Do it kindly and in love,
　That you both may dwell with Mamie
　In the shining land above."

Chorus

The Orphan Girl

This very popular song contains a remarkable number of features usually associated with melodrama: the dark and stormy night, the sneering rich man on his velvet couch, and the starving orphan girl in the tattered clothes who freezes to death on the steps of luxury. It was a hit on early radio shows and phonograph records, particularly as sung by Buell Kazee.

Sung by Miss Callie Craven, Gadsden, 11 August 1945.

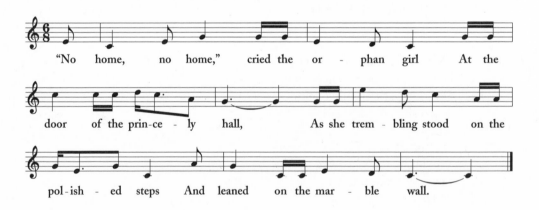

"No home, no home," cried the or - phan girl At the
door of the prin-ce - ly hall, As she trem - bling stood on the
pol-ish - ed steps And leaned on the mar - ble wall.

2 Her clothes were thin, her feet were bare,
　But the snow had covered her head.
　"Give me a home," she feebly said,
　"A home and a bit of bread.

3 "My father lost I never knew,"
   While the tears dimmed her eyes so bright.
   "My mother sleeps in a new-made grave;
   It is an orphan that begs tonight."

4 The night was dark and the snow fell fast,
   But the rich man shut his door,
   With his proud lips curved with scorn as he said,
   "No home, no bread, for the poor."

5 "I must freeze," she said, and sank to the floor
   And strove to cover her feet;
   Her faded dress all tattered and torn
   All covered in snow and sleet.

6 The rich man sleeps on his velvet couch
   And dreams of his silver and gold,
   While the orphan sleeps on a bed of snow,
   And Mama so cold, so cold.

7 The night was dark and the night wind blew,
   The hours rolled on like a funeral knell,
   The earth seems wrapped in a winding sheet,
   And the dizzling snow still fell.

8 The morning dawned and the orphan girl
   Still lay at the rich man's door,
   But her spirit had fled to a world above
   Where there's room and bread for the poor.

Put My Little Shoes Away

It is perhaps strange, but certainly true, that empty shoes are one of the most tear-jerking of all signs of a child's death in these sentimental pieces. Samuel N. Mitchell wrote the lyrics and Charles E. Pratt composed the tune for this hit of 1873. The song was popular on early radio and was recorded frequently in the first half of the twentieth century.

Sung by Miss Callie Craven, Gadsden, 26 August 1945.

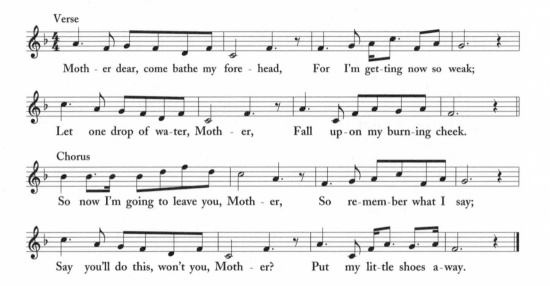

Moth - er dear, come bathe my fore - head, For I'm get-ting now so weak;

Let one drop of wa-ter, Moth - er, Fall up-on my burn-ing cheek.

So now I'm going to leave you, Moth - er, So re-mem-ber what I say;

Say you'll do this, won't you, Moth - er? Put my lit-tle shoes a-way.

2 Santy Claus he brought them to me
With another lot of things,
And I think he brought an angel
With a pair of golden wings.

Chorus

3 Tell my loving little schoolmates
That I never no more shall see;
Give them all my toys, Mother,
Put my little shoes away.

Chorus

4 Till my brother soon grows larger,
  Then they'll fit his little feet;
  He will look so neat and handsome
  As he runs along the street.

Chorus

The Blind Child's Prayer

This is one of the most popular of the sentimental pieces. It appeared in songsters of the 1860s and has been found in every section of the United States for at least a hundred years. The ballad's pursuit of pathos and melodrama is calculated and transparent, but still very effective for many singers and audiences. It was certainly popular with early "hillbilly" recording artists.

Sung by Mr. Lytle Burns, Florence, 9 June 1947.

"They tell me, Fa-ther, that to-night You wed an-oth-er bride, That you will clasp her in your arms Where my poor moth-er died.

2 "They say her name is Mary, too,
  The name my mother bore.
  Oh Father, is she kind and true
  Like the one you loved before?

3 "And is her step so soft and light,
  Her voice so sweet and mild?
  Oh Father, will she care for me,
  Your blind and helpless child?

4 "Oh Father, do not bid me come
   To meet your new-made bride.
   I cannot meet her in the room
   Where my poor mother died.

5 "There hangs her picture on the wall,
   Her books are lying there,
   And there is where her soft hands touched,
   And there's her vacant chair,

6 "The chair by which I used to kneel
   To say my evening prayer.
   Oh Father, it would break my heart;
   I cannot meet her there.

7 "I love you, but I long to go
   To that bright world so fair
   Where all God's love, and I am sure
   There'll be no blind ones there.

8 "Now let me kneel down by your side
   And to our Savior pray
   That God's right hand will you both guide
   Through life's long weary way."

9 The prayer was offered and a song.
   "I'm weary now," she said.
   Her father took her in his arms
   And laid her on the bed.

10 And as he turned to leave the room,
   One joyful cry was given.
   He turned to catch the last sweet smile;
   His blind child was in heaven.

11 They laid her by her mother's side,
   And engraved a marble there,
   And on it were these simple words:
   "There'll be no blind ones there."

Tying the Leaves

This song is unique among the sentimental pieces because it has a happy ending. Almost certainly of professional composition, the ballad has suffered somewhat in oral tradition, becoming awkward in its phrasing.

Sung by Mr. Sid Lanier, Point Clear, 7 July 1947.

Verses

Play - mates were they, girl and lad. She's ill to -
Lad with a tear climbs a tree. "I'll keep you

day, lad feels sad; Doc - tor calls forth, whis - pers
here," mur - murs he. Big man in blue stern - ly

1.
low: "When the last au - tumn leaves fall, then she must go."
2.
cries: "What are you do - ing?" The lad re - plies:

Chorus

"I'm ty - ing the leaves so they won't come down, So the wind won't blow them a -

way, For the best lit - tle girl in the wide, wide world Is

ly - ing so ill to - day. Her young life must go when the

last leaves fall, So I'm ty - ing them fast so they'll stay. I'm

ty - ing the leaves so they won't come down, So Nel - lie won't go a - way."

3   Sad were the griefs, day by day,
    Watching the leaves, hear the boy say:
    "You will not grieve for, you see,
    I've tied all the leaves fast up on the tree."

4   Doctor brings joy one glad day;
    Mother tells boy Nell will stay.
    Boy at girl's side cries in glee:
    "That's what I said one day in the tree:

    Chorus

Chapter 5
Pathos/Adults

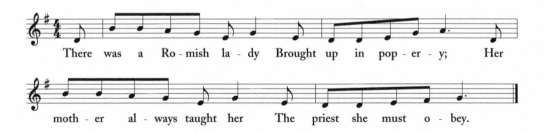

The Romish Lady
(Laws Q 32)

Dating back at least to the beginning of the seventeenth century in England, this ballad of a Protestant's revolt against the trappings of Catholicism is now almost forgotten in the British Isles. It maintains a moderate popularity in America, where it has been included in books of spirituals and of shape-note hymns, and where it is said to have been a favorite of the young Abraham Lincoln. Miss Craven's version is not so long or so complete as many recorded in the southern states. Here is a Missouri version of her incomplete eighth stanza:

> Soon as these words were spoken
> Up stepped the man of death
> And kindled up the fire
> To stop her mortal breath. (Belden, p. 453)

Sung by Miss Callie Craven, Gadsden, 11 August 1945.

There was a Ro - mish la - dy Brought up in pop - er - y; Her
moth - er al - ways taught her The priest she must o - bey.

2 Assisted by her handmaid,
   A Bible she concealed,
   And there she got instruction
   Till God His love revealed.

3 "I'll bow to my dear Jesus;
   I'll worship God unseen.

I'll live by faith forever;
The works of men are vain."

4 Then comes her raving mother,
Her daughter to behold,
And in her hand she brought her
Pictures decked with gold.

5 "Oh take from me these idols;
Remove them from my sight.
Restore to me my Bible,
Wherein I take delight."

6 The priests they soon assemble,
They for the maid did call,
And forced her in a dungeon,
To fright her soul withal.

7 The chains of gold so costly
They from this lady took,
And she, with all her spirit,
Her pride of life forsook.

8 Up steps the man of death
To kindle up the fire.

9 "Weep not, you tender ladies;
Shed not a tear for me,
While my poor body's burning,
My soul the Lord shall see."

The Letter Edged in Black

Some other versions contain a concluding stanza in which the father asks forgiveness for his harsh words that drove his son away and thus prevented Jack's being with his mother at her death. This song was written and copyrighted by Hattie Nevada in 1897, and versions were recorded by a number of early "hillbilly" artists, including Vernon Dalhart, whose 1925 recording was a best-seller. Although the ballad's treatment of plot is strongly literary, this song remains popular in oral tradition in the southern states.

Sung by Mr. Walter Black and Mr. Robert Lee, Troy, 13 August 1946.

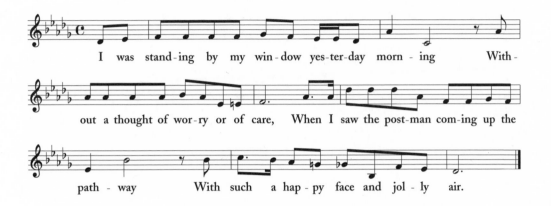

I was stand-ing by my win-dow yes-ter-day morn - ing With-

out a thought of wor-ry or of care, When I saw the post-man com-ing up the

path - way With such a hap-py face and jol-ly air.

2 He rang the bell and whistled as he waited,
   And then he said, "Good morning to you, Jack,"
   But he little knew the sorry that he brought me
   As he handed me this letter edged in black.

3 With trembling hands I took this letter from him;
   I broke the seal and this is what it read:
   "Come home, my boy, your dear old father wants you;
   Come home, my boy, your dear old mother's dead.

4 "The last words your mother ever uttered
   Was 'Tell my boy I want him to come back.'
   My eyes are blurred, my poor old heart is broken
   As I'm writing you this letter edged in black."

Darling, Soon I Will Be Sleeping

Although there were a number of professional recordings of this song in the 1920s and 1930s, Mrs. Burns clearly believed that it was her own. She claimed that she had composed it, both text and tune, with her sister when they were teenagers. She said that they had made up a number of songs but that this was the only one she had left, because she had saved a copy of the text.

Sung by Mrs. Delia Bates Burns, Florence, 9 June 1947.

Dar-ling, soon I will be sleep-ing In the church-yard o-ver there, Where the
grass and vines are creep-ing And the birds sing ev-'ry-where.

2   Where the grass grows above us
    And the springtide blossoms wave.
    Promise you will, if you love me,
    Plant sweet flowers on my grave.

3   From each other we'll be parted;
    Your dear face I cannot see.
    Dearest, do not be sad-hearted,
    For the flowers will speak of me.

4   I shall dream, perhaps, you are near me
    As the blossoms nod and wave.
    Grant me then this wish to cheer me:
    Plant sweet flowers on my grave.

5   When the golden thread is broken
    And I lay me down to sleep,
    This shall be the only token
    Of your love I wish to keep.

6   That when I shall leave you lonely,
    It's a little boon I crave,
    You will, for love's dear sake, only
    Plant sweet flowers on my grave.

Little Dove

Because the grieving widower here gains consolation from religion, this song is sometimes found in sacred contexts. It appears, for instance, in *The Social Harp* of 1855, but
is thought to enter print from folk tradition rather than making the opposite journey.

Its first two verses derive from the more fully traditional "Lonesome Dove," of which Mrs. Grace Hicks Ezell sings a much-reduced version (p. 125).

Sung by Mrs. Lena Hill, Lexington, 3 August 1945.

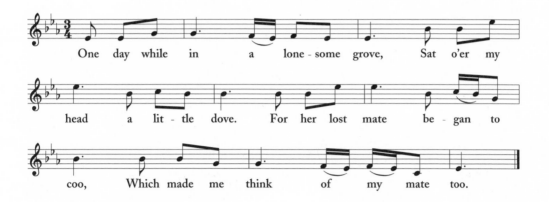

One day while in a lone-some grove, Sat o'er my head a lit-tle dove. For her lost mate be-gan to coo, Which made me think of my mate too.

2   Oh, little dove, you are not alone,
For like you I can only mourn.
Once like you I had a mate,
But now like you I am desolate.

3   Consumption seized my love severe
And preyed upon her one long year,
Till death came in a break of day
And my poor Mary he did slay.

4   Her sparkling eyes and cherry cheek
Withered like a rose and died;
The arms that once embraced me round
Lie mouldering under the cold ground.

5   But death, grim death, did not stop here.
I had one child, to me most dear;
He like a vulture came again
And took from me my little Jane.

6   But bless the Lord His words were given,
Declaring babes are heirs of heaven;
Then cease, my heart, to mourn for Jane,
Since my great loss is her great gain.

7 Oh have a hope that cheers my breast
   To think of loved one gone to rest,
   For, while her dying tongue could move,
   She praised the Lord for pardoning love.

Drunkard's Song

Usually called "The Drunkard's Doom," this is not just a song of pathos but also a weapon in the battle for temperance. In most versions, the first stanza's "drugshop" is "grogshop," "saying" in the third and fifth stanzas is "said," and the third and fourth lines of the fourth stanza are descriptive: "He drank while wife and child did starve / And ruined his own poor soul."

Sung by Mrs. Lena Hill, Lexington, 24 August 1945.

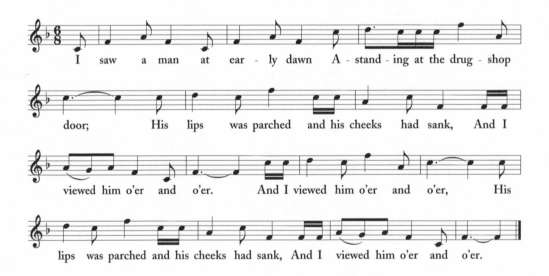

I saw a man at ear-ly dawn A-stand-ing at the drug-shop door; His lips was parched and his cheeks had sank, And I viewed him o'er and o'er. And I viewed him o'er and o'er, His lips was parched and his cheeks had sank, And I viewed him o'er and o'er.

2 He rose and to the drugshop went
   Where he had often been before,
   And in a faltering voice he cried:
   "Oh, give me one glass more,
   Oh, give me one glass more,"
   And in a faltering voice he cried,
   "Oh, give me one glass more."

3 His little son stands by his side
A-crying to him saying:
"Oh Poppa, Momma's sick at home,
And sister cries for bread,
And sister cries for bread,
Oh Poppa, Momma's sick at home,
And sister cries for bread."

4 The host obeyed at his command
And filled the sparkling bowl,
Saying: "Drink while wife and child do starve
And ruin your own poor soul,
And ruin your own poor soul,"
Saying: "Drink while wife and child do starve
And ruin your own poor soul."

5 His little son still by his side
A-crying to him saying:
"Oh Poppa, Poppa, please go home,
They say my Momma's dead,
They say my Momma's dead,
Oh Poppa, Poppa, please go home,
They say my Momma's dead."

6 One year ago I passed that way;
A crowd stood round the door.
I asked the cause, when one replied:
"The drunkard is no more,
The drunkard is no more."
I asked the cause, when one replied:
"The drunkard is no more."

7 I saw a hearse move slowly by,
No wife, no child was there;
They to a better world had gone
And left this world of care,
And left this world of care,
They to a better world had gone
And left this world of care.

Ragged Pat

This is another piece that uses pathos to enforce temperance.

Sung by Mrs. Corie Lambert, Mobile, 30 August 1945.

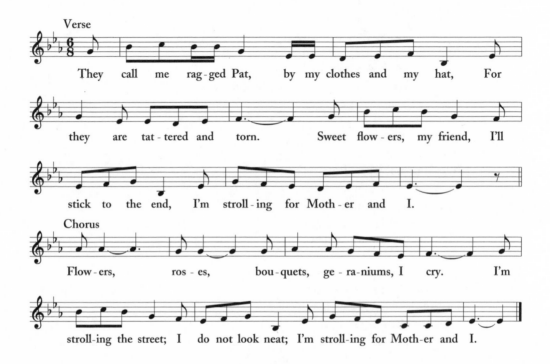

2 When I was a lad, I had a bad dad,
Bad in his ways was he;
Every dollar and cent for whiskey he spent
Till death came and stole him away.

Chorus

3 My mother took sick and was forced to her room,
And there she lingered in pain;
She called me to her bed, and this is what she said,
"You'll never see Mother again."

Chorus

4 One morning I rose, drew on my clothes,
   To sell sweet flowers for bread;
   When I returned, sad lesson I learned,
   I learned that my mother was dead.

Chorus

Chapter 6
Crimes and Criminals

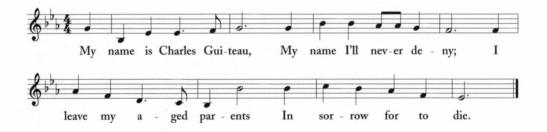

Charles Guiteau

(Laws E 11)

The title character, traditionally described as "a disappointed office-seeker," shot President James A. Garfield in Washington's Baltimore and Potomac railway station on 2 July 1881, and Garfield died on 19 September. Guiteau pleaded insanity but was found guilty of murder, condemned to death, and hanged on 30 June 1882. The basic form of the ballad predates the assassination, however, having been used to describe several earlier condemned murderers; only the names and a few details were changed to adapt it to each new situation. Because of that, there is no indication here that Garfield is anything other than a private citizen. "Jude" in the fourth stanza is normally "Judge."

Sung by Mrs. Corie Lambert, Mobile, 3 September 1945.

My name is Charles Gui-teau, My name I'll nev-er de - ny; I

leave my a - ged par - ents In sor - row for to die.

2 But little did I think
   While in my youthful bloom,
   That I'd be taken to the scaffold
   To meet my fatal doom.

3 Down at the old depot
   I tried to escape,
   But Providence being against me,
   I found it was too late.

4 Jude Clark, he read the sentence;
  The clerk he wrote it by:
  "For the murder of James A. Garfield
  You are condemned to die."

5 My sister came to the prison
  To bid me a last farewell;
  She threw her arms around me
  And wept so bitterly.

6 She said, "My darling brother,
  This day you are to die
  For the murder of James A. Garfield
  Upon the scaffold high."

7 The hangman is awaiting,
  It's a quarter after three;
  The black cap's on my forehead;
  I never more can see.

8 But when I'm dead and buried,
  Oh Lord, remember me.

Little Mary Phagan

(Laws F 20)

Fourteen-year-old Mary Phagan was killed on 26 April 1913 in Atlanta's National Pencil Factory, where her body was found the next day in a basement trash heap by Newt Lee, a watchman. Jim Conley, a black janitor, was arrested when he was found washing blood from a shirt. He swore that the girl had been killed by Leo M. Frank, the Jewish superintendent of the factory, and that, with Frank at his side, he had helped in disposing of the body. Although Frank staunchly denied any guilt for his employee's death, he was tried in a wave of anti-Semitism and convicted of murder on the strength of the testimony of Conley, who was sentenced to one year in the chain gang. Governor John M. Slaton commuted Frank's sentence to life imprisonment, but on 17 August 1915 a mob styled "The Knights of Mary Phagan" kidnapped Frank from the Milledgeville jail and lynched him. In 1982, Alonzo Mann, a former office boy at the National Pencil Factory, swore that on 26 April 1913 he had seen Conley taking the girl's body down a trapdoor to the basement. Contrary to Conley's testimony, he was alone, and the janitor threatened young Mann with death if he told anyone what he had seen. Believing these threats, Mann did not mention the incident in his trial testimony. At age eighty-three, and wanting to "clear the record" before he died, Mann passed two lie-detector tests and a psychological voice stress test with his story. Although sexual innuendoes surrounded the case, Mann believed that Conley had killed the girl only for the $1.20 pay she had just received from Frank, because the dissipated janitor had no money to buy beer, and Mann had already rejected his request for a dime. Leo Frank was granted a full pardon by the governor of Georgia in 1986. The case has been discussed in a book by Mary Phagan, the grandniece of the victim. Several different songs about the murder have been recorded by various artists since the mid-1920s. Here, Mrs. Hester's stanzas deal with the crime and its discovery, Mrs. Hill's fragment with sentencing and mourning. The first half of the last line in the fourth stanza is frequently confused. Other versions have "Solicitor New Dautry, he" and "The little girl you've brought me." The "holy day" of the last stanza is Confederate Memorial Day, April 26, when factories were closed.

A

Sung by Mrs. Myrtle Love Hester, Florence, 7 August 1945.

Lit-tle Ma-ry Pha-gan, she went to town one day, She went to the pen-cil fac-tory to get her lit-tle pay. She left her home at sev-en, she kissed her moth-er good-bye, But not one time did the poor child think that she was doomed to die.

2 Then Leo Franks he met her with brutish in his heart,
And now he said, "Little Mary, we soon will have to part."
He sneaked along behind her till she came to the middle room,
He laughed and said, "Little Mary, you have met your fatal doom."

3 Newt Lee was the watchman and when he wound the key,
Away down in the basement little Mary he could see.
He called for the policemen, their names I do not know;
They came to the pencil factory and told Newt that he must go.

B

Sung by Mrs. Lena Hill, Lexington, 3 August 1945.

4 Her mother sits a-weeping, she weeps and mourns all day.
She prays to meet her baby in a better world someday.
Judge Long he passed the sentence, you bet he did not fail;
Silester said you dortha and sent the brute to jail.

5 The people was astonished; the angels they did say,
"Why they killed poor Mary upon one holy day."
Come all you good people wherever you may be,
Supposing little Mary belonged to you or me.

Stagalee

(Laws I 15)

The gambler Stagalee, one of America's legendary black bad men, is best known for an event that may have historical basis: the killing of Bill O. Lion in a Memphis saloon. The cause of this fatal encounter is usually Bill's theft of Stagalee's Stetson, against which Lion's wife and children count for nothing in the eyes of the title character, who is not merely "bad" but "bad *with a gun*." The wonderful but confusing first stanza may be derived from versions that place the shooting on Christmas morning, while Lion's wife, "a terrible sinner," is home "a-preparin' Billy's dinner." The "hundred spot" Stagalee's woman extracts from her stocking seems to be intended for his bail, but, after finishing the song, Vera Hall told Byron Arnold: "She had to get more money." One of Alabama's finest singers, Hall was best known for her religious songs, thirteen of which are included in the "Spirituals" section.

Sung by Miss Vera Hall, Livingston, 17 June 1947.

Refrain

2 Don't you remember, you remember,
   One dark stormy night,
   Stagalee and Bill O. Lion
   They had an awful fight.

Refrain

3 Bill O. Lion told Stagalee,
   "Please don' take my life,
   I got three little children
   And a dear little lovin' wife."

Refrain

4 Stagalee told Bill O. Lion,
   "I don' care for your three little children
   Or even your lovin' wife;
   You stole my Stetson hat
   And I'm bound to take your life."

Refrain

5 Stagalee, Stagalee,
   Pulled out his forty-four;
   Wasn't long 'fore Bill O. Lion
   Were lyin' on the floor.

Refrain

6 Stagalee's woman she went to her boss,
   Said "Please give me some change.
   They got my baby in the stationhouse
   And my business must be 'ranged."

Refrain

7 Stagalee asked his woman,
   "How much change has you got?"
   She run her hand in her stockin' feet
   And pulled out a hundred spot.

Refrain

Boston City

(Laws L 16B, The Boston Burglar)

Unlike Jesse James or Stagalee, the criminal in "Boston City" is no rogue-hero but a rather pathetic young fellow who seems to have succeeded only in humiliating his family and who plans to reform when he is released from jail. This ballad is clearly derived from the British broadside "Botany Bay," in which an English convict is about to be transported to the Australian penal colony. The American version, however, is not only well known throughout the United States and Canada but has recrossed the seas to Ireland and Scotland, where it is sometimes found in folk tradition as "The Boston Smuggler." The song was popular with early recording artists and with radio singers on the first country music shows, such as WLS-Chicago's *National Barn Dance.* Instead of Mrs. Hill's "yonders" in the first two stanzas, most American versions have "honest." The serious confusion of her eighth stanza derives from a conflation of typical second and third lines into line two, leaving no story matter for line three. The stanza Sigmund Spaeth offers is typical:

> There goes the Boston burglar,
> In strong chains he is bound.
> For some crime or another,
> He is off to Charlestown. (177)

Mrs. Montgomery's version is almost identical to Hill's through the first seven stanza, but her conclusion, included here, is notably different.

A

Sung by Mrs. Lena Hill, Lexington, 3 August 1945.

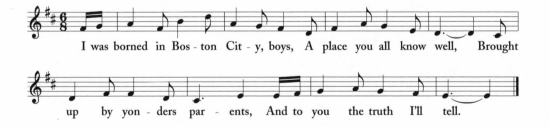

I was borned in Bos-ton Cit-y, boys, A place you all know well, Brought up by yon-ders par-ents, And to you the truth I'll tell.

2 Brought up by yonders parents, boys,
   And reared most tenderly,
   Till I became a sporting man
   At the age of twenty-three.

3 My character was then taken, boys,
   And I was sent to jail.
   My friends all thought it was vain
   To release me out on bail.

4 The jury found me guilty, boys,
   The clerk he wrote it down.
   The judge he passed the sentence,
   "You are bound for Charleston town."

5 My mother came to see me, boys,
   A-peeping through the bars;
   Likewise were my aged father,
   Pulling out the old gray locks.

6 Pulling out gray locks of hair, boys,
   With the tears a-rolling down.
   "My son, what have you done
   That you are bound for Charleston town."

7 They put me aboard a southern train, boys,
   One cold December day,
   And every station that I went through
   I heard those people say,

8 "Yonder goes some rambling burglar, boys,
   Or some strange crime he round
   The of here some obligation
   He is bound for Charleston town."

9 I have a girl in Boston City, boys,
   I girl that I love well;
   And if ever I gain my liberty
   I long with her to dwell.

10 And if ever I gain my liberty, boys,
Bad company I will shun,
Stop going around the streets at night,
And also drinking rum.

11 Young man, who have your character,
Pray keep it while you can,
For if you break the laws of man
Will now find yourself like me
A serving out your twenty-one years in the pen.

B

Probably sung by Mrs. Adele Harrison Montgomery, Tuscaloosa, 11 September 1945.

8 "There goes a Boston burglar,
For some chain gang he's bound;
For robbing of the Clifton train,
He's sent to Charlotte's town."

9 Come all ye men of liberty,
Take heed while you can,
Don't stand round on the corners
And break the laws of man.

10 For if you do you'll find yourself,
You'll find yourself like me,
A-serving out your twenty-one years
In the penitentiary.

Chapter 7
Humor

~

The Blue-Tail Fly
(Laws I 19)

This minstrel ballad was composed in the first half of the nineteenth century, probably by a white man adopting the black style. Also known as "Jimmy Crack Corn," the song has been used in play-party games, has attracted a large number of stanzas in different versions, and has become a standard fiddle and banjo piece. In its lyrics some sociologists have found subtle expression of the repressed hostility of the slave to his master, which these scholars consider an undercurrent of plantation society. Abraham Lincoln is said to have liked the tune.

Sung by Mrs. C. L. Forman, Birmingham, 1947.

Verse

When I was young I used to wait Up-on old Mass' and pass him de plate, And give him de bot-tle when he git dry, And bresh a-way de blue-tail fly.

Chorus

Jim-my crack corn an' I don't care, Jim-my crack corn an' I don't care, Jim-my crack corn an' I don't care, Old Mas-sa's gone a-way.

2 Then after dinner Massa sleep,
He bid me vigilance to keep;
He count upon me bein' very shy
To bresh away dat blue-tail fly.

Chorus

3 One day he ride aroun' de farm,
De flies so numerous they did swarm;
One chanced to bite him on de thigh.
The devil take dat blue-tail fly.

Chorus

4 That pony jumped, he run, he pitch,
He throw ole Massa in the ditch.
He died and the jury wondered why;
The verdict was that blue-tail fly.

Chorus

5 They buried him under the 'simmon tree;
His epitaph am there to see:
"Beneath this stone I'm forced to lie,
All because of a blue-tail fly."

Chorus

Springfield Mountain/Rattle-um Snake

(Laws G 16, Springfield Mountain)

This may well be the first native American ballad. On 3 August 1761, Timothy Myrick of Springfield Mountain, Massachusetts, died of a snakebite. A ballad memorializing the youth and his tragic demise was created, and several serious versions moved into folk tradition where they lived a vigorous life through the nineteenth century, and a considerably less vigorous life after 1900. The song is popular today among the folk because it has been converted from a serious to a comic ballad, evidently by the music hall minstrels of the middle decades of the nineteenth century. It has taken a number of different forms, two of which are represented by our Alabama versions. Mrs. Beck sang the first line of each couplet with doleful slowness, the second with as much bright speed as her tongue could manage. Her "love-lie" is "lovely." Mrs. Hester sang a "stuttering" version that is remarkable for the length to which each line is drawn out and also for the cogent "moral" of its last stanza.

Springfield Mountain

Sung by Mrs. May Randlette Beck, Mobile, 8 July 1947.

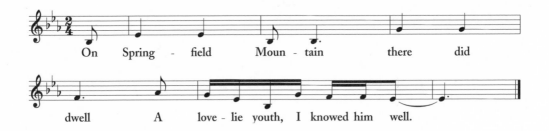

On Spring - field Moun - tain there did
dwell A love - lie youth, I knowed him well.

2 On Monday morning he did go
  In a meadow for to mow.

3 While standing there he did feel
  A big black snake bite him on the heel.

4 "Daddy, Daddy, fetch the rake,
  I'm bitten by a big black snake."

5 Daddy took him by the hand;
  He went for to see Mollie Brand,

6 Singin', singin' as he went,
  "I'm bitten by the ser-pie-ent."

Rattle-um Snake

Sung by Mrs. Myrtle Love Hester, Florence, 8 June 1947.

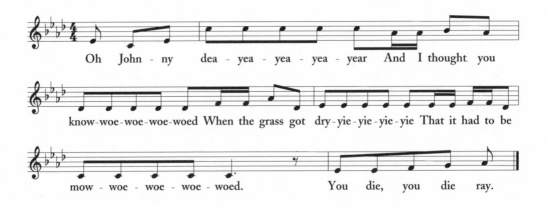

Oh John - ny dea - yea - yea - yea - year And I thought you
know-woe-woe-woe-woed When the grass got dry-yie-yie-yie-yie That it had to be
mow - woe - woe - woe - woed. You die, you die ray.

2 And he had not mow-woe-woe-woe-woed
   But half around the fie-yee-yee-yee-yield
   When a rattle-um sna-yay-yay-yay-yake
   Came and bit him on the hee-yee-yee-yee-yeel.
   You die, you die ray.

3 Oh Johnny dea-yea-yea-yea-year
   Won't you get my ga-ya-ya-ya-yal
   For I think I'll die-yie-yie-yie-yie
   And I know I sha-ya-ya-ya-yall.
   You die, you die ray.

4 Now all young me-yeh-yeh-yeh-yen
   Come a warning tay-yay-yay-yay-yake
   And don't get bi-yi-yi-yi-yit
   By a rattle-um snay-yay-yay-yay-yake.
   You die, you die ray.

Billy Grimes

This has the sound of a stage song, but its precise origin has not been determined. The idea that a match's suitability can be measured on a monetary barometer is a very old source of humor. Mrs. Grace Hicks Ezell of Birmingham (26 June 1947) remembered an additional stanza of the mother's objection:

Oh daughter dear, I'll not allow
Your cutting up such capers.
So forthwith send Old Grimes's son
His fastest walking papers.

Sung by Mrs. May Randlette Beck, Mobile, 8 July 1947.

"To-mor-row morn I'm sweet six-teen, And Bil-ly Grimes the dro-ver   Has

popped the ques-tion to me, Ma, And wants to be my lov-er.

2 "Tomorrow morn, he says, Mama,
He's coming here quite early,
To take a pleasant walk with me
Across the fields of barley."

3 "You shall not go, my daughter dear,
There ain't no use a-talking.
You shall not go with Billy Grimes
Across the fields a-walking.

4 "To think of his presumption too,
That dirty, ugly drover!
I wonder where your pride has gone
To think of such a lover."

5 "Old Grimes is dead, you know, Mama,
And Billy is so lonely;
Besides they say of Grimes' estate
That Billy is the only

6 "Surviving heir to all that's left,
And that, they say, is nearly
A good ten thousand dollars, Ma,
At least six hundred yearly."

7 "I did not hear, my daughter dear,
Your last remark quite clearly,
But Billy is a clever lad;
No doubt he loves you dearly.

8 "Remember then, tomorrow morn,
To be up bright and early,
And take a pleasant walk with him
Across the fields of barley."

Squire Jones's Daughter

Although this has all the hallmarks of professional composition, I have been unable to locate any other versions of the ballad.

Sung by Mrs. Julia Greer Marechal, Mobile, 6 July 1947.

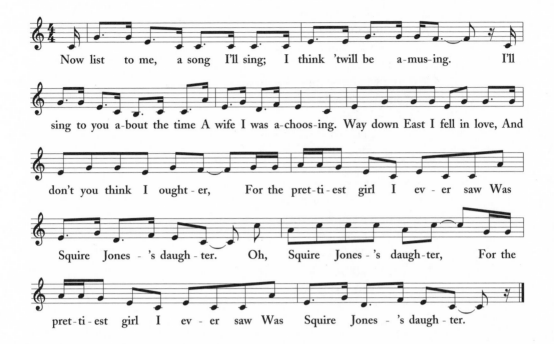

Now list to me, a song I'll sing; I think 'twill be a-mus-ing. I'll sing to you a-bout the time A wife I was a-choos-ing. Way down East I fell in love, And don't you think I ought-er, For the pret-ti-est girl I ev-er saw Was Squire Jones-'s daugh-ter. Oh, Squire Jones-'s daugh-ter, For the pret-ti-est girl I ev-er saw Was Squire Jones-'s daugh-ter.

2 Red are the roses posies here
   That grow down in the hollow,
   Red as Sister Sally's bonnet
   That cost a hundred dollars.
   But redder still were the blushing cheeks
   Of Squire Jones's daughter.
   Oh, Squire Jones's daughter,
   But redder still were the blushing cheeks
   Of Squire Jones's daughter.

3 Her beauty sent me raving mad
   At Cupid's bow and quiver.
   I swore that I would have that gal
   And never, never leave her.
   I spent my money rather free,
   And lots of jewels bought her.
   But still I could not reach the heart
   Of Squire Jones's daughter.
   Oh, Squire Jones's daughter,
   But still I could not reach the heart
   Of Squire Jones's daughter.

4 One night to serenade that gal
I went with my old fiddle,
And 'neath the window began to scratch
Tee yum, tee yum, tum diddle.
When something fell upon my head,
It must have been hot water,
And out of the window popped the head
Of Squire Jones's daughter.
Oh, Squire Jones's daughter,
And out of the window popped the head
Of Squire Jones's daughter.

5 One night I gathered up my spunk,
And round the waist I clasped her,
And in a low and trembling voice,
If she'd be mine I asked her.
Then suddenly I saw more stars
Than I really thought I oughter,
And both of my ears were soundly boxed
By Squire Jones's daughter.
Oh, Squire Jones's daughter,
And both of my ears were soundly boxed
By Squire Jones's daughter.

The Old Man Lived in the West

(Child 277, The Wife Wrapped in Wether's Skin)

This lively ballad tells the story of a husband who disciplines his wife for failing to wait on him properly. When she threatens to complain to her relatives about the beating he has administered, he replies that he was not beating her at all but was merely tanning a sheepskin he had happened to place on her back. The nonsense refrain, internal and external to each stanza, adds to the song's high spirits.

Sung by Mrs. Corie Lambert, Mobile, 3 September 1945.

2 This old man came in from plow,
   Von doo, von doo,
   This old man came in from plow,
   He said "My dear, it's breakfast now."

   Chorus

3 "There's a bit o' bread upon the shelf,
   Von doo, von doo,
   There's a bit o' bread upon the shelf,
   If you want any more you may cook it yourself."

   Chorus

4 He wrapped the hide around her back,
   Van doo, von doo,
   He wrapped the hide around her back,
   And made his hickory go whick a-to-me whack.

   Chorus

5 "I'll tell my father and brothers three,
   Von doo, von doo,
   I'll tell my father and brothers three,
   Such a whipping you gave me."

Chorus

6 "You may tell your father and all your kin,
 Von doo, von doo,
 You may tell your father and all your kin,
 That I was a-tanning my sheepskin."

Chorus

Father Grumble

(Laws Q 1)

This widely distributed comic ballad details the inevitable results of spousal chore-swapping. It is more frequently sung by women than by men. Although "Father Grumble" appeared early as a broadside, it might well have originated in an oral folk tradition. Among early recordings of the song is one by Gene Autry, done for Montgomery Ward. Ms. Kirk's stanzas would follow the second stanza of Miss Goldsby's version.

A

Sung by Ms. Louise Goldsby, Daphne, 10 July 1947.

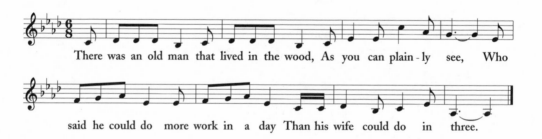

There was an old man that lived in the wood, As you can plain-ly see, Who said he could do more work in a day Than his wife could do in three.

2 "So very well," the old woman said,
 "All this I will allow,
 If you will stay at home today
 While I go follow the plow."

3 The old woman took the staff in her hand
And went to follow the plow,
While the old man took the pail in his hand
And went to milk the cow.

4 "Whoa Teeny, and so Teeny,
My pretty little cow stand still.
If ever I come to milk you again,
'Twill be against my will."

5 Teeny winced and Teeny flinched
And Teeny curled her nose.
She gave the old man such a kick in the face,
That the blood ran down to his toes.

6 He went to feed the brindle pigs
That lay within the sty;
The old sow ran between his legs
And threw him in the mire.

7 He went to feed the speckled hen
For fear she'd lay astray,
And forgot to wind the bobbin of thread
That his wife spun yesterday.

8 He swore by all the leaves on the trees
And all the stars in heaven,
That his wife could do more work in a day
Than he could do in seven.

B

Recited by Miss Mary Wallace Kirk, Tuscumbia, 10 June 1947.

3 And you must milk the brindle cow
For fear she will go dry,
And you must feed the little pigs
That are in the sty.

4 And you must watch the speckled hen
For fear she lay astray,
And don't forget the bobbin thread
That I spun yesterday.

The Frog He Would A-Courting Ride

This is an old story. A broadside ballad titled "A Moste Strange Weddinge of the Frogge and the Mouse" was registered for publication with the London Company of Stationers on 21 November 1580. Some allege that this version refers to the courtship of Queen Elizabeth by the Duke of Anjou and contains veiled references to important political figures, including Sir Walter Ralegh. But the song had likely been sung long before 1580, and it has since had a continuous existence both in print and in oral tradition. In fact, it is probably the most frequently recovered of all folksongs. Certainly that is true in Alabama. The story is dramatic, the tune is lively, and the song's structure lends itself to any number of additions or variations. Miss Pillans's is the longest version collected by Arnold, but other versions contain interesting stanzas, some of which are presented here.

A

Sung by Miss Laura Pillans, Mobile, 23 July 1947.

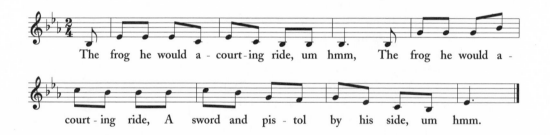

The frog he would a-court-ing ride, um hmm, The frog he would a-court-ing ride, A sword and pis-tol by his side, um hmm.

2   He rode down to Miss Mousie's hall, um hmm,
    He rode down to Miss Mousie's hall
    To pay Miss Mouse a morning call, um hmm.

3   Then down he stooped upon his knee, um hmm,
    Then down he stooped upon his knee
    "Pray, Miss Mouse, will you have me? um hmm."

4   "Not without Uncle Rat's consent, um hmm,
    Not without Uncle Rat's consent
    I would not marry the President, um hmm."

5 Old Uncle Rat he laughed and cried, um hmm,
Old Uncle Rat he laughed and cried
To think his niece would be a bride, um hmm.

6 Then her mother went to town, um hmm,
Then her mother went to town
To find Miss Mouse a wedding gown, um hmm.

7 Where, oh where will the wedding be? um hmm,
Where, oh where will the wedding be?
Right down there in that hollow tree, um hmm.

8 Well, the first that came was little Miss Moth, um hmm,
The first that came was little Miss Moth
She laid the wedding tablecloth, um hmm.

9 The next that came was Bumblebee, um hmm,
The next that came was Bumblebee
With his fiddle on his knee, um hmm.

10 The next that came was little Miss Flea, um hmm,
The next that came was little Miss Flea
She danced a jig with the Bumblebee, um hmm.

11 The next that came was Parson Crow, um hmm,
The next that came was Parson Crow
He tied the knot with feather and bow, um hmm.

12 The frog went sailing on the lake, um hmm,
The frog went sailing on the lake
And he was swallowed by a big black snake, um hmm.

13 The big black snake he went to land, um hmm,
The big black snake he went to land
And he was killed by a big black man, um hmm.

14 The big black man he went to France, um hmm,
The big black man he went to France
And that's the end of a long romance, um hmm.

B

Sung by Mrs. May Randlette Beck, Mobile, 8 July 1947.

3 "Oh, pray, Miss Mouse, are you within? um hmm,
Oh, pray, Miss Mouse, are you within?"
"Oh yes, kind sir, won't you please walk in, um hmm."

4 He took Miss Mouse upon his knee, um hmm,
He took Miss Mouse upon his knee
Says he, "Miss Mouse, will you marry me? um hmm."

6 Old Rat he came a-tearing home, um hmm
Old Rat he came a-tearing home
Says "Who's been here since I've been gone? um hmm."

7 "Oh a nice young gentleman, Uncle Rat, um hmm
Oh a nice young gentleman, Uncle Rat,
With a willow cane and a beaver hat, um hmm."

8 "Go put that gentleman's horse away, um hmm,
Go put that gentleman's horse away
And feed him well on corn and hay, um hmm."

9 "Oh, Mister Rat, may I have Miss Mouse? um hmm,
Oh, Mister Rat, may I have Miss Mouse?
And I will build her a very fine house, um hmm."

10 "Oh take her, oh take her with all your heart, um hmm,
Oh take her, oh take her with all your heart
And may you never, never part, um hmm."

C

Sung by Mrs. Emma Craig, Florence, 31 July 1945.

5 Uncle Rat came riding home, um hmm,
Uncle Rat came riding home
"Who's been here since I've been gone? um hmm."

6 "A tall and a straight and a handsome man, um hmm,
A tall and a straight and a handsome man.
May I marry him if I can? um hmm."

7 Then where shall the wedding supper be? um hmm.
Then where shall the wedding supper be?
Away down yonder in the juniper tree, um hmm.

8 And what shall the wedding supper be? um hmm,
And what shall the wedding supper be?
Two big beans and a black-eyed pea, um hmm.

9 The first to come was the bumblebee, um hmm,
The first to come was the bumblebee,
Bow and fiddle on his knee, um hmm.

10 And the last to come was the old gray cat, um hmm,
And the last to come was the old gray cat,
And the first to leave was Uncle Rat, um hmm.

11 Little Miss Mouse she ran up the wall, um hmm,
Little Miss Mouse she ran up the wall,
Her foot slipped and she did fall, um hmm.

12 Mr. Frog he jumped in the lake, um hmm,
Mr. Frog he jumped in the lake,
He got swallowed by a big black snake, um hmm.

13 And that's the end of one, two, three, um hmm,
And that's the end of one, two, three,
The mouse and the frog and the bumblebee, um hmm.

D

Sung by Mrs. Addye Goldsmith, Atmore, 13 August 1946.

5 When shall the wedding supper be? um hmm,
When shall the wedding supper be?
Tomorrow afternoon at half past three, um hmm.

7 What shall the wedding supper be? um hmm,
What shall the wedding supper be?
A grain of rice and a black-eyed pea, um hmm.

8 What shall the wedding supper be? um hmm,
What shall the wedding supper be?
Dog-wood soup and cat-wood tea, um hmm.

E

A fragment sung by Mrs. Jane Peavy, Atmore, 11 July 1947.

First to come was Captain Redbug, um hmm,
First to come was Captain Redbug
He swore he had a very fine jug, um hmm.

Next to come was Parson Flea, um hmm,
Next to come was Parson Flea
And he danced a jig with the bumblebee, um hmm.

F

Sung by Miss Callie Craven, Gadsden, 27 July 1945.

8 What do you reckon they'll have for supper? um hmm,
What do you reckon they'll have for supper?
Two black beans and not a speck of butter, um hmm.

The Fox

Almost certainly descended from a British broadside ballad of the late eighteenth century, "The Fox" was frequently printed in the next century and is well known throughout America today. More than most ballads, it appeals to children with its good humor and high spirits and has often served as a nursery song or lullabye. The obscure phrase at the end of Mrs. Carleton's second line appears, equally obscurely, in several other American versions.

Sung by Mrs. Laurie C. Carleton, Grove Hill, 5 July 1947.

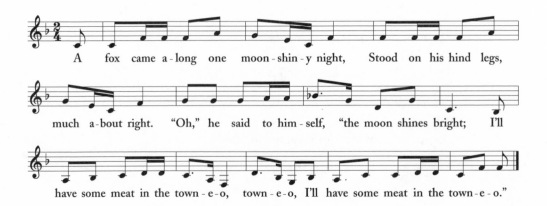

A fox came a-long one moon-shin-y night, Stood on his hind legs, much a-bout right. "Oh," he said to him-self, "the moon shines bright; I'll have some meat in the town-e-o, town-e-o, I'll have some meat in the town-e-o."

2 The fox ran down by the farmer's house;
  Looked at the gate and there sat a goose.
  Oh he gave the goose a snatch and slung her across his back;
  I thought I heared her go quarleyo, quarleyo,
  I thought I heard her go quandeo.

3 Old Molly Nick Nack lying in the bed,
  Hoisted her heels and down came her head,
  "Old man, our gray goose is gone;
  I thought I heard her go quarleyo, quarleyo,
  I thought I heard her go quandeo."

4 The old man jumped up with a right good will;
  Ran to the gate but the music was still.
  "Oh, old fox, now don't you go along so fast."
  "I'll have some meat in the towneo, towneo,
  I'll have some meat in the towneo."

5 The fox ran down by the river at his den;
  Called out his young ones, eight, nine, and ten.
  And while the fox was gnawing on the old gray goose,
  The young ones were gnawing on the boneo, boneo,
  The young ones were gnawing on the boneo.

The Clerks of Parch's Cove

The best possible introduction to this and the next song is provided by their singer, Mrs. Janie Barnard Couch, cited by Arnold in *Folksongs of Alabama.*

    Great-grandfather, Joseph B. Barnard, must have come to this territory about the time of the War of 1812, for he was here before the Indians were moved, and was a friend and associate of Parch Corn, for whom the Cove was named. Parch Corn had so many friends among the white settlers he would not move with the Indians, so was allowed to stay.

    Parch's Cove is a small valley running into the Tennessee River. It is bounded by Blue Rock Bluff up river and Bean Rock down river. This cove was one of the earliest settled valleys in North Alabama. The Cove is just below the Tennessee Valley Authority's Guntersville Dam. Up and down the Tennessee River from Parch's Cove were Barnard's Landing; Cotaco (an Indian name) Creek and Valley; Guess's Cove, below Bean Rock; and Bean Rock Hollow. Another hollow was Wash Cotton Sinks. Water came down off the mountain and sank into the sand, coming up again at Beach Springs where there was a church. There are no houses left at the Spring, only a few at Barnard's Landing and one in Parch's Cove. These formerly rich valleys were deserted for new land on top of Sand Mountain.

My grandfather, Robert W. Barnard, built the old log house [which] had three large rooms with a dog-trot between, and a long porch extending from the dog-trot to the kitchen wing. In this home Bill Gross also lived for about twelve years as hired man and member of the family as was the rule in those days. He lived the latter part of his life in Scottsboro. He made up ballads on lots of things in the Cove and was known by my mother and father. Uncle Bill Gross made the song, "The Clerks of Parch's Cove," about a bunch of drunken young fellows who came down to the Cove in the absence of Colonel Sheffield and Uncle Charlie Carter, who owned the store, and sold out the entire stock. He wrote a number of rollicking ballads. Since he has been dead only a few years, his wife may have the written songs.

Arnold found Bill Gross's widow in Scottsboro. She told him that after her husband "got religion" he figured his ballads were silly and burned the whole box of them. Mrs. Gross could remember neither the tunes nor the words of any.

Sung by Mrs. Janie Barnard Couch, Guntersville, 26 July 1945.

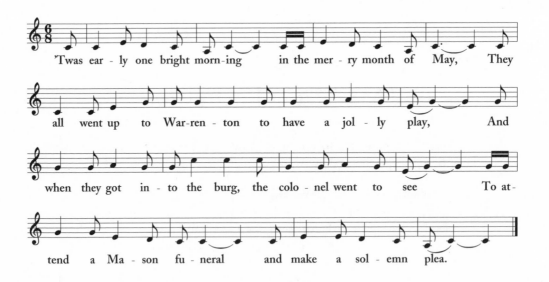

'Twas early one bright morning in the merry month of May, They all went up to Warrenton to have a jolly play, And when they got into the burg, the colonel went to see To attend a Mason funeral and make a solemn plea.

2 He left his doors wide open in care of Johnny Wood,
   To wait upon his customers the best way that he could.
   Before he got a mile from town all on his solemn road,
   His house was filled entirely with the clerks of Parch's Cove.

3 While some went down to Roper's to take a morning dram,
   The rest were in the sugar, a handful at a cram.
   And the time will be remembered by the price mark that was lost,
   Brought down the trade of Jasper Smith by selling goods at cost.

4 The first clerk was George Allen, who walked and sweetly glide,
   Who clerked for just two dollars and a pair of boots beside.
   There was little Jim Releford, a dirty little booger,
   Ate a box of candy, a half a barrel of sugar.

5 There was little Charlie Carter, the best clerk of all,
   He had a pen and pencil and couldn't write at all;
   Twenty-five pounds of flour, the best was ever ground,
   He couldn't tell its value at four cents a pound.

6 There was old Waffle Eye, so drunk he couldn't go;
   He gave away the candy and ate the indigo.
   He stood behind the counter so loud as he could holler
   And auctioned off the coffee nine pounds to the dollar.

7 The colonel at the burial sends up his solemn plea,
   The will of God accomplished and so amote it be.
   When he heard the sad news he sighed with a sob,
   And swore he was ruined by a darn drunken mob.

8 And now to you young ladies and ere you wish to trade,
   When there's another funeral you then can make a raid,
   Against monopolism the working class to strove;
   You'll make a better bargain with the clerks at Parch's Cove.

<hr/>

The Wedding of Bean Rock Hollow

Mrs. Janie Barnard Couch told Byron Arnold that this "song was made up by Uncle Bill Gross, the ballad maker of the community. This incident took place at the wedding of Rachel Blake and George Kerbo. The persons mentioned in the song were well-known members of the community." Mrs. Couch identified H. G. as her great-uncle H. G. Williams, Captain Martin as her husband's grandfather, and Dr. Hinds as a physician whose practice was located in New Hope. See the headnote to the preceding song for more local background information. Variants of the third stanza's last two lines are included in many square dance and play-party songs, such as "Old Joe Clark." The fourth stanza's last two lines appear as the conclusion of a number of different songs, most of them more suggestive than this.

Sung by Mrs. Janie Barnard Couch, Guntersville, 26 July 1945.

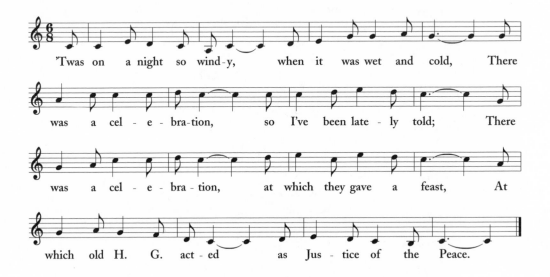

2 Oh there was Captain Martin so yawningly at times
Got choked on apple dumplings and sent for Doctor Hinds.
The Doctor came with a cork screw and a probe six inches long;
With all his skill and surgery he changed the Captain's song.

3 Steamer Jackson coming and bellowed for the mail.
. . . .
Old Aunt looked up in Bean Rock and gave his horn a blow.
Miss Dicey clapped her hands and cried, "Yonder comes my beau."

4 But when she found the greenhorn a-laying by her side
She wept aloud most bitterly and wrung her hands and cried,
"In your arms my true love, once and twice about
Come roll me in your arms, my love, and blow the candle out."

PART 2
FOLKSONGS

This is a catch-all section, because it is defined by negatives. Its entries can be anything so long as they are not basically narrative in form or religious in content. These folksongs give us a cross section of the concerns, moods, and delights of the singers of Alabama. They move from seriousness to humor, from work to play, from the South to the world. Here are songs passed from professional music halls into tradition, and here are the intimate lullabies composed for an audience of one.

We begin with songs of the Civil War and of nostalgia for the way of life it killed. The vision of the good old South found in songs like "Rosalee" and "I'm Gwine from the Cotton Fields" probably owes its existence more to the imagination of professional singers and composers than to intimate contact with existence below the Mason-Dixon Line. In fact, the influence of the minstrel lies behind many of the songs in this section. By the 1840s the blackface singers were scoring hits with pseudo-black material, a white man's interpretation of a black man's experience, and such entertainment remained greatly popular through World War I. Some of the "burnt cork" pieces were based on true folksongs, but were made catchier and more clever. Many of these professional reworkings reentered folk tradition and enliven our traditional singers' repertoires.

On the other hand, here are also some songs absolutely true to the black folk experience in Alabama. With mournful lyricism and powerful silences, Miss Vera Hall creates one of the finest folksongs in her famous version of "Another Man Done Gone." Mr. Stence Crozier's railroad work songs are at once art, encouragement to the gandy dancers, and insurance of efficient labor.

Certainly influenced by professional minstrels are the songs of love. The serious treatments embody rejection and abandonment in images of the mountaintop castle or cabin, the cuckoo or turtledove, the withering flower or willow. The gayer pieces deal with skirmishes in the ongoing battle between the sexes. Some of the oldest and most frequently found of traditional songs are the dialogues of courtship such as "Paper of Pins" and "La La Trudom." Opinions on wedlock range from "I Wish I Was Single Again" to the seven-times-married woman's rather broad declaration: "I'm Satisfied."

The "grown-up" section here continues with a few ditties about slightly risqué characters, a group of humorous and satiric songs probably derived from the minstrel stage, and a handful of rousing banjo and fiddle tunes. Like the songs of rejection that include

"Old Smoky," these last pieces swap stanzas back and forth with wild abandon, paying little attention to logic or to the niceties of polite society. As a bridge between the worlds of adult and child, we have a few songs featuring creatures of fur and feather, notably the impudent, sly, and raucous jaybird.

The game songs begin with those for choosing partners and continue with those whose movements are most like the dance. These games were not the sole property of children. Rather, in many communities of conservative morality and fundamentalist religion, where dancing was forbidden and the banjo and fiddle considered the instruments of the devil, the young folks of courting age would adopt these games for play-parties. These were dancing parties in everything but the name, during which the "games" would be played to the accompaniment of the singing of the participants. "Answering-back" and miscellaneous children's songs follow, and the section concludes with the tender lullabies that have helped generations of Alabama children "Go to Sleepy."

Chapter 8
The Civil War and After

Old Abe's Elected

The pure optimism of this song places the time of its composition before the first bloody battles of the Civil War. More precisely, a reference in the second stanza may date it in the last weeks of 1860 or the first of 1861 when groups of local "minutemen" were forming. Shortly thereafter, and still before secession, the southern governors called up their state militias. "Darky Shamblin" is Lincoln's radical abolitionist vice-president, Hannibal Hamlin of Maine. The tune is "Yankee Doodle."

Sung by Mrs. Julia Greer Marechal, Mobile, 6 July 1947.

Verse

Old Abe's e - lec - ted so they say And so is dark - y Sham - blin. The

Yan - kees think they've gained the day By nig - ger votes and gam - blin'.

Chorus

So let 'em have a hap - py time With pump - kin pies and clam - bakes; Be -

fore they're through I'll bet they'll find There are two sides to pan - cakes.

2 Our minutemen are gathering round
   Their firesides and their altars.
   Their blood is up, their hearts are touched,
   Their hands will never falter.

   Chorus

3 But if they come across the line
   To gamble, act uncivil,
   Or undertake to whip us back,
   We'll thrash 'em like the devil.

Chorus

In the Year '61

As optimistic as the preceding song, this fragment celebrates the Confederate victory at the First Battle of Manassas, or Bull Run, on 21 July 1861. A broadside ballad, of which this was the first stanza and chorus, appeared almost immediately. It was full of the names of generals and the details of specific engagements, just those things most likely to disappear in oral transmission. We are left with Mrs. Marechal's stanzas' patriotic confidence, to swift destruction doomed.

Sung by Mrs. Julia Greer Marechal, Mobile, 6 July 1947.

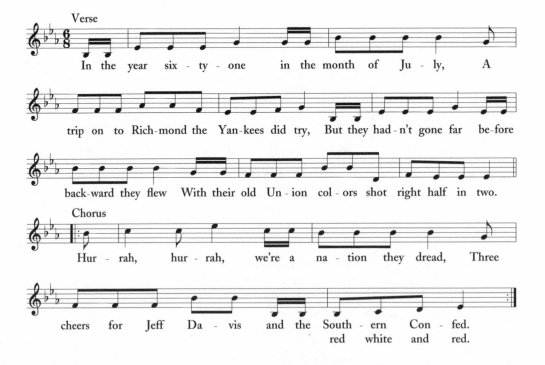

The Year of Jubilo

This song was written and copyrighted by Henry Clay Work at the beginning of the Civil War. It gained an immediate popularity in oral tradition, and was also frequently printed as a penny broadside. During the war, a "contraband" was a black slave who escaped to or was brought within the Union lines. Mrs. Marechal's last narrative lines are derived from the refrain. A fuller conclusion is provided by Mrs. Laurie Cater Carleton (Grove Hill, 5 July 1947):

> There's wine and cider in the cellar
> And the darkies there have some,
> But I guess it'll all be confiscated
> When the Lincoln gunboats come.

Sung by Mrs. Julia Greer Marechal, Mobile, 6 July 1947.

Say, dark-ies, have you seen old Mas-ter With a mus-tache on his face Go

'long this road some-time this morn-ing Like he's gwine to leave this place? He

seen the smoke way up the riv-er Where the Lin-coln gun-boats lay; He

picked up his hat and he left real sud-den. I think he's run a-way.

Mas-ter run, ha ha, Dark-ies say hee hee; It

must be now that the king-dom am a-com-in' In the year of Ju-bi-lee.

2 He's six foot one way and he's two foot another
   And he weighs three hundred pounds.
   His coat's so big that he wouldn't pay a tailor,
   So it couldn't go halfway round.
   He drilled so much they called him Captain
   And his face so dreadful tan.
   I suspect he'll fool them gunboat sailors
   And pass for contraband.
   Master run, ha ha,
   Darkies say ho ho;
   It must be now that the kingdom am a-comin'
   In the year of Jubilo.

3 The darkies they got tired of living
   In the log house on the lawn;
   They moved their things into Master's parlor,
   Gonna keep it while he's gone.
   There's wine and cider in the cellar
   And the darkies there have some,
   But it must be now that the kingdom am a-comin'
   In the year of Jubilo.
   Master run, ha ha,
   Darkies say ho ho;
   It must be now that the kingdom am a-comin'
   In the year of Jubilo.

Before This War Broke Out

I have found no other versions of this pseudo-black minstrel song set during the Civil War and urging the "marsa" of the singer to give up fighting for the South and thereby "save the old plantation."

Sung by Mrs. Julia Greer Marechal, Mobile, 6 July 1947.

Verse

Be - fore this war broke out, Mis-tress dressed in sat - ins fine; Now she wears old shirt With - out an - y crin - o - line.

What this war is all a-bout, This dark-y does-n't know, But he thinks ole Mar-sa Dav-is Has a might-y slim show.

Chorus

Then come back, Mar-sa, come back, Oh, come back, Mar-sa, come back. Shake hands with Un-cle Sam, and be a Un-ion man, And save the old plan-ta-tion.

2 Since Marsa's been away,
On the devil has been to play;
All the cotton picking darkies
Have gone and run away.
Some are down to Richmond,
The good-for-nothing scamps,
And some are digging muck
In the Union Army camps.

Chorus

❧

The Soldier's Fare

This was the first song collected by Arnold, and it gives a lengthy and detailed picture of military life. Miss Craven's belief that it is a Civil War song is supported by the "Yankees" in the third stanza, but this may be called into question by the "foreign land" in the sixth. "Grog" is a mixture of alcoholic liquor and water, and "calomel" was the age's purgative panacea. I have found only one other version of this in print, a four-stanza text from Mississippi. Apart from the information conveyed by his song, nothing is known of J. P. Hite.

Sung by Miss Callie Craven, Gadsden, 26 July 1945.

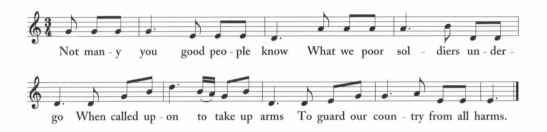

Not man-y you good peo-ple know What we poor sol - diers un-der-
go When called up-on to take up arms To guard our coun-try from all harms.

2 Sometimes we lie on the cold ground
  Where there's no shelter to be found.
  Sometimes it rains, sometimes it snows;
  The howling wind through the tempest blows.

3 At break of day the Yankees come,
  They play their fife, they beat their drum,
  Disturb the soldier's sweet repose;
  He rouses up, puts on his clothes.

4 Our sergeant comes and goes about:
  "Sing 'hurrah' boys and turn out,
  Sing 'hurrah' boys and form a line."
  Our instruments how they do shine.

5 As right and left and ready at a word,
  Our captain then presents his sword.
  Our sergeant then takes out the roll;
  Their names are called, their absence told.

6 Our officers, how bad they are,
  Wear out their men for want of care,
  And bring them to some desperate plan,
  And bury them in foreign land,

7 Where there's no friends nor relatives near
  To shed a sympathizing tear,
  Nor nurse them on their dying bed,
  Nor bury them when they are dead.

8 But as to grog we get enough,
  Although our beef is lean and tough;
  But as to that we'll not complain.
  We hope to get good beef again.

9 Our doctor is a man of skill
And every day he gives a pill,
And if that pill does not prove well
He gives a dose of calomel.

10 You want to know who composed this song,
I'll tell you now it won't take long.
It was composed by J. P. Hite
On his post one rainy night.

My Southern Home

Although Mrs. McClure was unaware that this piece was written in 1864 by Will S. Hays of Louisville, Kentucky, she associated this sentimental parlor song with the Civil War. She told Arnold that her mother and friends would gather around the piano almost every evening and that in these circumstances she learned "My Southern Home."

Sung by Mrs. Venetia Danner McClure, Mobile, 8 July 1947.

Oh Moth-er dear, I have come home to the home I love so true, But
I'm un-hap-py all is changed, yet there's no change in you. Each
flow-er lifts its blush-ing head, the birds are glad I've come, But
na-ture seems to weep a-round my south-ern sun-ny home.

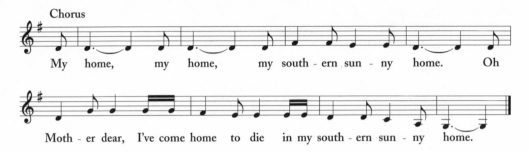

Chorus

My home, my home, my south-ern sun-ny home. Oh

Moth-er dear, I've come home to die in my south-ern sun-ny home.

2 It seems a few short years ago, oh we were happy then,
  Oh Mother dear, I weep not now for we'll be glad again.
  There is a place beyond the skies where angels love to roam,
  Where you and I are sure to find a happier sunnier home.

Chorus

Tombigbee River

Also known as "The Gum-Tree Canoe," this idyllic ditty was written by S. S. Steele and A. F. Winnemore in the nineteenth century. Although it is found in tradition with moderate frequency, most versions do not vary greatly one from another, perhaps because it was a radio favorite and was recorded by numerous "hillbilly" artists, including several from Alabama. This was the favorite song of Mrs. Wilson's father-in-law.

Sung by Mrs. Julia T. Wilson, Grove Hill, 22 August 1946.

Verse

On the Tom-big-bee Riv-er so bright I was born In a hut made of gum trees and

tall yel-low corn; 'Twas there that I met with my Ju-lia so true, And at

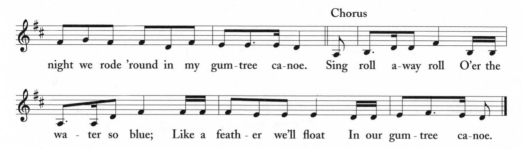

night we rode 'round in my gum-tree ca-noe. Sing roll a-way roll O'er the

wa – ter so blue; Like a feath – er we'll float In our gum – tree ca-noe.

2 All day in the fields of soft cotton I hoe;
   I think of my Julia and sing as I go.
   I'll catch her a bird with wings of true blue,
   And at night sail around in my gum-tree canoe.

   Chorus

Dixie

This stanza sounds like a chorus from a late-nineteenth- or early-twentieth-century song celebrating the delights of the South. Sheet music for a song titled "I'se Gwine Back to Dixie" credited to James A. Bland was published by White, Smith & Company in Boston in 1879, but I have not been able to locate a copy of it.

Sung by Mrs. Janie Barnard Couch, Guntersville, 13 June 1947.

I'm go – ing back to Dix – ie; no more I'm going to wan – der. My

heart's turned back to Dix – ie; I can't stay here no long – er. I

miss the old plan-ta – tion, my home, and my re – la – tions; My

heart's turned back to Dix – ie, and I must go.

Rosalee

An incomplete version of this sentimental "plantation" song was singled out for great praise by one reviewer of Arnold's *Folksongs of Alabama*. An 1880 piece of sheet music lists this as "composed and sung by Happy Billy Radcliffe." It had some popularity over early radio and was recorded several times in the 1920s and 1930s. The chorus is sung to the same tune as the verse.

Sung by Mrs. Janie Barnard Couch, Guntersville, 8 August 1945.

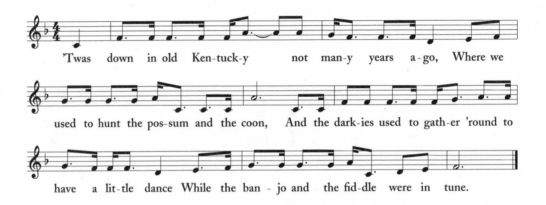

'Twas down in old Ken-tuck-y not man-y years a-go, Where we used to hunt the pos-sum and the coon, And the dark-ies used to gath-er 'round to have a lit-tle dance While the ban - jo and the fid-dle were in tune.

2 No more we hear the merry sound nor see the days of yore,
Nor the little darkies playing on the green,
Nor the merry smiles of Rosalee, the only flower that blooms,
In my little old log cabin by the stream.

Chorus
Then hang up your banjo and your fiddle on the wall,
Lay away your bones and tambourine,
Since death has taken Rosalee, the only flower that blooms,
In my little old log cabin by the stream.

3 I never shall forget the happy hours we spent
As we wandered together o'er the hills,
And sat beneath the willow and watched the rolling stream,
And listened to the clatter of the mill.

4 And when the night was coming on, the darkies' work was done,
How we used to gather on the green;
The banjo and the fiddle would make the forest ring
In the little old log cabin by the stream.

Chorus

5 The stream is running just the same; the willows on its banks
  Are bending o'er the grave of Rosalee;
  And here I sit and weep and pass the hours away,
  And wonder when the same shall shelter me.

6 My steps are growing feeble and my hair is turning gray,
  Still the grass is growing fresh and green;
  And here I sit till death shall take me to my Rosalee
  From my little old log cabin by the stream.

Chorus

I'm Gwine from the Cotton Fields

This obviously professional and sentimental composition attempts to pass itself off as a former slave's farewell to his longtime home as he leaves for better prospects in the West. Mrs. Lambert says: "Miss Alice Walthall, my schoolteacher in Pineapple, Alabama, taught us this song."

Mrs. Corie Lambert, Mobile, 3 September 1945.

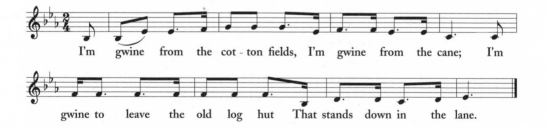

I'm gwine from the cot-ton fields, I'm gwine from the cane; I'm gwine to leave the old log hut That stands down in the lane.

2 The boats are on the river;
  They're gwine to take me off.
  I'm gwine to join the exodus
  That's making for the North.

3 They tell me out in Kansas,
  So many miles away,
  The colored folks are flocking
  'Cause they're getting better pay.

4 I don't know how they found it out,
But still I'm bound to try,
For when the sun goes down tonight
I'm gwine to say good-bye.

5 There's Dinah, she don't want to go;
She says she's growing old.
She's 'fraid that she will freeze to death
'Cause the country am so cold.

6 Talk about your work and play;
You don't believe it's true,
But she don't want to do the things
That I am bound to do.

7 I sold my little log cabin,
My little patch of ground,
The kind old master gave me
When the Yankee troops came down.

8 Now my hair is turning gray;
The tears are in my eyes,
For when the sun goes down tonight
I'm gwine to say good-bye.

Come, My Love, Come

This fragment is the chorus from a long sentimental serenade designed to encourage a woman to forsake her parents for her lover.

Sung by Ms. Mary Vance, Guntersville, 27 July 1945.

Chapter 9
Blues

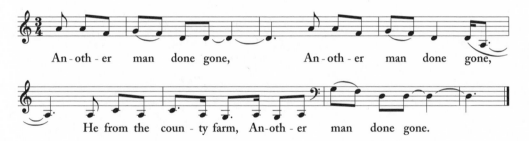

Another Man Done Gone

Vera Hall's version of this blues song about an escaped convict may well be the most famous folksong to come out of Alabama. She was first recorded in 1937 by John Lomax, who later called her rendition "an Afro-American classic." Visiting the Lomaxes in Texas, Carl Sandburg listened in fascination at least a dozen times to "one of the strikingly original creations of Negro singing art." Hall's first recorded version was played in the Library of Congress as part of the celebration of the seventy-fifth anniversary of the Emancipation Proclamation and was included on the Library's "Afro-American Blues and Game Songs" recording in its "Folk Music of the United States" series. In the odd idiom of Hall's last stanza, the convict threatens his listener with violence if a rendezvous (no doubt of assistance in escape) is not kept.

Sung by Vera Hall, Livingston, 16 June 1947.

An-oth-er man done gone, An-oth-er man done gone,

He from the coun-ty farm, An-oth-er man done gone.

2 I didn't know his name,
   I didn't know his name,
   I didn't know his name,
   I didn't know his name.

3 He killed another man,
   He killed another man,
   He killed another man,
   He killed another man.

4 He has a long chain on,
   He has a long chain on,
   He has a long chain on,
   He has a long chain on.

5 He from the county farm,
   He from the county farm,
   He from the county farm,
   He from the county farm.

6 I'm gonna walk your log
   If you don't meet me
   At the waterfall.
   I'm gonna walk your log.

Chain Gang Song

The singer told Arnold that there were more verses to this convict blues song than she remembered. She added: "This used to be sung to the tune of a banjo."

Sung by Mrs. Mary Holly, Parch's Cove, 24 August 1945.

2 As I was coming a-down the street,
   I met a policeman; he asked me my name.

Refrain

3 Ninety-five dollars and ninety days,
   Right around my leg with a ball and chain.

Refrain

4 Boys, boys, I'm going home,
  Stay with Mamma every night.

Refrain

Deep Blue Sea

The origin of this song is unknown. It shares verses with several less-than-serious songs, notably "Old Blue," and its tone seems related to that of some spirituals. Other versions replace "Mama" with "Baby" and conclude with the stanza: "Lower him down with a golden chain." Its tune, which may bear West Indian influences, is simple and moving.

Sung by Mrs. C. L. Forman, Birmingham, 1947.

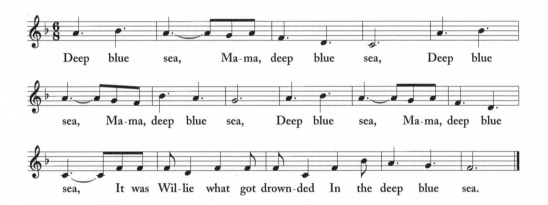

Deep blue sea, Ma-ma, deep blue sea, Deep blue sea, Ma-ma, deep blue sea, Deep blue sea, Ma-ma, deep blue sea, It was Wil-lie what got drown-ded In the deep blue sea.

2 Wrap him up in a silken gown,
  Wrap him up in a silken gown,
  Wrap him up in a silken gown,
  It was Willie what got drownded
  In the deep blue sea.

3 Dig his grave with a silver spade,
  Dig his grave with a silver spade,
  Dig his grave with a silver spade,
  It was Willie what got drownded
  In the deep blue sea.

Chapter 10
Railroad Work Songs

Lining Track

Mr. Crozier was a gandy dancer and a straw boss of gandy dancers. The special tools used by railroad section gangs were made almost exclusively by the Gandy Manufacturing Company of Chicago, and all the track laborers had to move in unison as they used those tools—hence the term. The foreman gave his orders to the straw boss, who passed them on to the crew and then led the song that provided the rhythm for the work. The chain of improvised, and not always sensible, verses is endless as the gandy dancers line (straighten out) the railroad track. In time with the song, they lean their weight into and shake the lining bars thrust under the rails. The "L and N" is the Louisville and Nashville Railroad. "Jack the rabbit, Jack the bear" appears in several other track-lining songs.

Sung by Mr. Stence Crozier, Gadsden, 13 June 1947.

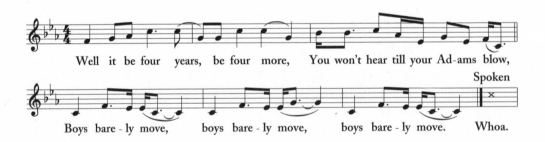

Well it be four years, be four more, You won't hear till your Ad-ams blow,

Boys bare-ly move, boys bare-ly move, boys bare-ly move. Whoa.

2 Now I'm going to town, going to spread the news,
   Bama women won't wear no shoes,
   Boys barely move, boys barely move, boys barely move.
   Whoa. (spoken)

3 I don't know but I believe I will
   Stay all night in a Jackson jail,
   Boys barely move, boys barely move it, boys barely move.
   Whoa. (spoken)

4 Well, down the curve around the bend,
  Yonder comes that L and N,
  Boys barely move, boys barely move, boys barely move it.
  Whoa. (spoken)

5 I don't know but I had to swear,
  Jack the rabbit, and Jack the bear,
  Boys can't you move it, boys can't you move, boys can't you move it.
  Whoa. (spoken)

6 I don't know I believe I will,
  Believe my job'll go cross the hill,
  Boys barely move it, boys barely move, boys barely move.
  Whoa. (spoken)

7 I grew up to be a railroad man,
  Get your learning on the L and N,
  Boys barely move, boys barely move it, boys barely move.
  Whoa. (spoken)

8 Shout, shout, the devil's about,
  Shut the door and you'll keep him out,
  Boys barely move it, boys barely move, boys barely move it.
  Whoa. (spoken)

9 I don't know Colonel Bell, don't go with me,
  Going back to Tennesee,
  Boys barely move, boys barely move it, boys barely move.
  Whoa. (spoken)

10 Who is that? Susie Bline.
   That's a pretty girl just like mine,
   Boys barely move, boys barely move, boys barely move.
   Whoa. (spoken)

11 Well peach and honey and rock and rye,
   You can line it, boys, if you try,
   Boys barely move, boys barely move, boys barely move.
   Whoa. (spoken)

Laying Rails

A regulation length of rail weighs over a ton, and the men who handle it must work together perfectly so as not to strain themselves or get in the way of a falling iron. The singer carefully dictates each step in the process of laying the rail, from grabbing it with the Gandy tool, the dog, to jointing it with its neighbor. Mr. Crozier gave Arnold a long and detailed description of this operation, and it is all included here.

Sung by Mr. Stence Crozier, Gadsden, 13 June 1947.

Now this layin' rails what I'm fixin' to tell you about. As we lays this rail we heave the same amount, six on each end. Well, I bees on the back end, you see, where we joins at. Well, you see, I sings:

Let your dog bite his man. Then pick him up. Deal him all long, man.
Set him in the bed, man. Joint i-ron. This joint meet all right. Move on.

You see, you move down to the next joint, then say:

Let your dog bite his man.
Now pick him up all long.
Set him in the bed, man.
Joint iron.

You joint the iron on one. Well then move down to the next one, you see. What I say?

Let your dog bite his man.
So deal him all long.
Set him in the bed, man.
Joint your irons.

You see, we going to throw old rails here now. You see, we done went down to where we going to throw out old rails.

Well, set down 'deed, man.
I'll set down.

I'm going outside say.

> Move down.
> Joint one all right.
> Set down.
> Lead men in the outside iron.
> The outside iron all right, sir.
> Well move back now.
> Say now.
> Let your dog bite him.
> Set him in the bed, man.
> Joint him.

They joint the iron then. I say:

> The joint's made all right.
> Move on, move to the next joint.
> Let your dog bite his man.
> Let's pick him up all along.
> Set him in the bed, man.
> Let's joint irons.
> That joint meet all right now.

I'm a going to change now.

> Set down on the old rail, man.
> Outside iron, man.
> Well the outside iron, say well.
> That's all right.
> Move on.
> Said'll set down, 'deed man, set down.
> Say outside iron,
> Says outside all right, sir.

Now move back, going to get a new rail.

> Let your dog bite his man.
> Say pick him up all long.
> Set him in the bed, son.
> Joint iron.
> Joint meet all right.
> Move on.

When they get to the next joint.

Let your dog bite his son.
Say pick him up all along.
Set him in the bed, man.
Joint iron.
Joint meet all right.

Now say:

Set down the old rails, outside irons.
Outside again.
I take you outside iron.
It's all right.
Move back now.
Let your dogs bite him now.
Pick him up all long.
Set him in the bed, son.
Join on one.
The joint meet all right.

That's the record of that.

Tamping Ties

Mr. Crozier told Arnold that "this is a song for tamping ties." After removing an old worn crosstie, the laborers would tug the new one into position and then each would work his tamp, a long iron crowbar with a spatulated nose, to shove cinders under the tie until it was solidly in place. The "Cap'n" would be the foreman rather than the straw boss, and the "Southern" is the Southern Railroad. I can find no specific "great big wreck" to which the second stanza might refer.

Sung by Mr. Stence Crozier, Gadsden, 13 June 1947.

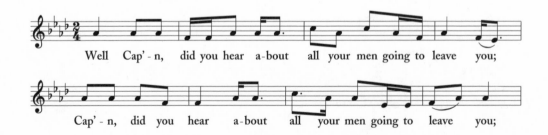

Well Cap'-n,   did you hear a-bout all your men going to leave you;

Cap'-n, did you   hear   a-bout all your men going to leave you;

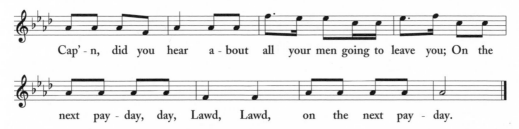

Cap'-n, did you hear a-bout all your men going to leave you; On the
next pay-day, day, Lawd, Lawd, on the next pay-day.

2 Cap'n, did you hear about a great big wreck on the Southern,
Say Cap'n, did you hear about a great big wreck upon the Southern,
Cap'n did you hear about a great big wreck upon the Southern,
Killed a hundred men, Lawd, Lawd, killed a hundred men.

Picking and Grading

The title refers to the shaping and smoothing of the gravel of the railroad bed. After completing the second stanza of his song for picking and grading, Mr. Crozier noted its relation to the first by telling Arnold: "That sort of don't go with the other."

Sung by Mr. Stence Crozier, Gadsden, 13 June 1947.

Lit-tle girl, I heard ev-ery word you said 'bout me; Lit-tle
girl, I heard ev-ery word you said 'bout me; I was
stand-ing on your door-step the day you thought that I was gone; Lit-tle
girl, I heard ev-ery word you said 'bout me.

2 Sinner man, you must be borned again,
Sinner man, you must be borned again,
Have your sins done forgiven, and your soul done set free,
Sinner man, you must be borned again.

Chapter 11
Serious Songs of Love

Old Smoky

One of the advantages of building a song out of stanzas of lyric emotion rather than of linear narration is that the stanzas can be arranged in any number of different ways, creating new perspectives on an emotional theme at the same time that the theme's components remain reassuringly familiar. "Old Smoky" and the four songs that follow it are clearly related. They share emotions, images, lines, stanzas, and portions of tune. And these five songs are just as clearly different one from another, for no two achieve quite the same effect. One of several forerunners of these love songs is a British broadside ballad called "The Wagoner's Lad." The girl's sorrow at the departure of her wagoner lover is a common feature of the ballad and of this lyric, the most popular of the forms into which these love stanzas fall.

Sung by Mr. Robert Wallace, Tuscaloosa, 18 June 1948.

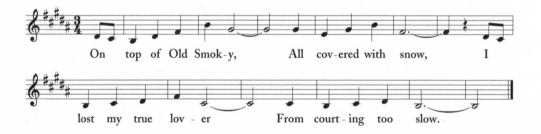

On top of Old Smok-y, All cov-ered with snow, I lost my true lov-er From court-ing too slow.

2 A-courting is a pleasure,
   And a pleasure and a pain,
   But a false-hearted true lover
   Will send you to your grave.

3 Your grave will encave you
   And turn you to dust;
   Not a boy in a hundred
   A poor girl can trust.

4 "Go on hitch your horses,
   And feed them some hay,
   And set down beside me
   As long as you may."

5 "My horses ain't hungry;
   They won't eat your hay.
   I'll drive on a little farther
   And eat on my way.

6 "Your parents aren't willing
   And mine are the same,
   Go deep down in your heart
   And blot out my name."

7 "I'll go back to Old Smoky,
   To the mountaintops high,
   Where the wild birds and turtledoves
   Can hear my sad cry."

Long Ways from Home

The poor damsel here has been especially badly treated because she has clearly left her parents, relatives, and friends against their wishes and advice to follow her unconstant Johnnie. Abandoned now in the desert, she longs not so much for a return to her family as for a retreat to a castle, an image of fantasy, of safety, and of an independent life in which close and messy interpersonal relationships are not required. Almost certainly, the third line of the third stanza should repeat that of the second stanza.

Sung by Mrs. Lena Hill, Lexington, 3 August 1945.

One morn-ing, one morn-ing, one morn-ing in spring,

Out in the des-ert the birds so lone-ly did sing;

I heard a poor dam-sel all weep-ing and mourn,

"Oh," she said, "I'm a poor lost girl and a long ways from home."

2 "Oh Johnnie, oh Johnnie, oh Johnnie," said she,
"You see what I have come to by the making of thee,
By the making of thee in the desert so lone.
Oh," she says, "I am a poor lost girl and a long ways from home."

3 I stepped up to her, her feature to see;
I asked her pardon by the making of thee,
By thee in the desert so lone.
"Oh," she says, "I am a poor lost girl and a long ways from home.

4 "I left my dear father without his command,
I left my dear mother a-wringing her hands,
I left my friends and relatives all weeping and mourn.
Oh," she says, "I am a poor lost girl and a long ways from home.

5 "I'll build me a castle on the mountaintop high,
So the wild geese can see me as they go roving by,
So the wild geese can see me and help me to mourn.
Oh," she says, "I am a poor lost girl and a long ways from home."

A-Walking, A-Talking

Again the woman is forsaken, but her demeanor is very different in our two versions. From rejection, Mrs. Hill's "poor girl" has drawn bitter resignation, while Mrs. Trotter's "fair maiden" boldly asserts her worth and independence. The praises of the cuckoo ring ironically, for it is a conventional symbol of inconstancy in love. The song is widespread in oral tradition and has been recorded frequently.

A

Sung by Mrs. Lena Hill, Lexington, 10 June 1947.

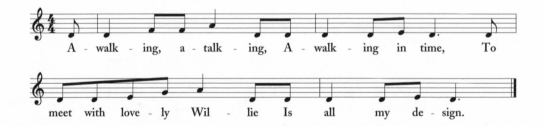

A - walk - ing, a - talk - ing, A - walk - ing in time, To
meet with love - ly Wil - lie Is all my de - sign.

2 To meet him in the meadows
  Is a delight;
  I'll walk and talk with him
  From morning till night.

3 A meeting is a pleasure,
  A parting is a grief;
  An unconstant lover
  Is worse than a thief.

4 A thief can but rob you
  And take what you possess;
  An unconstant lover
  Can bring you to the grave.

5 The grave it will mold you
  And turn you to dust.
  There is not one boy in twenty
  A poor girl may trust.

6 They'll tell you fine stories
  That you may deceive;
  There is not one boy in fifty
  That you may believe.

7 A cuckoo is a pretty bird,
  She sings as she flies;
  She brings us glad tidings,
  She tells us no lies.

8 She sucks the sweet flowers
  To make her voice clear,
  And never sings "cuckoo"
  Till spring of the year.

B

Sung by Mrs. Pearl Trotter, Troy, 22 July 1946.

1 A-walking and talking,
  A-walking goes I;
  I'll meet with my true love,
  I'll meet him by and by.

2 I'll meet him in the meadow.
   He is my heart's delight;
   I'll walk and talk with him
   From morning till night.

3 Come all you fair maidens,
   Take warning from me,
   Never cast your affections
   On a green willow tree.

4 The leaves they will wither,
   The roots they will die,
   And if I am forsaken,
   I can't tell for why.

5 I'll dress myself in the finest,
   In the finest degree;
   I'll walk as like by him
   As he does by me.

6 If I am forsaken,
   I know who's forsworn,
   And you're badly mistaken
   If you think that I'll mourn.

Pretty Mollie

This song's originality lies in the speaker and situation presented in its first stanza and chorus. Here the woman has rejected the man after he has driven himself into irredeemable financial debt in pursuit of her hand, and, most likely, at her instigation. His bitterness undermines the normal effects of the images in the familiar and conventional second and third stanzas, and it ironically sets the two halves of the chorus against each other.

Sung by Miss Callie Craven, Gadsden, 11 August 1945.

Verse

I'm trav'-ling a long jour-ney, O'er the moun-tain I go; I'm leav-ing my coun-try For the mon-ey I owe.

Chorus

Fare you well, pret-ty Mol-lie, I will bid you a-dieu; I am ru-ined for-ev-er By the lov-ing of you.

2 On top of yon mountain
There stands a green tree;
The leaves are all wilted,
And the roots are decayed.

Chorus

3 I'll build my fine building
On some mountain high,
Where the spring birds do holler
And the wild geese fly by.

Chorus

Bertha

This last in the line of songs stretching from "Old Smoky" marshals the whole tradition in support of temperance. The first, fourth, and fifth stanzas could also be expanded in the same way that the third stanza expands the second.

Sung by Mrs. Grace Hicks Ezell, Birmingham, 26 June 1947.

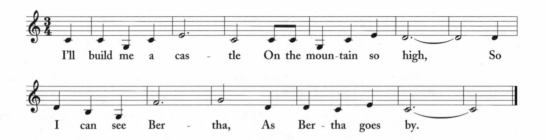

I'll build me a cas - tle On the moun-tain so high, So
I can see Ber - tha, As Ber - tha goes by.

2 If all the young ladies
   Were placed in a row,
   Little Bertha'd outshine them
   Like a mountain of snow.

3 Like a mountain of snow, love,
   Like a mountain of snow,
   Little Bertha'd outshine them
   Like a mountain of snow.

4 I wrote her a letter,
   'Twas only one line:
   "I will be yours, love,
   If you will be mine."

5 She wrote me an answer,
   'Twas only one line:
   "The lips that touch liquor
   Shall never touch mine."

Lonesome Dove

The dove is a traditional symbol of constancy in love, and the impossibilities of the second and third stanzas reinforce the idea of the lover's faithfulness. The first stanza appears in a number of different folksongs, such as "Winter's Night" (p. 35).

Sung by Mrs. Grace Hicks Ezell, Birmingham, 26 June 1947.

Oh, don't you see that lone-some dove That flies from pine to pine? It's mourn-ing for its own true love Just like I mourn for mine.

2 The blackest crow that ever flew
   Will surely turn to white,
   If ever my love prove false to you
   Bright day will turn to night.

3 Bright day will turn to night, my love,
   The elements will mourn,
   If ever my love prove false to you
   The roaring sea will burn.

Chapter 12
Courting

⌒

Paper of Pins

One of the most popular dialogue songs in America, "Paper of Pins" derives from the old British song "The Keys of Heaven" and recalls a time in this country when the object of its title was of considerable value. The song can have several different endings: the young woman rejects all of her suitor's offers, she finally accepts "the key to my heart," she accepts "the key to my chest" and they marry, she accepts "the key to my chest" but the young man rejects the now-revealed gold digger. Mrs. Craig's version is of this last sort. Like most dialogue courting songs, "Paper of Pins" has been performed dramatically on social occasions and used often as a singing game or play-party song. Mrs. Pearl Trotter (Troy, 22 July 1946) updates the second gift here: "I'll give to you a dress of green / Stitched all around with a sewing machine."

Sung by Mrs. Emma Craig, Florence, 9 June 1947.

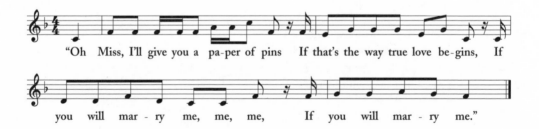

"Oh Miss, I'll give you a pa-per of pins If that's the way true love be-gins, If you will mar - ry me, me, me, If you will mar - ry me."

2 "I'll not accept your paper of pins
   If that's the way true love begins,
   And I'll not marry you, you, you,
   And I'll not marry you."

3 "Oh Miss, I'll give you a dress of green
   That you may look as any queen,
   If you will marry me, me, me,
   If you will marry me."

4 "I'll not accept your dress of green
That I may look as any queen,
And I'll not marry you, you, you,
And I'll not marry you."

5 "Oh Miss, I'll give you a dress of red
All trimmed around with golden thread,
If you will marry me, me, me,
If you will marry me."

6 "I'll not accept your dress of red
All trimmed around with golden thread,
And I'll not marry you, you, you,
And I'll not marry you."

7 "Oh Miss, I'll give you a coach and six,
With horses black as any pitch,
If you will marry me, me, me,
If you will marry me."

8 "I'll not accept your coach and six,
With horses black as any pitch,
And I'll not marry you, you, you,
And I'll not marry you."

9 "Oh Miss, I'll give you a little lapdog
That you may carry when you go abroad,
If you will marry me, me, me,
If you will marry me."

10 "I'll not accept your little lapdog
That I may carry when I go abroad,
And I'll not marry you, you, you,
And I'll not marry you."

11 "Oh Miss, I'll give you the key to my heart,
That we may lock and never part,
If you will marry me, me, me,
If you will marry me."

12 "I'll not accept the key to your heart,
That we may lock and never part,
And I'll not marry you, you, you,
And I'll not marry you."

13 "Oh Miss, I'll give you the key to my chest
 That you may spend money at your request,
 If you will marry me, me, me,
 If you will marry me."

14 "Oh, I'll accept the key to your chest
 That I may spend money at my request,
 And I will marry you, you, you,
 And I will marry you."

15 "Ha, ha, ha, money ain't all,
 A lady's love is nothing at all,
 And I'll not marry you, you, you,
 And I'll not marry you."

I'll Have No Drunkard to Please

As in the preceding "answering-back" song, so here the man has the last word but, ironically, it seals his defeat and shows the woman to have been right all along. This is one of the finest American versions of what is often called "The Courting Case." This song was one of the most popular items in the repertoire of WLS-Chicago radio stars Lulu Belle and Scotty.

Sung by Mrs. Myrtle Love Hester, Florence, 8 June 1947.

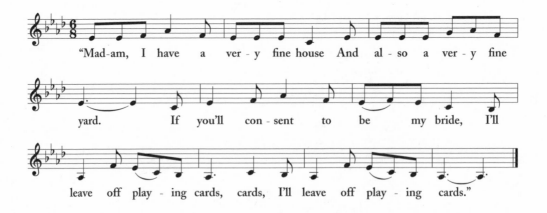

"Mad-am, I have a ver-y fine house And al-so a ver-y fine yard. If you'll con-sent to be my bride, I'll leave off play-ing cards, cards, I'll leave off play-ing cards."

2   "Oh Sir, I know you've a very fine house
    And also a very fine yard,
    But who will sit by the side of my bed
    When you're off playing cards, cards,
    When you're off playing cards?"

3   "Madam, I quit that long ago;
    I never did think it was right.
    If you'll consent to be my bride,
    I'll never stay out at night, night,
    I'll never stay out at night."

4   "Oh Sir, I know you'll promise me that,
    And think to take me in,
    But if I consent to be your bride,
    Then you'll go gambling again, again,
    Then you'll go gambling again."

5   "Madam, I have a very fine horse,
    And he paces like a tide,
    And you can have him at your command
    Whenever you wish to ride, ride,
    Whenever you wish to ride."

6   "Yes Sir, I know you've a very fine horse;
    He stands in yonders barn,
    But his master loves to tilt his glass,
    And I'm afraid he can't learn, learn,
    And I'm afraid he can't learn."

7   "Madam, you're a very proud miss
    And very hard to please.
    When you get old and shiver in the cold,
    I hope to the Lord you freeze, freeze,
    I hope to the Lord you freeze."

8   "Oh Sir, I know I'm a very proud miss,
    And very hard to please.
    But when I get old and shiver in the cold,
    I'll have no drunkard to please, please,
    I'll have no drunkard to please."

9   "Madam, I'll take my very fine horse,
    For he pulls my buggy well;
    I'll drink my dram and throw my cards,
    And you can go to hell, hell,
    And you can go to hell."

Courting Song

In this short version of the song often called "The Quaker's Courtship," the man who perceives wooing as a duty rather than a delight is flatly rejected by the woman who wants more spirit than sobriety in her beau. In longer versions, the man and woman usually alternate stanzas.

Sung by Mrs. Grace Hicks Ezell, Birmingham, 26 June 1947.

Young man

"My fath - er sent me here a - court-in', oh, oh, oh, Oh
"You are tall and you are slen - der, oh, oh, oh, And
"I've got a ring that cost twenty shil-lings, oh, oh, oh, You

when I come it's not for sport-in', oh, oh, oh.
I know your heart is ten - der, oh, oh, oh.
may have it if you are will-ing, oh, oh, oh."

Young woman

"I don't want your ring or your mon-ey, I don't want your house or your land,

I want a man that will call me hon-ey, And I'll get him if I can."

La La Trudum

This mother-daughter dialogue frequently ends with the mother not only agreeing to her daughter's marriage but also deciding that she will marry too.

Sung by Mrs. J. K. Estes, Fort Payne, 12 June 1947.

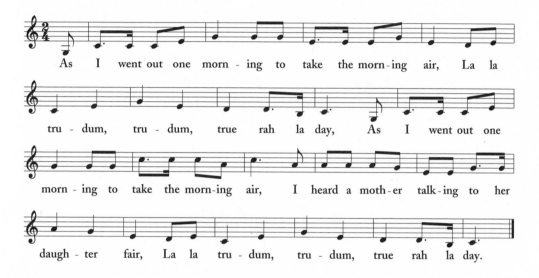

As I went out one morn-ing to take the morn-ing air, La la tru-dum, tru-dum, true rah la day, As I went out one morn-ing to take the morn-ing air, I heard a moth-er talk-ing to her daugh-ter fair, La la tru-dum, tru-dum, true rah la day.

2 "Hush your foolish talking and hold your idle tongue,
   La la trudum, trudum, true rah la day,
   Hush your foolish talking and hold your idle tongue,
   Talking now of marrying and you know you are too young,
   La la trudum, trudum, true rah la day."

3 "Mama, I am sixteen and you know I'm nearly grown,
   La la trudum, trudum, true rah la day,
   Mama, I am sixteen and you know I'm nearly grown,
   La la, Mama, just consider case your own,
   La la trudum, trudum, true rah la day."

4 "Suppose I was consented, where'd you get your man?
   La la trudum, trudum, true rah la day,
   Suppose I was consented, where'd you get your man?"
   "La la, Mama, there's handsome little Sam,
   La la trudum, trudum, true rah la day."

5 "Suppose he was to fool you, as you know he's done before,
La la trudum, trudum, true rah la day,
Suppose he was to fool you, as you know he's done before."
"La la, Mama, there's a half dozen more,
La la trudum, trudum, true rah la day."

6 "Johnny's gone out for the license, the preacher for to get,
La la trudum, trudum, true rah la day,
Johnny's gone for the license, the preacher for to get;
I'll be married before the sun is set,
La la trudum, trudum, true rah la day."

7 "My daughter's gonna get married, what shall I do?
La la trudum, trudum, true rah la day,
My daughter's gonna get married, what shall I do?
La la, Johnny boy, it's better for me too,
La la trudum, trudum, true rah la day."

Teddy O'Hussey

Mrs. Elebash learned this comic song from her father, who had learned it from his father in Virginia.

Sung by Mrs. Belzora Parrish Elebash, Selma, 14 August 1946.

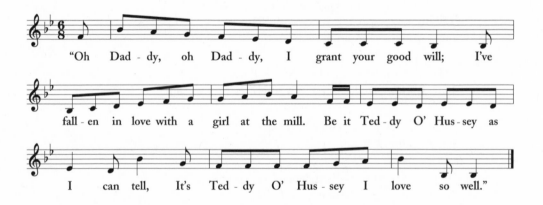

"Oh Dad-dy, oh Dad-dy, I grant your good will; I've fall-en in love with a girl at the mill. Be it Ted-dy O' Hus-sey as I can tell, It's Ted-dy O' Hus-sey I love so well."

2 "Oh Son, oh Son, that never can be;
  Go marry an old woman, make puddings for thee,
  Go marry an old woman, make puddings and pies,
  And you will live well all the days of your lives."

3 "Oh Daddy, oh Daddy, that never can be,
  To marry an old woman, make puddings for me,
  For the lips are thick and the cheeks are thin,
  Old woman makes pudding and her nose drips in."

4 "Oh Son, oh Son, you speak very bold,
  Oh don't you know your mother is old."
  "Oh Daddy, oh Daddy, oh hold your tongue,
  You married my mother when she was young."

5 "I'll make my will, and I'll leave you but little,
  And what shall it be but an old brass kettle,
  For you are the worst boy that a man ever had."
  "Oh hold your tongue, Daddy, for you've been as bad."

Old Shiboots and Leggins

The courtship of a young woman by an old man, with or without her mother's encouragement, has long been a staple of comedy. Its form also contributes to this song's considerable popularity in Alabama and throughout the United States. Singers can add any and all the horrible details they want. "Shiboots" are shoe-boots or dress boots.

A

Sung by Miss Callie Craven, Gadsden, late 1945 or early 1946.

My moth-er told me to ask him in, Oh, but I shan't have him, I asked him in with a drip-ping chin, With his old shi-boots and leg-gins.

2 My mother told me to give him a chair,
   Oh, but I shan't have him,
   I gave him a chair and he called me his dear,
   With his old shiboots and leggins.

3 My mother told me to give him something to eat,
   Oh, but I shan't have him,
   I gave him something to eat, Good Lord how he eat,
   With his old shiboots and leggins.

4 My mother told me to put him to bed,
   Oh, but I shan't have him,
   I put him to bed and he slept like he's dead,
   With his old shiboots and leggins.

5 My mother told me to wake him up,
   Oh, but I shan't have him,
   I woke him up and he quacked like a duck,
   With his old shiboots and leggins.

6 My mother told me to light his pipe,
   Oh, but I shan't have him,
   I lit his pipe and he smoked like a snipe,
   With his old shiboots and leggins.

7 My mother told me to saddle his horse,
   Oh, but I shan't have him,
   I saddled his horse and I saddled him off,
   With his old shiboots and leggins.

8 My mother told me to bid him farewell,
   Oh, but I shan't have him,
   I bid him farewell and I wished him in the well,
   With his old shiboots and leggins.

B

Sung by Mrs. Pearl Trotter, Troy, 22 July 1946.

1 My mother told me to open the door,
   With his old gray beard a-shaking,
   I opened the door and he fell on the floor,
   With his old gray beard a-shaking.

2 My mother told me to give him a seat,
   With his old gray beard a-shaking,
   I gave him a seat and he stripped his feet,
   With his old gray beard a-shaking.

3 My mother told me to buckle his shoe,
   With his old gray beard a-shaking,
   I buckled his shoe and he fell in the stew,
   With his old gray beard a-shaking.

4 My mother told me to put him to bed,
   With his old gray beard a-shaking,
   I put him to bed and I wish he was dead,
   With his old gray beard a-shaking.

C

Sung by Miss May H. Wilson of Selma, Florence, 2 August 1946.

1 My mother told me to give him some fish,
   I gave him the fish and he ate up the dish.

2 My mother told me to put him to bed,
   I put him to bed and chopped off his head.

D

No information on informant.

1 My mama told me to look down the road,
   I won't have him,
   I looked down the road and he came like a toad,
   With his old shoes a-draggin.

2 My mama told me to ask him in,
   I won't have him,
   I asked him in and he clucked like a hen,
   With his old shoes a-draggin.

Chapter 13
Marital Relations

Niggljy Naggljy

Because they both deal humorously with less-than-perfect wives and contain nonsense refrains, this song and "The Wife Wrapped in Wether's Skin" (p. 82) have frequently been grouped together, but there are significant differences between the two pieces. Instead of the ballad's wife who refuses to work, here the wife works in the worst fashion imaginable; instead of the ballad's linear and closed narrative, here the form is capable of great expansion through the singer's or group's adding stanzas dealing with other reprehensible qualities, features, and activities of this awful woman. The "child's old clout" is a diaper, and the "pot hooks," which held kettles over the open fire, were likely to be pretty filthy.

Sung by Mrs. Janie Barnard Couch, Guntersville, 8 August 1945.

I bought my wife three milk-ing cows, Nig-gl-jy, nag-gl-jy, now, now, now, And she milked them till they all went dry, Nig-gl-jy, nag-gl-jy, ben-jy-bo rig-gl-jy, Ruf-fl-jy, ruf-fl-jy, now, now, now.

2 She milked her milk in the old slop pail,
Niggljy, naggljy, now, now, now,
She strained her milk through the child's old clout,
Niggljy, naggljy, benjy-bo riggljy,
Ruffljy, ruffljy, now, now, now.

3 She churned her milk in an old boot,
Niggljy, naggljy, now, now, now,

She took up her butter with the old pot hooks;
Niggljy, naggljy, benjy-bo riggljy,
Ruffljy, ruffljy, now, now, now.

4   She had two eyes like two rotten pears,
Niggljy, naggljy, now, now, now,
And she had two teeth like two wiry pins,
Niggljy, naggljy, benjy-bo riggljy,
Ruffljy, ruffljy, now, now, now.

I Wish I Was Single Again

The joke here is that the man would repeat his marital mistake. The song is found frequently in all portions of the United States except New England. There were a number of early "hillbilly" recordings, including a popular one made in Birmingham in 1926 by John Foster and J. D. James.

Sung by Mrs. Myrtle Love Hester, Florence, 7 August 1945.

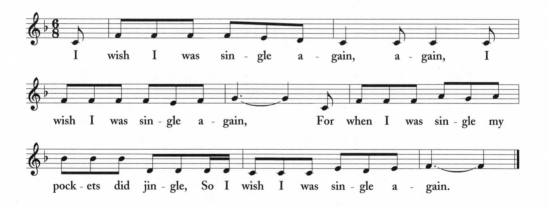

2   I married me a wife, oh then, oh then,
I married me a wife, oh then,
I married me a wife and I loved her for my life,
But I wished I was single again.

3   She beat me, she banged me, oh then, oh then,
She beat me, she banged me, oh then,
She beat me, she banged me, she swore she would hang me,
So I wished I was single again.

4 She spun the rope, oh then, oh then,
   She spun the rope, oh then,
   She spun the rope my neck for to choke,
   So I wished I was single again.

5 She tied it to the joist, oh then, oh then,
   She tied it to the joist, oh then,
   But the rope it did break and my neck did escape,
   But I wished I was single again.

6 So then she died, oh then, oh then,
   So then she died, oh then,
   So then she died and I laughed till I cried,
   But I wished I was single again.

7 I married me another, oh then, oh then,
   I married me another, oh then,
   I married me another; she was the devil's grandmother,
   Oh I wished I was single again.

I Wish I Were a Single Girl Again

Certainly more serious than the preceding, this is often listed among temperance songs. Other versions have "and them to maintain" in place of "all obtain" in the third stanza.

Sung by Mrs. Pearl Trotter, Troy, 22 July 1946.

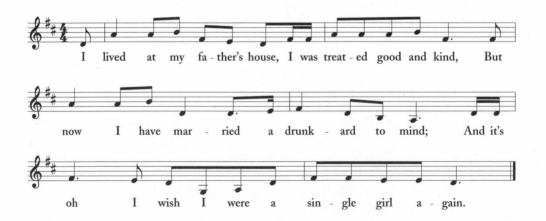

I lived at my fa-ther's house, I was treat-ed good and kind, But

now I have mar-ried a drunk-ard to mind; And it's

oh I wish I were a sin-gle girl a-gain.

2 Between midnight and daylight
  Comes staggering in at home
  Who would it be but a drunk man alone;
  And it's oh I wish I were a single girl again.

3 Three little children
  All obtain
  Nary one large enough to do anything;
  And it's oh I wish I were a single girl again.

I'm Satisfied

This song provides a different view of the "marriage debate" from the preceding.

Sung by Mrs. Mae White, Lexington, 24 August 1945.

I'm a wom-an been mar-ried sev-en men, An' if I get rid of this 'un, I'll mar-ry a - gain. But I'm sat - is - fie - hie-hied, I'm sat - is - fied.

2 First I married a lawyer, he stayed gone,
  Making love to other women, Lawd, he done me wrong.
  But I'm satisfie-hie-hied, I'm satisfied.

3 Next I married a doctor and a doctor was he;
  He cured the other women and tried to kill me.
  But I'm satisfie-hie-hied, I'm satisfied.

4 Next I married a preacher, he preached the stuff;
  He got a divorce; said I 'as too rough.
  But I'm satisfie-hie-hied, I'm satisfied.

5 Next I married a butcher, blood over his clothes;
  Can't say that he loved me, for, Lawd, I don't know.
  But I'm satisfie-hie-hied, I'm satisfied.

6 Next I married a baker, the baker of the town;
   He hugged the other women as he turned the damper down.
   But I'm satisfie-hie-hied, I'm satisfied.

7 Next I married a farmer, the farmer was he;
   He raised pintos and old speckled peas.
   But I'm satisfie-hie-hied, I'm satisfied.

8 Now I'm living with a bum, a dad-gum bum;
   When he says scat I mean I run.
   But I'm satisfie-hie-hied, I'm satisfied.

All for the Men

This is an old English children's singing game that seems to have taken on a slightly satiric tinge among both blacks and whites in the United States. The structure of each stanza's last three lines is reminiscent of that of "Old MacDonald Had a Farm." Mrs. Ruby Pickens Tartt was an early and highly effective collector of folk material in Alabama. Although Arnold lists her as the informant for this song, it was almost certainly collected by her from a singer, or singers, in the Livingston area. Arnold may have copied it from the Tartt material in the state archives in Montgomery, or Mrs. Tartt may have given it to him directly.

Mrs. Ruby Pickens Tartt, Livingston, 1945.

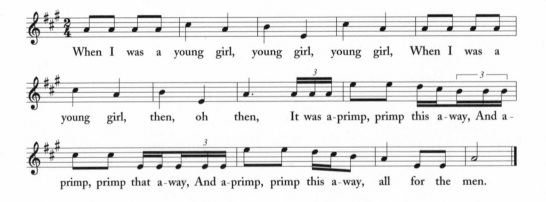

2 The boys come a-courtin', courtin', courtin',
The boys come a-courtin', then, oh then.
It was a-kiss, kiss this a-way,
And a-kiss, kiss that a-way,
This way, that way, all for the men.

3 Then we quarreled, quarreled, quarreled,
Then we quarreled, then, oh then.
And it was a-yow, yow this a-way,
And a-yow, yow that a-way,
This way, that way, all for the men.

4 Pretty soon we made it up, made it up, made it up,
Pretty soon we made it up, then, oh then.
It was "My love" this a-way,
"My love" that a-way,
"My love" this a-way, all for the men.

5 Then we married, married, married,
Then we married, then, oh then.
And a-ha, ha this a-way,
And a-ha, ha that a-way,
This way, that way, all for the men.

6 Then he died, died, died,
Then he died, then, oh then.
And it was a-boo hoo this a-way,
Boo hoo that a-way,
This way, that way, then, oh then.

Chapter 14
Risqué Characters

~

Rosen the Beau

This was an extremely popular song in the mid–nineteenth century, largely because of its tune, which was borrowed for at least four political campaign songs between 1832 and 1872. It appeared in dozens of songsters and was a pillar of the sheet music industry. Rosen, or Rosin, is often identified as a "Bow," but most versions present him more clearly as a ladies' man than as a musician. Like the spelling of its hero's name, the country of this song's origin is uncertain. Also uncertain is the meaning of "donnicks," which appears in the last stanza of most versions. Mr. Jacks confessed ignorance, and scholars divide over whether it means "tombstones" or "drinking mugs." The chorus following each stanza is composed of the stanza's last line repeated twice followed by the stanza's third and last lines.

Sung by Mr. Joe M. Jacks, Jr., Sheffield, 10 June 1947.

Verse

I've trav-eled this coun-try all o - ver, And now to an-oth-er I'll go; I
know there's good quar-ters a - wait-ing To wel-come old Ros-en the beau.

Chorus

To wel-come old Ros-en the beau, To wel-come old Ros-en the beau, I
know there's good quar-ters a - wait-ing, To wel-come old Ros-en the beau.

2 And when I'm laid on the counter
   The ladies would all like to know;

Just raise up the lid of the coffin
And look at old Rosen the beau.

Chorus

3 And get you a dozen good fellows,
And stand them all up in a row,
And drink out of a big bellied bottle
The health of old Rosen the beau.

Chorus

4 Just get you a couple of donnicks;
Place one at my head and my toe,
And do not forget to scratch on it
The name of old Rosen the beau.

Chorus

Till I Die

In form and content, this appears to be a professional minstrel parody of the spiritual. The singer said that "we learned this old song from our Negro nurse about 1912 in Bullock County." In 1926, Charlie Poole had a smash hit on Columbia records with a version of this song titled "Coon from Tennessee."

Sung by Leigh Harrison, Tuscaloosa, autumn 1945.

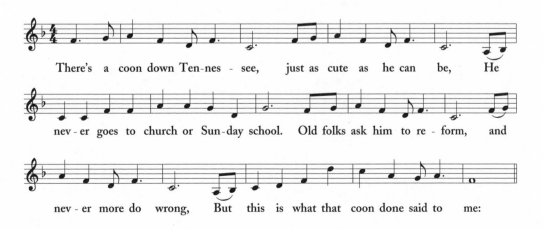

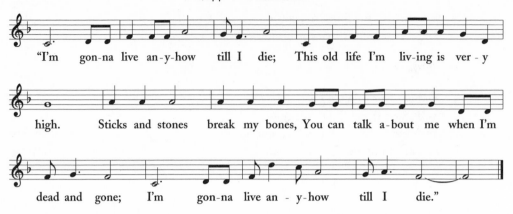

"I'm gon-na live an-y-how till I die; This old life I'm liv-ing is ver - y high. Sticks and stones break my bones, You can talk a-bout me when I'm dead and gone; I'm gon-na live an - y-how till I die."

No! No! No!

This vigorous and vehement song eloquently testifies to the fact that the crusade for temperance did not always find willing converts.

Sung by Mr. James Kidd, Lower Peachtree, 20 July 1947.

No! No! No! No! Ain't gon-na lay my liq-uor down. No! No! No! No! Ain't gon-na lay my liq-uor down. Got my war cap on my head, Ain't gon-na lay my liq-uor down; Ain't gon-na put it off till I'm dead, Ain't gon-na lay my liq-uor down.

Negro Demimonde Song

This and the next song are good examples of bordello blues. The singer's comment on this song clearly establishes the source of both: "As a school kid I used to be scared to pass by the 'brick house,' a Negro sporting joint for white men. I heard a high brown singing this song while playing the piano." The tinge of self-pity characteristic of blues songs rules this fragment.

Sung by Mr. John Proctor Mills, Montgomery, 10 August 1946.

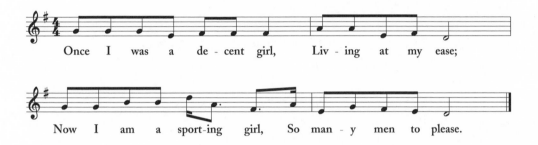

Once I was a de - cent girl, Liv - ing at my ease;

Now I am a sport-ing girl, So man - y men to please.

Hesitatin' Whiskey

Whiskey, gin, and the doctor's pronouncement appear in several brothel blues songs of the 1920s. "Hesitatin'" may be derived from the "Hesitation Waltz," popular around 1914, or from W. C. Handy's "Hesitating Blues," published in 1926. Apart from that word, however, neither song has anything in common with Mr. Mills's fragment.

Sung by Mr. John Proctor Mills, Montgomery, 10 August 1946.

Hes - i - tat - in' whis - key, Hes - i - tat - in' gin,

Doc - tor said 't'ud kill me But he did - n't say when.

Chapter 15
Humor

The Smeller Song

Mrs. Hester learned this from her father, who sometimes called it "The Proboscis Song." It is almost certainly of professional origin, and its chorus is very close to that of the well-known "Irish Lullaby."

Sung by Mrs. Myrtle Love Hester, Florence, 6 August 1945.

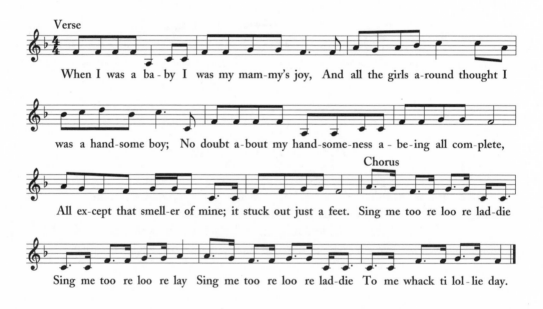

2 I grew to be a big boy, I wasn't worth a darn.
My daddy sent me off to school, I had no sense to learn;
The schoolbooks and me fell out, and I burnt my daddy's stack of wheat.
He cotched me by that smeller of mine and stretched it another feet.

Chorus

3 Then I went a-walking, a-walking down the street;
   There I saw my true love, and her I went to meet.
   I made a dash to kiss her, would have kissed her all complete,
   Except my smeller hooked her bonnet off, and I missed her just a feet.

Chorus

4 Then I went a-courting, a-courting down the street;
   She asked me in the parlor, and bade me take a seat,
   And there I sat so awkwardly a-looking at my feet,
   The old lady sniggered right out, "Tee hee, his nose sticks out a feet."

Chorus

Jolly Neighbor

The jollity of this piece derives from the singer's trying to fit longer and longer lines into the same musical phrase. It becomes a ferociously paced tongue twister. Mrs. Hester said that "Plymouth Rock" was a brand of cloth. A few versions of this song are found in recordings for children and in lessons for beginning guitarists.

Sung by Mrs. Myrtle Love Hester, Florence, 8 June 1947.

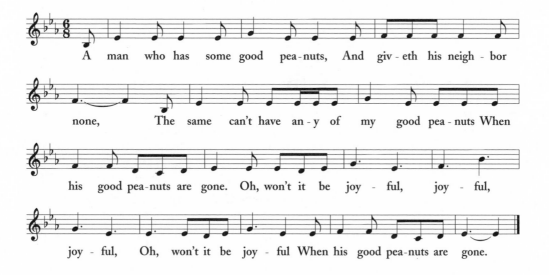

2 A man who has some soft sweet soda crackers,
  And giveth his neighbor none,
  The same can't have any of my soft sweet soda crackers
  When his soft sweet soda crackers are gone.
  Oh, won't it be joyful, joyful, joyful,
  Oh, won't it be joyful
  When his soft sweet soda crackers are gone.

3 A man who has some rich red ripe rare strawberry shortcake,
  And giveth his neighbor none,
  The same can't have any of my rich red ripe rare strawberry shortcake
  When his rich red ripe rare strawberry shortcake is gone.
  Oh, won't it be joyful, joyful, joyful,
  Oh, won't it be joyful
  When his rich red ripe rare strawberry shortcake is gone.

4 A man who has some three-dollar Plymouth Rock all wool and a yard wide
     guaranteed not to rip nor tear pants,
  And giveth his neighbor none,
  The same can't have any of my three-dollar Plymouth Rock all wool and a
     yard wide guaranteed not to rip nor tear pants
  When his three-dollar Plymouth Rock all wool and a yard wide guaranteed
     not to rip nor tear pants are gone.
  Oh, won't it be joyful, joyful, joyful,
  Oh, won't it be joyful
  When his three-dollar Plymouth Rock all wool and a yard wide guaranteed
     not to rip nor tear pants are gone.

Fifty Cents

This saga of a young swain's monetary embarassment in the face of his young lady's appetite appeared in numerous songsters of the later nineteenth century and was a favorite of many singers in the early decades of the recording industry. Because of its popularity, texts of almost all recovered versions are very similar. The half line forgotten by Mr. Ladnier in the fifth stanza appears in other versions as "it made me shake with fear."

Sung by Mr. John Ladnier, Point Clear, 7 July 1947.

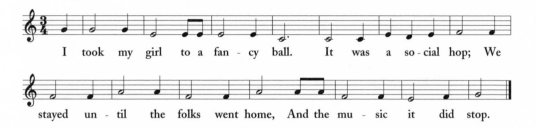

I took my girl to a fan-cy ball. It was a so-cial hop; We
stayed un-til the folks went home, And the mu-sic it did stop.

2 To a restaurant we went,
Best one in the street.
She said she wasn't hungry,
But this is what she eat:

3 Dozen raw, plate of slaw,
Chicken and a roast,
Sparagrass and applesauce
With a soft-shell crab on toast,

4 Big box stew and crackers too.
Her appetite was immense.
When she called for pie I thought I'd die,
For I had but fifty cents.

5 She said she wasn't thirsty,
But this is what she drank:
Whiskey skin, glass of gin

. . . .

Some ginger pop with rum on top,
A schooner of lager beer,

6 A glass of ale, a gin cocktail.
She oughta had more sense.
She called for more; I fell on the floor
For I had but fifty cents.

7 You bet I wasn't hungry,
I didn't care to eat,
Expecting every moment
To be kicked out in the street.

8 She said she'd bring her family round
Someday and we'd have fun,
And I gave the man my fifty cents,
And this is what he done:

9 He mashed my nose, he tore my clothes,
   He hit me in the jaw,
   He gave me the prize of a pair of black eyes,
   And with me swept the floor,

10 He took me where my pants hung loose
   And fired me over the fence.
   Take my advice and don't try it twice
   When you have but fifty cents.

Hard Times

Although many versions of this satiric song have been recovered, and although they all follow the same basic structural pattern, very few versions share many of the same details. Even when singers attack the same occupation, they usually do so from quite different perspectives. Evidently the popularity of the song is based upon its form's adaptability to whatever targets the singer might choose.

Sung by Mrs. J. K. Estes, Fort Payne, 31 July 1946.

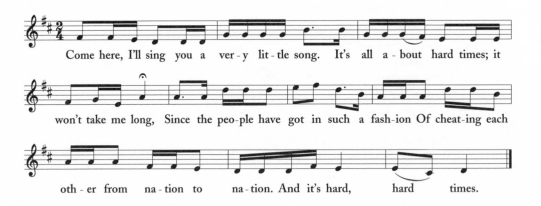

Come here, I'll sing you a ver-y lit-tle song. It's all a-bout hard times; it won't take me long, Since the peo-ple have got in such a fash-ion Of cheat-ing each oth-er from na-tion to na-tion. And it's hard, hard times.

2 Here's the old preacher, the worst of all,
   Preachin' for the money but not for the soul.
   He rides at his circuit some twelve times a year;
   If your soul's lost you may be sure he don't care.
   And it's hard, hard times.

3 Here's the old merchant, the worst of all,
   He cheats his customers in his sugar and his salt.
   He tells his tales from evening till night,
   But he'll charge you five dollars when a dollar was the price.
   And it's hard, hard times.

4 Here's the old shoemaker, the worst of all,
   Sits and sews with his braces and his awls.
   He takes his stitches an inch at a clip
   And then he'll vow that the shoes won't rip.
   And it's hard, hard times.

5 Here's the old miller I like to forgot,
   Sits all day and pecks on his rock.
   Sometimes he takes half and sometimes all,
   And then he'll vow that he didn't toll at all.
   And it's hard, hard times.

6 Here's the young girls to church they'll go;
   They ruffle and puffle and try to make a show,
   Play ruffle and a puffle to try and look neat
   And make the boys think they are so sweet.
   And it's hard, hard times.

7 Here's the young boys to church they'll go;
   They ruffle and puffle and try to make a show.
   To town they'll go for the brandy and wine;
   All such boys the ladies will find.
   And it's hard, hard times.

8 Here comes the end of my song,
   Very well worded but not very long,
   And I hope that you all your attention will give,
   For the devil gets all that the Lord won't forgive.
   And it's hard, hard times.

The Watermelon Song

This delightful tune and silly lyric almost certainly come to us from the vaudeville stage
in the first decade of the twentieth century. Some other versions have three more lines

at the beginning: "There was a watermelon / A-growing in the garden / And in the garden wall there was a hole."

Sung by Mrs. Helen Thigpen, Troy, 22 July 1947.

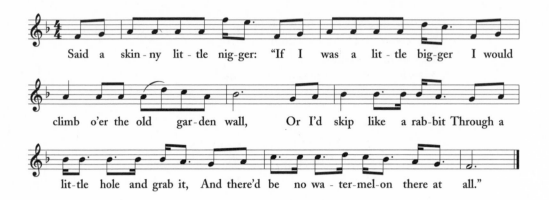

Said a skin-ny lit-tle nig-ger: "If I was a lit-tle big-ger I would climb o'er the old gar-den wall, Or I'd skip like a rab-bit Through a lit-tle hole and grab it, And there'd be no wa-ter-mel-on there at all."

Work Song

This is the chorus from an early-twentieth-century vaudeville tune that was popularized in the South over the radio by the Johnson Brothers Band from Sand Mountain. Although Mrs. King used the title "Work Song," the song is better known by its first four words.

Sung by Mrs. Irma Smith King, Selma, 15 August 1945.

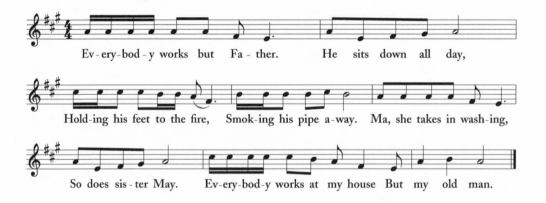

Ev-ery-bod-y works but Fa-ther. He sits down all day, Hold-ing his feet to the fire, Smok-ing his pipe a-way. Ma, she takes in wash-ing, So does sis-ter May. Ev-ery-bod-y works at my house But my old man.

Melissa

I have found no other versions of this comic song, which is pretty obviously of professional origin.

Sung by Mrs. Kate Newton Middleton, Mobile, 21 August 1946.

First time I saw Me - lis - sa she was sit - ting in the
cel - lar, Sit - ting in the cel - lar shell - ing peas (shell - ing
peas), And when I stooped to kiss her, she said she'd tell her
fa - ther, For she was such an aw - ful girl to tease. Oh,
was-n't she sil - ly, you bet she was; She said she'd nev - er leave me. But
did-n't she do it, you bet she did; She has - tened to de - ceive me. And be -
cause she was so cru - el, From the flame she took the fu - el, And I
nev - er saw Me - lis - sa an - y - more, you bet.

2 We were almost to be married, and yet we ever tarried,
   Content to revel in our dream of joy (dream of joy),

But our dream of joy was busted for she got up and dusted,
And ran off with an awful butcher boy (butcher boy).
Oh, wasn't it rough, you bet it was tough,
It couldn't have been any tougher.
And wasn't she silly, you bet she was,
To go with such a duffer.
And because she was so cruel,
From the flame she took the fuel,
And I never saw Melissa anymore, you bet.

Bible Tales

A burlesque of spirituals, this song once enjoyed great favor with college glee clubs and drinking societies. Other versions contain many more stanzas than this, but relatively few of the tales are ever drawn from the New Testament. Arnold's manuscript notebook includes a variant reading, attributed only to "Underwood," for the last two words in the fourth stanza: "him in the ear."

Sung by Mr. Donald Mead, Russellville, 3 August 1945.

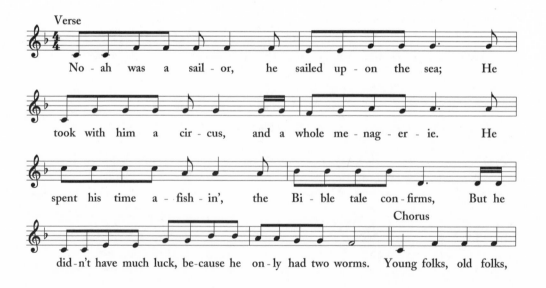

Verse

No - ah was a sail - or, he sailed up - on the sea; He

took with him a cir - cus, and a whole me - nag - er - ie. He

spent his time a - fish - in', the Bi - ble tale con - firms, But he

Chorus

did-n't have much luck, be-cause he on-ly had two worms. Young folks, old folks,

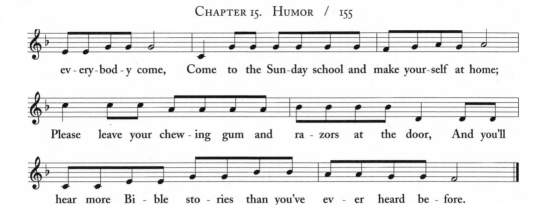

ev-ery-bod-y come, Come to the Sun-day school and make your-self at home;

Please leave your chew-ing gum and ra-zors at the door, And you'll

hear more Bi-ble sto-ries than you've ev-er heard be-fore.

2 Jonah was a sailor, so runs the Bible tale;
   He took an ocean voyage on a transatlantic whale.
   The whale was overcrowded, which put Jonah to distress,
   So Jonah pushed the button and the whale did all the rest.

   Chorus

3 Meshach, Shadrach and Abednego
   Disobeyed the king, and so they had to go
   Into the fiery furnace to be burned out like chaff,
   But they wore asbestos B.V.D.'s and gave the king a laugh.

   Chorus

4 Salome was a dancer, she danced the hootchy kootch;
   The people didn't like her 'cause she didn't wear so mooch.
   The king said, "My dear, we cannot have you here."
   But Salome said, "The heck you can't," and kicked the chandelier.

   Chorus

5 Daniel was a naughty man, he wouldn't mind the king.
   The people said they never heard of such a silly thing;
   They put him in a den with the lions underneath,
   But Daniel was a dentist and he pulled the lions' teeth.

   Chorus

Chapter 16
Frolic Tunes

Boil Them Cabbage Down

Many of the most popular southern American fiddle and banjo tunes swap verses back and forth with wild abandon, and the verses are rarely sung in the same order twice. It is often very difficult to separate "Boil Them Cabbage Down," "Cindy," "Lynchburg Town," "Old Joe Clark," and a half dozen other songs. Many of the stanzas of these pieces are sheer nonsense, providing little more than a verbal rationale to keep on plucking or bowing, but they are full of the high spirits appropriate to square dances or, in the absence of musical instruments, to play-parties. Combining elements of the musical traditions of the slaves, of the pseudo-black minstrels, and of the backwoods whites, these songs are uniquely American. "Boil" is often pronounced "bile," and all singers indiscriminately substitute the baking biscuits for the boiling cabbage whenever they feel like doing so.

A

Sung by Mrs. Josie O. Estes, Fort Payne, 12 June 1947.

Chorus: Boil them cab-bage down, Bake them bis-cuits brown; All in the world that I can sing Is boil them cab-bage down.

Verse: Wish I was in Ten-nes-see A-sit-ting on a rail, Sweet po-ta-to in my hand And a pos-sum by the tail.

Chorus

2 I wish I had a nickel,
 I wish I had a dime,
 I wish I had a pretty little girl
 To kiss and call her mine.

Chorus

3 I wish I had a needle
 As fine as I could sew;
 I'd sew my true love to my side
 And down the road I'd go.

Chorus

4 I wish I had a nickel,
 I wish I had a dime;
 I'd go and buy a pretty little watch
 To give that gal of mine.

Chorus

B

Sung by Mrs. Ethel Lake, Elba, 23 July 1947.

1 Ol' Masta had a barn,
 'Twas eighteen stories high,
 And every story in that barn
 Was full o' chicken pie.

 Chorus
 I wish that gal was mine,
 I wish that gal was mine;
 All the tunes that I can play
 Is I wish that gal was mine.

2 Oh if I had a banjo
 And all the strings would twang,
 All the tunes that I could play
 Was I wish that gal was mine.

 Chorus

C

Sung by Mr. Orie Neighbors, Brewton, 15 August 1946.

Raccoon up the 'simmon tree,
Possum on the groun';
Says the possum to the raccoon,
"Shake them 'simmons down."

D

Sung by Mr. John L. Hatley, Russelville, 27 July 1946.

I wished I was in Tennessee,
Never more to roam,
Wished somebody'd have my hand,
And boil the cabbage down.

Cindy

Mrs. Lambert said that she learned the words to this song from her black mammy and that her paternal grandfather frequently played the tune on his fiddle. "Cindy" was recorded in the mid-1920s by "Fiddlin'" John Carson, who, as Old Dan Wheeling, loses the famous fiddling contest in Stephen Vincent Benét's poem "The Mountain Whip-poorwill."

A

Sung by Mrs. Corie Lambert, Mobile, 3 September 1945.

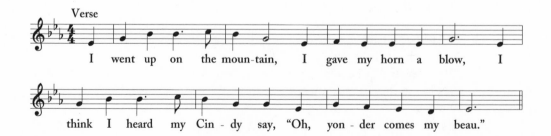

I went up on the moun-tain, I gave my horn a blow, I
think I heard my Cin-dy say, "Oh, yon-der comes my beau."

Oh, hop a-long home, my Cin - dy, Oh, hop a-long home I say, Oh, hop a-long home, my Cin - dy, A - long the rug - ged way.

2 Oh, when I owned a white house,
   A horse and buggy fine,
   I courted all the pretty gals;
   I always called them mine.

   Chorus

3 Cindy is a good gal,
   I knowed her all my life;
   If ever I get married,
   Cindy will be my wife.

   Chorus

4 Oh, hop along home, Cindy,
   And lay your hand in mine;
   And you shall live a lady
   As long as you are mine.

   Chorus

B

Sung by Mr. John L. Hatley, Russelville, 27 July 1946.

I went up on the mountain
An' I give my horn a blow,
An' every girl in Georgia
Came a-runnin' to the do'.

Chorus
Get on board, little children,
Get on board, little children,
Get on board, little children,
There's room for many mo'.

Melinda

Mrs. Middleton said that "this was sung by John Hull, a patent lawyer who was on the seas for a long time. He had a tremendous mouth, an awful cave, and we children used to shout and holler when he'd sing these to us. His eyes kept getting bigger and bigger."

Sung by Mrs. Kate Newton Middleton, Mobile, 21 August 1946.

Me - lin - da she   is hand - some, Just   as   fair   as an - y lamb;   Her

mouth   is like   a cel - lar door,   Her ear   is like   a ham.

2 She's seven feet and over
   And her hair is awful red,
   And she has to stand upon a chair
   When she wants to scratch her head.

3 First time I saw an elephant,
   How happy I should be;
   I'd lock Melinda in my trunk
   And always keep the key.

4 Or else an alligator,
   And whene'er I went to swim,
   I'd open wide my alligate
   And scoop Melinda in.

Buckeye Rabbit

This banjo/fiddle/dance tune is pretty surely of minstrel-show origin, perhaps derived from an old song called "Lucy Long."

Sung by Miss Laura Pillans, Mobile, 3 September 1945.

Verse

I want-ed sug-ar ver-y much, I went to sug-ar town; I

climbed up in the sug-ar tree And I shook shook sug-ar down.

Chorus

Buck-eye rab-bit, shoo, shoo, Buck-eye rab-bit, shoo dah,

Buck-eye rab-bit, shoo, shoo, shoo, Buck-eye rab-bit, shoo dah.

2 The raccoon's tail is ringed around,
   The possum's tail is bare,
   The rabbit's got no tail at all,
   Just a little bunch of hair.

   Chorus

3 I went down to my sweetheart's house;
   I ain't been there before.
   She fed me out of an old dog's trough,
   And I won't go there no more.

   Chorus

4 If I had a scolding wife,
   I'd whip her sure's you're born;
   I'd take her down to Mobile town
   And trade her off for corn.

   Chorus

5 I went down to New Orleans,
   I'd not been there before;
   A nigger knocked me in the eye,
   And I won't go there no more.

Chorus

Walk Tom Walker

This "coon song" from the blackface minstrel stage is a particularly good banjo tune, and as such it has been popular with radio and recording artists. Mrs. Couch notes that "the chorus is where the real banjo picking comes in."

Sung by Mrs. Janie Barnard Couch, Guntersville, 13 June 1947.

2 I slipped up behind him,
I slipped up behind him,
I slipped up behind him,
And catched him by the tail, catched him by the tail,
Catched him by the tail, and throwed him on the ground.

Chorus

3 That old coon he fought and scratched,
I gave him two licks all my might,
I bummed his eyes I spoiled his sight,
And I'm the chil' to fight, I'm the chil' to fight,
I'm the chil' to fight, and play the banjo too.

Chorus

Lank Dank

A version of this nursery song is included in the Sloane manuscript 1489 which was written in 1627, and it may well be older than that. It is usually called "The Carrion Crow." Mrs. Couch sang the chorus after the second and fourth stanzas.

Sung by Mrs. Janie Barnard Couch, Guntersville, 13 June 1947.

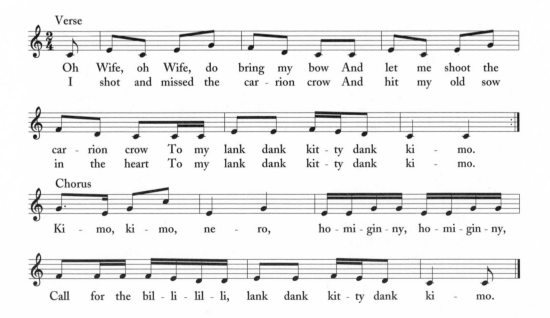

Verse

Oh Wife, oh Wife, do bring my bow And let me shoot the
I shot and missed the car - rion crow And hit my old sow

car - rion crow To my lank dank kit - ty dank ki - mo.
in the heart To my lank dank kit - ty dank ki - mo.

Chorus

Ki - mo, ki - mo, ne - ro, ho - mi - gin - ny, ho - mi - gin - ny,

Call for the bil - li - lil - li, lank dank kit - ty dank ki - mo.

3 Oh Wife, oh Wife, go bring some rum
And let me give the old sow some
With a lank dank kitty dank kimo.

4 Oh bring it in a silver spoon
For this old sow's in a mighty tune
With a lank dank kitty dank kimo.

Chorus

Carve Dat Possum

Both words and melody of this popular folksong are credited to Samuel Lucas, a black man born of free parents in Ohio in 1840. After serving in the Union army he performed onstage for almost fifty years, moving from minstrel troupes to vaudeville to musical comedy. Lucas's original version also contained stanzas dealing with the preparation and the deliciousness of possum meat. The song achieved some popularity with early "hillbilly" recording artists.

Sung by Mrs. Kate Newton Middleton, Mobile, 7 July 1947.

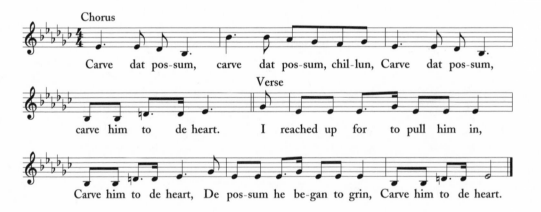

Chorus

Carve dat pos-sum, carve dat pos-sum, chil-lun, Carve dat pos-sum,

Verse

carve him to de heart. I reached up for to pull him in,

Carve him to de heart, De pos-sum he be-gan to grin, Carve him to de heart.

Chorus

2 I carried him home and dressed him off,
Carve him to de heart,
I hung him dat night in de frost,
Crave him to de heart.

Chorus

Run, Nigger, Run

It has been suggested that the refrain here refers to a time when slaves were required to be on their own plantations after dark and patrols roamed abroad to enforce this curfew, but there is no reason why the runner could not be a slave seeking freedom or a criminal evading the law. These serious possibilities, however, seem to have little to do with the nonsense that fills many versions of this song. Miss Pillans's second, third, and fourth stanzas simply repeat the first couplet's melody for the second.

A

Sung by Miss Laura Pillans, Mobile, 3 September 1945.

Chorus

2 A jaybird sittin' on a hickory limb,
   He winked at me and I winked at him.
   I picked up a rock and I hit him on the shin.
   Said he, "Lookee here, don't you do that again."

Chorus

3 Old cow died by the fork of the branch,
   Jaybird whistle and the blackbird dance.
   Creek's all gone, the pond's all dry;
   If it weren't for the tadpole, we would die.

Chorus

4 Old Miss Pembleton sittin' on a log,
Her finger on a trigger and her eye on a hog;
Up jump a tadpole, thought it was a crane,
Said he, "Lordy mercy, how we all need rain."

Chorus

B

Sung by Mrs. J. R. Aplin, Mobile, 3 September 1945.

Some folks say a nigger won't steal,
But I caught one in my cornfield;
That nigger run, that nigger flew,
That nigger tore his shirt in two.

The Jaybird Song

The impudent and raucous jaybird rises from a supporting role in the preceding song to a starring one here. Although there is an obvious influence of the spiritual on its chorus, this song is determinedly secular, quite possibly of minstrel origin. Mrs. Carleton's pronunciation of "mourner" is close to "mona." Mrs. Peavy's verse, which shares tune and bird and some phrasing with Mrs. Carleton's, appears to have been adapted to some sort of children's game.

A

Sung by Mrs. Laurie Cater Carleton, Grove Hill, 22 August 1946.

Verse
A - way down yon - der, some-where off, The jay - bird died of the
whoop - ing cough; He whooped so hard with the whoop - ing cough Till he
whooped his head and his tail both off. Oh mourn - er, you shall

be free, In the morn-ing, you shall be free, Sis-ter Liz-zie, you shall be

free, Un-cle Mo-ses, you shall be free, When the good Lord sets you free.

2 Away down yonder on Sycamore Street,
The niggers grow to be ten feet;
They go to bed, but it ain't no use,
For their feet stick out for the chickens to roost.

Chorus

3 A jay flew in the grocery store,
Right through the transom over the door;
He pecked at the coffee and he pecked at the tea;
If I hadn't been quick he'd a-pecked at me.

Chorus

B

Sung by Mrs. Jane Peavy, Atmore, 15 August 1946.

Away down yonder in the white oak branch,
The jaybirds whistle and the buzzards dance.
If you can't thread the needle, come wind the ball,
If you can't thread the needle, come wind the ball.

We Whooped and We Hollered

Early versions of this humorous hunting song are found in seventeenth-century England. The song has not changed greatly in form since its first appearance, though the things discovered vary considerably from singer to singer. Mrs. Kirk did not sing "booger" in the last stanza, but shouted it quite forcefully. Some other versions, less loud but more specific, identify the bogey as "the devil."

Sung by Mrs. Mary Wallace Kirk, Tuscumbia, 10 June 1947.

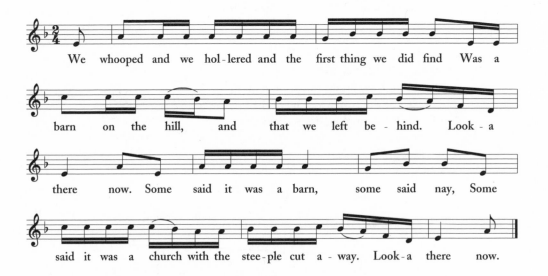

We whooped and we hol-lered and the first thing we did find Was a barn on the hill, and that we left be-hind. Look-a there now. Some said it was a barn, some said nay, Some said it was a church with the stee-ple cut a-way. Look-a there now.

2 So we whooped and we hollered and the next thing we did find
Was a pig in the lane, and that we left behind.
Look-a there now.
Some said it was a pig, some said nay,
Some said it was an elephant with his snout cut away.
Look-a there now.

3 We whooped and we hollered and the next thing we did find
Was the moon in the trees, and that we left behind.
Look-a there now.
Some said it was the moon, some said nay,
Some said it was a cheese with its half cut away.
Look-a there now.

4 So we whooped and we hollered and the next thing we did find
  Was a frog in the well, and that we left behind.
  Look-a there now.
  Some said it was a frog, some said nay,
  Some said it was a jaybird with the feathers washed away.
  Look-a there now.

5 So we whooped and we hollered and the next thing we did find
  Was an owl in the trees, and that we left behind.
  Look-a there now.
  Some said it was an owl, some said nay,
  Some said it was a booger and we all ran away.
  Look-a there now.

Chapter 17
Children Choosing Partners

Hog Drovers

Descended from an old English game-song called "Three Dukes A-Riding," "Hog Drovers" seems to have served often as a "pairing-off" song at the beginning of play-parties. One boy and one girl sit in the room's center as father and daughter, the rest of the girls sit or stand around the walls of the room, and the rest of the boys sing the first stanza while moving in a circle around the pair. The father replies with the second stanza, and the boys answer back with the third, snapping their fingers as they sing "that" and "here" in its first line. Changing his mind, the father, in the fourth stanza, pairs his daughter with one of the hog drovers. Another girl then approaches to take the daughter's position, and the game continues until all possible partnerships are formed. The father figure clearly has considerable matchmaking powers.

Sung by Mrs. Myrtle Love Hester, Florence, 2 August 1946.

"Hog dro - vers, hog dro - vers, hog dro - vers we are, A - court-ing your daugh-ter so neat and so fair, And we want lodg - ing here, oh here, And we want lodg - ing here."

> 2 "Oh this is my daughter who sits by my side,
> And no hog drover can have her for a bride,
> So you can't get lodging here, oh here,
> So you can't get lodging here."

> 3 "Take that for your daughter and here for yourself;
> I'll travel on farther and better myself,

And I don't want lodging here, oh here,
And I don't want lodging here."

4   "Oh this is my daughter who sits by my side,
And this young fellow can have her for a bride,
And you can have lodging here, oh here,
And you can have lodging here."

Little Gentleman from the Spring

This is pretty certainly another pairing-off game in which different singers alternate pairs of lines. Succeeding stanzas begin with successive numbers: the second stanza—"Two little gentleman," the third—"Three little gentleman," and so on. Unfortunately, Ms. Longmire seems to have given Arnold no description of the game.

Sung by Ms. Mozelle Longmire, Atmore, 17 July 1947.

"One lit-tle gen-tle-man just from the spring, To court your lov-ing

daugh-ter Jane." "My daugh-ter Jane, she most too young To be con-trolled by

an - y - one." "Oh, let her be old or let her be young, It

is her du - ty and it must be done." "Get back, get back, you

sass - y man To the fair - est in the land." "The fair - est one that

I can see, So come Miss ———— and walk with me."

Here Comes Someone A-Roving

Mrs. Richardson describes this game for choosing partners: "A line of players is formed, and one player, the rover, comes up to the line as they sing the first two verses. On the fifth verse he chooses someone whose name is filled in and the game goes on with this couple coming toward the line. The girl now chooses a partner, substituting 'Mr.' for 'Miss' in the fifth verse and the boy's name. Continue playing until all players are chosen." Although the structure here is very similar to that of "Hog Drovers," there is a major difference in that the individual chooses his or her own partner, rather than abiding by the dictates of the father figure. The rover, of course, sings the third stanza as well as the fifth.

"Here comes some-one a - rov - ing, a - rov - ing, a - rov - ing,
Here comes some-one a - rov - ing, Ran - som, han - som, tid - dy, bo-peep."

Sung by Mrs. Pansy Richardson, Mobile, 30 August 1945.

2 "What are you roving here for, here for, here for?
What are you roving here for?
Ransom, hansom, tiddy, bo-peep."

3 "I'm roving here to get married, married, married,
I'm roving here to get married.
Ransom, hansom, tiddy, bo-peep."

4 "Who do you reckon would have you, have you, have you?
Who do you reckon would have you?
Ransom, hansom, tiddy, bo-peep."

5 "I guess Miss ——— would have me, would have me, would have me,
I guess Miss ——— would have me.
Ransom, hansom, tiddy, bo-peep."

Come Over the Heather

This may be the most widely known of all play-party songs, and its figures are clearly those of the dance rather than of any sort of game. Several scholars contend that it is really a Virginia reel danced to unaccompanied song. The lack of fiddle or other instrument makes it a play-party game acceptable to members of all religious denominations, even those who frown most severely on dancing to instrumental music. The song is of particular interest because its Charlie seems pretty surely descended from the Bonnie Prince Charlie of the Jacobite ballads, the pretender to the throne of England. Certainly a high proportion of this song's singers are of Scottish highland stock.

A

Sung by Sayre [only identification], Montgomery, between 2 and 10 August 1946.

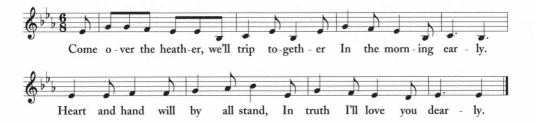

Come o-ver the heath-er, we'll trip to-geth - er   In the morn-ing ear - ly.

Heart and hand will by all stand, In truth I'll love you dear - ly.

2 I won't have any of your weevily wheat;
  I won't have any of your barley.
  Give me some of your good wheat
  To make a cake for Charlie.

3 Charlie is a handsome man,
  Charlie is a dandy,
  Charlie loves to court the girls
  Because it comes so handy.

B

Sung by Mr. M. C. Oliver, Valley Head, between March and June 1948.

1 Over the river . . .
  Over the river Charlie,
  Over the river to feed my sheep
  And measure up my barley.

2 Charlie's this and Charlie's that,
  Oh, Charlie he's a daisy.

Charlie, he's a very young man
Who looks so awful lazy.

3 Charlie's this and Charlie's that,
Oh, Charlie he's a dandy.
Charlie, he's a very young man
Who brings the girls some candy.

Acorns Grow on White Oak Trees

The boys and girls sing this as they dance in a ring around one person chosen for the center. At the appropriate moment, that person chooses a partner. The second time through the verse the couple chooses another couple to join them in the center, and the numbers would be changed accordingly: "Four in the middle and they can't get out." But four is the largest number we ever find in the middle, and the next line would be: "Four in the middle and we knock two out." The original inner couple returns to the outer circle. Depending upon the ages, inclinations, and chaperones of the participants, there may be more going on here than just singing and dancing. The "little sugar" taken could well be a kiss. In other versions, the second line is "The river flows with brandy."

Sung by Mrs. Pearl Trotter, Troy, 22 July 1946.

A - corns grow on white oak trees; The riv - er flows
like branch-es free. Go choose the one that you like best, And
take a lit - tle sug - ar in your cof - fee. Two in the mid - dle and they
can't get out, Two in the mid - dle and they can't get out,
Two in the mid - dle and they can't get out, As we go swing-ing a - round.

Bower of Roses

An equal number of boys and girls form lines facing each other. The girls sing the verse below, and the boys repond in the affirmative: "If you build me . . . I will come today," and so forth. Then the couples join hands and raise their arms, as in "London Bridge." One couple on the end skips through the "bower of roses" and begins skipping in a circle around the room. They are followed by the second couple, the third, and so on, until the whole company is skipping a circular pattern. When the last couple completes the circuit of the room, the game ends.

Sung by Mrs. Martha N. Drisdale, Sheffield, 10 June 1947.

Chapter 18
Children Playing Games

Green Gravel

The players stand either in a line, with each child facing in the same direction, or in a circle, with each child facing the center. As each child's name is called, he or she must turn around, and the song continues until all the children have turned. Several Alabama versions substitute for Mrs. Drisdale's first line: "Green crabapple tree where the grass grows so green." Mrs. Richardson indicated that her text was sung exclusively by girls.

A

Sung by Mrs. Martha N. Drisdale, Sheffield, 10 June 1947.

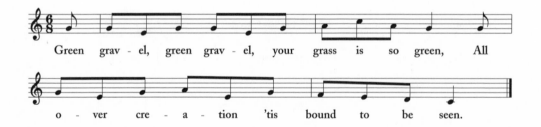

Green grav - el, green grav - el, your grass is so green, All o - ver cre - a - tion 'tis bound to be seen.

2 Dear ——, dear ——, your sweetheart is dead;
He wrote you a letter, so turn back your head.

B

Sung by Mrs. Pansy Richardson, Mobile, 30 August 1945.

1 Green gravel, green gravel, your dress is so green,
The prettiest fair maiden I ever have seen.

2 Miss ——, Miss ——, your sweetheart is dead;
He sent you a letter, so turn back your head.

My Pigeon House

Mrs. Drisdale describes the game: "One group of children stand in a ring holding hands, making the pigeon house, and another group of children, usually with a leader, are inside the ring of children who are the pigeon house, and they are the little pigeons. While the song is being sung, and it comes to the place where it says the pigeon house is open wide, the children on the outside of the ring lift their hands high, and the pigeons fly out, and then as they are supposed to come back in they fly back in, and the children lower their hands to keep them in the ring."

Sung by Mrs. Martha N. Drisdale, Sheffield, 10 June 1947.

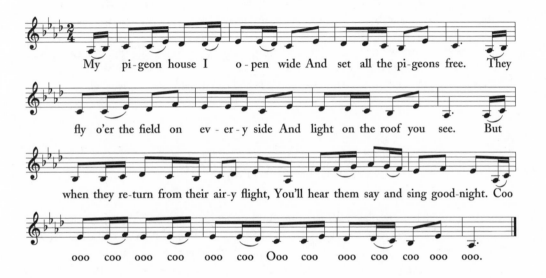

Riggety Jig

Mrs. Drisdale describes the game: "One child is chosen to walk down the street first. At the end of the verse where he says he chooses a playmate, then he chooses a child (joins crossed hands with him or her) and skips. After those two children have skipped around the room once, they walk down the street in single file and choose another playmate until the whole group of children has played the game." Mrs. Drisdale also told Arnold that the children "walk sedately" until they choose partners and then they skip a little faster.

Sung by Mrs. Martha N. Drisdale, Sheffield, 10 June 1947.

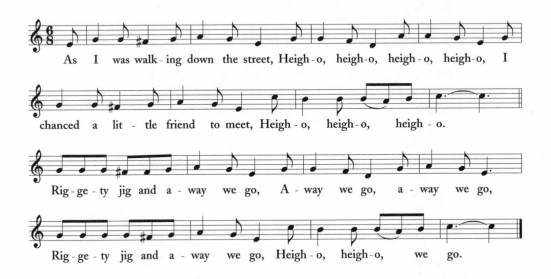

As I was walk-ing down the street, Heigh-o, heigh-o, heigh-o, heigh-o, I chanced a lit-tle friend to meet, Heigh-o, heigh-o, heigh-o.

Rig-ge-ty jig and a-way we go, A-way we go, a-way we go,

Rig-ge-ty jig and a-way we go, Heigh-o, heigh-o, we go.

The Old Gray Cat

In this game, Mrs. Drisdale tells us, "one child pretends to be the old gray cat and sits in front of the other children who are the little mice. Then he sings the song after everything has become very quiet. He continues to sing as the 'mice' move closer and then looks up and grabs the first child he can grab. That child then becomes the old gray cat."

Sung by Mrs. Martha N. Drisdale, Sheffield, 10 June 1947.

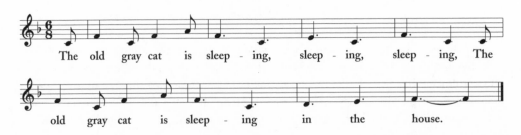

The old gray cat is sleep-ing, sleep-ing, sleep-ing, The old gray cat is sleep-ing in the house.

2 The little mice come creeping, creeping, creeping,
   The little mice come creeping through the house.

Like a Leaf or Feather

Mrs. Drisdale indicated that this game has no set pattern. Children can stand in a circle, a line, or just scattered about as they act out the words they sing.

Sung by Mrs. Martha N. Drisdale, Sheffield, 10 June 1947.

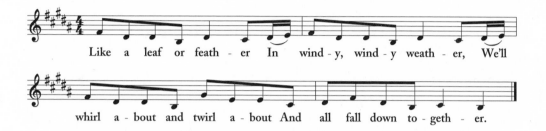

Little Sally Walker

This is a popular children's game with many variations in its words, tune, and action. In Ms. Longmire's version, the song is sung by a group of children standing (or moving) hand in hand in a circle around the seated "Little Sally Walker" (or "Little Tommy Walker" if a boy is in the center). Normally the child in the center pretends to be crying and rises at the appropriate moment to wipe her "weeping eyes." She then does a very agitated dance, as the other children request. The "best loved" child in the ring, to whom it is "shaken" last, becomes the next "Sally" or "Tommy" and the game continues, until all the children have danced. When Ms. Longmire sang the words a second time, she substituted "do the Mobile dip" for "let your backbone slip."

Sung by Ms. Mozelle Longmire, Atmore, 17 July 1947.

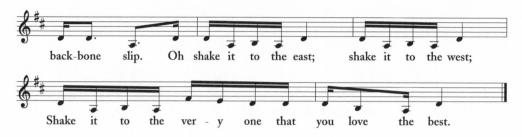

back-bone slip. Oh shake it to the east; shake it to the west;

Shake it to the ver - y one that you love the best.

Smoke Goes Up the Chimney

Children singing this song work the imaginary damper with their hands, and they turn around to indicate the smoke spiraling up the chimney.

Sung by Mrs. Kate Newton Middleton, Mobile, 7 July 1947.

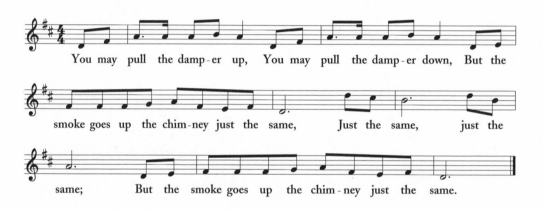

You may pull the damp-er up, You may pull the damp-er down, But the

smoke goes up the chim-ney just the same, Just the same, just the

same; But the smoke goes up the chim-ney just the same.

2 You may push the damper in,
   You may pull the damper out,
   But the smoke goes up the chimney just the same,
   Just the same, just the same;
   But the smoke goes up the chimney just the same.

Chapter 19
Answering-Back Songs

The Little White Daisies

The children sit in a ring, except for the one who is "it," who sits in the center, and that child's first and last names begin the first and second stanzas. The first name is used in the third stanza. When the game starts, the name of the first widow or widower must be selected arbitrarily, but after the first time the name of the child who was previously "it" is used. The new person to be "it" is chosen by the child in the center counting around the circle until twenty-four is reached.

Sung by Mrs. Pansy Richardson, Mobile, 10 July 1947.

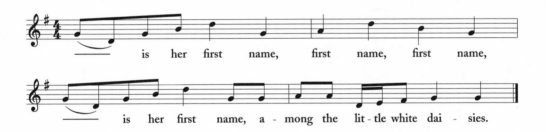

2 —— is her second name, second name, second name,
   —— is her second name, among the little white daisies.

3 Now poor —— is dead and gone, dead and gone, dead and gone,
   Now poor —— is dead and gone, among the little white daisies.

4 Left poor —— a widower, a widower, a widower,
   Left poor —— a widower, among the little white daisies.

5 Twenty-four children out in a field, out in a field, out in a field,
   Twenty-four children out in a field, among the little white daisies.

Old Pompey

The singing children march in a circle around the dead Old Pompey until they reach the end of the third stanza. Here they stop in place and the child nearest the head of Pompey becomes the old woman who must move into the circle, pretending to pick up apples. As the fifth stanza begins, Pompey rises and chases the old woman, trying sometimes to kick ("pop") her but often merely to touch her before the stanza ends. If he fails, he must resume his place in the grave and the song begins again. If he succeeds, the old woman must act out the sixth stanza as the children sing it, after which she becomes the new Old Pompey and the former Pompey takes his place in the ring.

Sung by Mrs. Pansy Richardson, Mobile, 10 July 1947.

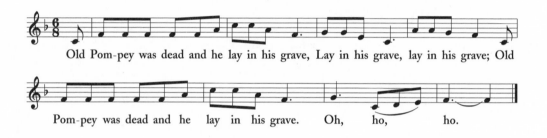

Old Pom-pey was dead and he lay in his grave, Lay in his grave, lay in his grave; Old Pom-pey was dead and he lay in his grave. Oh, ho, ho.

2 There grew an old apple tree over his head,
    Over his head, over his head;
    There grew an old apple tree over his head.
    Oh, ho, ho.

3 The apples got ripe and begun to fall,
    Begun to fall, begun to fall;
    The apples got ripe and begun to fall.
    Oh, ho, ho.

4 There came an old woman a-picking them up,
    Picking them up, picking them up;
    There came an old woman a-picking them up.
    Oh, ho, ho.

5 Old Pompey got up and he gave her a pop,
    Gave her a pop, gave her a pop;
    Old Pompey got up and he gave her a pop.
    Oh, ho, ho.

6 And made the old woman go hippity hop,
   Hippity hop, hippity hop;
   And made the old woman go hippity hop.
   Oh, ho, ho.

Miss Jennie O. Jones

Two lines of players face each other with the "Jennie O. Jones" standing or seated between them. She pantomimes the actions of the opening stanzas. The first line skips forward and back singing the first stanza. Jennie speaks, and then the second line skips forward and back singing the second stanza. This pattern continues until Jennie shouts "Ghost," and then the lines scatter. Whomever Jennie catches takes her place for the next round.

Sung by Mrs. Pansy Richardson, Mobile, 10 July 1947.

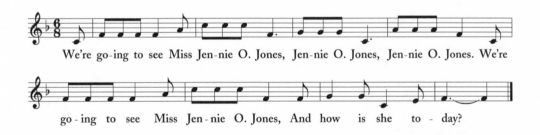

We're go-ing to see Miss Jen-nie O. Jones, Jen-nie O. Jones, Jen-nie O. Jones. We're
go-ing to see Miss Jen-nie O. Jones, And how is she to - day?

Spoken: I'm washing.

2 We're very glad to hear it,
   Hear it, hear it.
   We're very glad to hear it;
   We'll call another day.

3 We're going to see Miss Jennie O. Jones,
   Jennie O. Jones, Jennie O. Jones.
   We're going to see Miss Jennie O. Jones,
   And how is she today?

Spoken: I'm ironing.

4 We're very glad to hear it,
   Hear it, hear it.
   We're very glad to hear it;
   We'll call another day.

5 We're going to see Miss Jennie O. Jones,
   Jennie O. Jones, Jennie O. Jones.
   We're going to see Miss Jennie O. Jones,
   And how is she today?

Spoken: I'm sick.

6 We're very sorry to hear it,
   Hear it, hear it.
   We're very sorry to hear it;
   We'll call another day.

7 We're going to see Miss Jennie O. Jones,
   Jennie O. Jones, Jennie O. Jones.
   We're going to see Miss Jennie O. Jones,
   And how is she today?

Spoken: She's worse.

8 We're very sorry to hear it,
   Hear it, hear it.
   We're very sorry to hear it;
   We'll call another day.

9 We're going to see Miss Jennie O. Jones,
   Jennie O. Jones, Jennie O. Jones.
   We're going to see Miss Jennie O. Jones,
   And how is she today?

Spoken: She's dead.

10 We're very sorry to hear it,
   Hear it, hear it.
   We're very sorry to hear it;
   We'll call another day.

11 What shall we bury her in,
   Bury her in, bury her in,

What shall we bury her in?
We'll call another day.

Spoken: Blue.

12   Blue is for babies,
For babies, for babies,
Blue is for babies,
And that will never do.

13   What shall we bury her in,
Bury her in, bury her in,
What shall we bury her in?
We'll call another day.

Spoken: Red.

14   Red is for firemen,
For firemen, for firemen,
Red is for firemen,
And that will never do.

15   What shall we bury her in,
Bury her in, bury her in,
What shall we bury her in?
We'll call another day.

Spoken: White.

16   White is for angels,
For angels, for angels,
White is for angels,
And that will have to do.

17   We're going to her funeral,
Her funeral, her funeral,
We're going to her funeral . . .

Shouted: Ghost.

Jenny Jane

An answering-back song imported from Britain and now found throughout America, this piece may well be related to "Miss Jennie O. Jones" both by the girls' names and by the progression of colors. But "Jenny Jane" is clearly simpler than "Miss Jennie O. Jones," and our version, like most versions found in America, is simpler than the British texts. They frequently conclude with blue, which Jenny will wear because "my [or your] love is true."

Sung by Mrs. Mary Wallace Kirk, Tuscumbia, 10 June 1947.

2 "Jenny Jane, won't you wear black?"
   "I won't wear black, it's the color of my back."

   Refrain

3 "Jenny Jane, won't you wear blue?"
   "I won't wear blue, it's the color of my shoe."

   Refrain

4 "Jenny Jane, won't you wear brown?"
   "I won't wear brown, it's the color of the groun'."

   Refrain

5 "Jenny Jane, won't you wear green?"
   "I won't wear green, it's a color too mean."

   Refrain

6 "Jenny Jane, won't you wear yeller?"
  "I won't wear yeller, it's a color too meller."

Refrain

Feed the Animals

The first half of each line is sung by one person, the latter half by another, and the designations (girl, boy, Sir, Ma'am) depend on the participants. The game, of course, lies in the respondent's ability to think of food appropriate for the animal named by the questioner, and the game can go on indefinitely. Two people can play by themselves, or many can be included, with a child having to stop playing if he or she repeats the name of an animal already used or if a sensible food cannot be thought of in time. Mrs. Richardson's is an interesting variation of the game. She said she played this game with her old black mammy, Aunt Emma, and that the response to the last question was action rather than words: "Then I'd have to flop my arms like buzzard's wings circling around the room."

A

Sung by Mrs. Mae Erskine Irvine, Florence, 9 June 1947.

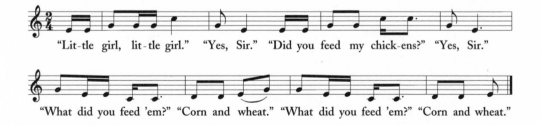

"Lit-tle girl, lit-tle girl." "Yes, Sir." "Did you feed my chick-ens?" "Yes, Sir."

"What did you feed 'em?" "Corn and wheat." "What did you feed 'em?" "Corn and wheat."

2 "Little boy, little boy." "Yes, Ma'am."
  "Did you feed my horse?" "Yes, Ma'am."
  "What did you feed 'im?" "Oats and barley."
  "What did you feed 'im?" "Oats and barley."

3 "Little girl, little girl." "Yes, Sir."
  "Did you feed my cow?" "Yes, Sir."
  "What did you feed 'er?" "Oats and hay."
  "What did you feed 'er?" "Oats and hay."

4 "Little boy, little boy." "Yes, Ma'am."
  "Did you feed my sheep?" "Yes, Ma'am."
  "What did you feed 'em?" "Oats and barley."
  "What did you feed 'em?" "Oats and barley."

5 "Little girl, little girl." "Yes, Sir."
  "Did you feed my cat?" "Yes, Sir."
  "What did you feed 'er?" "Bread and milk."
  "What did you feed 'er?" "Bread and milk."

B

Sung by Mrs. Pansy Richardson, Mobile, 10 July 1947.

"Did you feed my pony?" "Yes, Ma'am."
"Did the pony eat?" "Yes, Ma'am."
"Did the pony die?" "Yes, Ma'am."
"Did the buzzards come?" "Yes, Ma'am."
"How'd they come?"

Mr. Carpenter

Mrs. Irvine said she learned this delightful answering-back song from her grandfather, Dr. A. R. Erskine of Huntsville. The reason for the nonsense here may be suggested by the last stanza.

Sung by Mrs. Mae Erskine Irvine, Florence, 9 June 1947.

Spoken: Hello, Mr. Carpenter, how'll I get across the river?

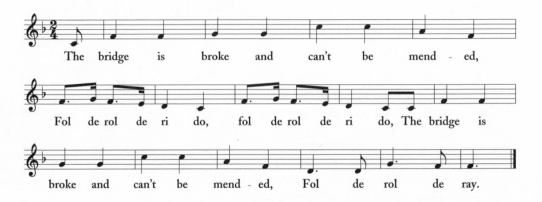

The bridge is broke and can't be mend - ed,
Fol de rol de ri do, fol de rol de ri do, The bridge is
broke and can't be mend - ed, Fol de rol de ray.

Spoken: But Mr. Carpenter, how deep is the river?

2 Throw a rock, it will sink to the bottom,
   Fol de rol de ri do, fol de rol de ri do,
   Throw a rock, it will sink to the bottom,
   Fol de rol de ray.

Spoken: But Mr. Carpenter, how can I get across the river?

3 The ducks and the geese they all swim over,
   Fol de rol de ri do, fol de rol de ri do,
   The ducks and the geese they all swim over,
   Fol de rol de ray.

Spoken: Mr. Carpenter, whose fine house is that you're building?

4 It's none of yours, I can tell by the asking,
   Fol de rol de ri do, fol de rol de ri do,
   It's none of yours, I can tell by the asking,
   Fol de rol de ray.

Spoken: Mr. Carpenter, have you got any wine at your house?

5 Some of the best you've ever tasted,
   Fol de rol de ri do, fol de rol de ri do,
   Some of the best you've ever tasted,
   Fol de rol de ray.

Chapter 20
Songs Appealing to Children

Mister Tick-Tock

Ms. Mary Chapman, the black nurse employed by the Carleton family, used to sing this to the delight of her little charges.

Sung by Ms. Mary Chapman, Grove Hill, 5 July 1947.

Mis-ter Tick-tock, Tick-tock, Please hur-ry up, Mis-ter Clock.

Oh you count the hours so slow; Can't you make them fas-ter, fast-er go? Mis-ter

Tick-tock, Tick-tock, Please hur-ry up, Mis-ter Clock.

Bullfrog Jumped

Children may have acted out this song.

Sung by Mrs. Laurie Cater Carleton, Grove Hill, 5 July 1947.

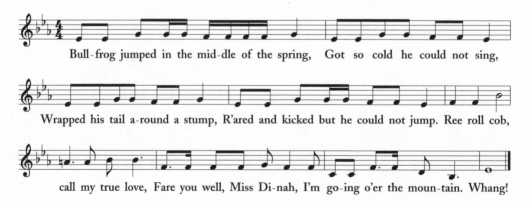

Bull-frog jumped in the mid-dle of the spring, Got so cold he could not sing,

Wrapped his tail a-round a stump, R'ared and kicked but he could not jump. Ree roll cob,

call my true love, Fare you well, Miss Di-nah, I'm go-ing o'er the moun-tain. Whang!

The Black Cat

Relatively few versions of this nursery song have been recovered from folk tradition. Its origin is unknown, but it seems to be found only in the southern states.

Sung by Mrs. Laurie Cater Carleton, Grove Hill, 5 July 1947.

Verse

Who's so full of fun and glee, Hap-py as a cat can be?

All his sides so nice and fat, Oh I love my old black cat.

Chorus

Oh, oh, kit-ty, oh, poor kit-ty, Sit-ting so co-zy, close by the fire.

2 Pleasant, purring, pretty kitty,
   Frisky, full of fun, and fussy,
   Not a fear of mouse and rat,
   Oh I love my old black cat.

   Chorus

Dance to Your Daddy

Mrs. Middleton learned this song from her mother.

Sung by Mrs. Kate Newton Middleton, Mobile, 22 August 1946.

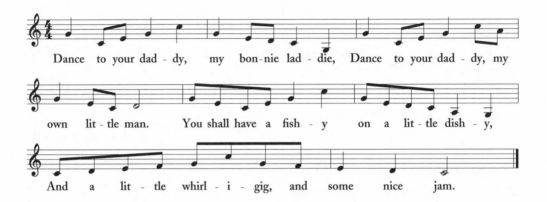

Dance to your dad - dy, my bon-nie lad - die, Dance to your dad - dy, my own lit - tle man. You shall have a fish - y on a lit - tle dish - y, And a lit - tle whirl - i - gig, and some nice jam.

Bobby Bumble

Miss Milner learned this song from her mother and found it useful in teaching kindergarten.

Sung by Miss Josie Milner, Florence, 23 August 1945.

Hur - rah for Bob - by Bum - ble, He nev - er minds a tum - ble, But up he jumps and rubs his bumps And does - n't e - ven grum - ble.

Short'nin' Bread

On 16 August 1945, Arnold copied this song from material collected by Mrs. Tartt in 1938 and 1939 and later deposited in the state archives in Montgomery. The origins of "Short'nin' Bread" have been lost. It may be a legitimate black plantation song or a product of the blackface minstrel stage. It has been used as a children's ring-game song, as a lullaby, and even as a concert song in the arrangement by Jacques Wolfe. Sometimes called "cracklin' bread," shortening bread was made of water-ground meal to which bacon gravy and bits of crisp bacon—the "cracklins"—had been added to make it especially rich.

Mrs. Ruby Pickens Tartt, Livingston.

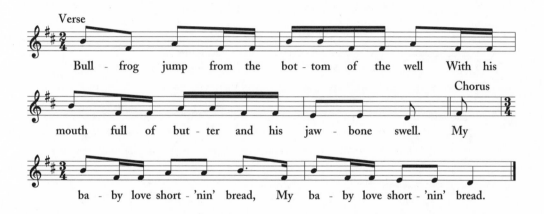

2 Put on the skillet, take off the lid,
 Mamma gonna cook some short'nin' bread.

Chorus

3 Bullfrog jump from out the well,
 Swore by God he was just from hell.

Chorus

Chapter 21
Nonsense Songs, Rocking Songs, and Lullabies

Here We Go Up

Although Mrs. Middleton called this a trotting song, or lullaby, she told Arnold that it was really a song sung to her just before bedtime by her father, who would swing her up and down and back and forth on his foot.

Sung by Mrs. Kate Newton Middleton, Mobile, 7 July 1947.

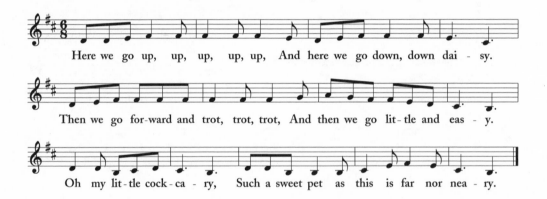

Here we go up, up, up, up, up, And here we go down, down dai - sy.

Then we go for-ward and trot, trot, trot, And then we go lit - tle and eas - y.

Oh my lit-tle cock - ca - ry, Such a sweet pet as this is far nor nea - ry.

Oh My Little Boy

Mrs. Irvine recalled that her grandfather would take her on one knee and her brother on the other and trot the children while singing this song.

Sung by Mrs. Mae Erskine Irvine, Florence, 9 June 1947.

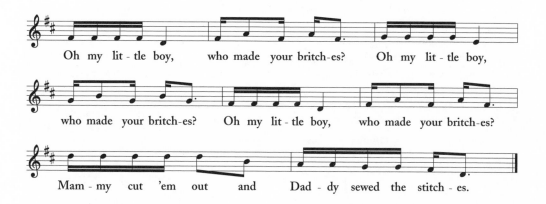

Rod a Rinc-tum

Mrs. Sawyer said that she learned this lullaby from her black nurse.

Sung by Mrs. Sarah Sawyer, Fort Payne, 31 July 1946.

Little Lapdog

Sung by Miss Vera Hall, Livingston, 16 June 1947.

Ma-ma's gon-na buy him a lit-tle lap-dog, Ma-ma's gon-na buy him a lit-tle lap-dog, Ma-ma's gon-na buy him a lit-tle lap-dog, Gon-na put him in his lap when she go 'broad. Come up horse-y, hey, hey, Come up horse-y, hey, hey. Go to sleep and don't you cry, Ma-ma's gon-na give you some ap-ple pie. Come up horse-y, hey, hey, Come up horse-y, hey, hey.

My Mama's Sweet Baby Boy

Sung by Ms. Zimmer Holding, Huntsville, 10 June 1947.

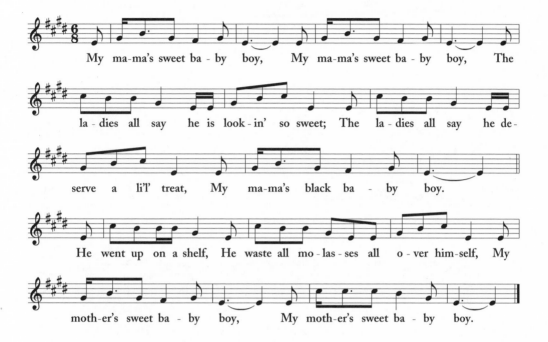

My ma-ma's sweet ba-by boy, My ma-ma's sweet ba-by boy, The
la-dies all say he is look-in' so sweet; The la-dies all say he de-
serve a li'l' treat, My ma-ma's black ba-by boy.
He went up on a shelf, He waste all mo-las-ses all o-ver him-self, My
moth-er's sweet ba-by boy, My moth-er's sweet ba-by boy.

2 My mother's sweet baby boy,
   My mother's sweet baby boy,
   The ladies all say that he deserves a li'l' treat.
   They gave him a ten cents to buy him a little drum;
   He take a li'l' ten cents and bought him a li'l' rum,
   My mother's sweet baby boy,
   My mama's black baby boy.

3 My mama's sweet baby boy,
   My mama's sweet baby boy,
   The ladies all say he is lookin' so sweet;
   The ladies all say that he deserves a li'l' treat,
   My mother's black baby boy.

Alabama Coon

A product of the late-nineteenth-century minstrel stage, this song has moved into tradition as a lullabye. In most versions the child is less precocious than here and his mammy watches him "grow" rather than "hoe."

Sung by Mrs. Emma Craig and Mr. Donald Mead, Florence, 31 July 1945.

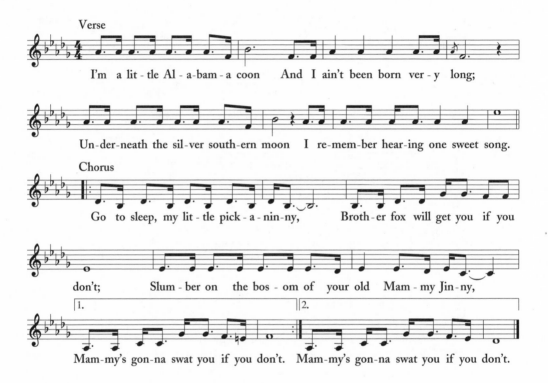

I'm a lit-tle Al-a-bam-a coon   And I ain't been born ver-y long;

Un-der-neath the sil-ver south-ern moon   I re-mem-ber hear-ing one sweet song.

Go to sleep, my lit-tle pick-a-nin-ny,   Broth-er fox will get you if you

don't;   Slum-ber on the bos-om of your old Mam-my Jin-ny,

1. Mam-my's gon-na swat you if you don't. 2. Mam-my's gon-na swat you if you don't.

2 When my mammy take me down to the cotton patch,
  I roll and I tumble in the sun;
  My daddy pick the cotton and my mammy watch me hoe,
  And this am the song she'd sing.

  Chorus

Bones

Mrs. Turner learned this lullabye as a child and used it to rock her own baby to sleep. It is found quite frequently throughout the American South, sometimes as a stanza of "Go to Sleepy." Like the similar old English song "The Twa Corbies," "Bones" keeps its macabre nature in all versions. Mrs. Louise D. Harris (Tuscaloosa, 10 September 1945) had a different third line: "Buzzards and the flies picking out his eyes."

Sung by Mrs. Bertha Turner, Florence, 7 August 1945.

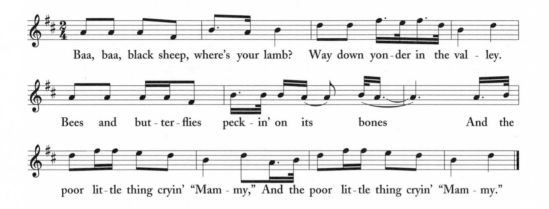

Baa, baa, black sheep, where's your lamb? Way down yon-der in the val - ley.

Bees and but - ter - flies peck - in' on its bones And the

poor lit-tle thing cryin' "Mam - my," And the poor lit-tle thing cryin' "Mam - my."

Come, Butter, Come

This is a churning song that evidently was also used as a lullabye.

Sung by Mrs. Janie Barnard Couch, Guntersville, 8 August 1945.

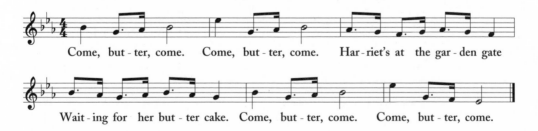

Come, but - ter, come. Come, but - ter, come. Har-riet's at the gar - den gate

Wait - ing for her but - ter cake. Come, but - ter, come. Come, but - ter, come.

Raccoon and Possum

Miss Kathryn Barnard, Mrs. Couch's sister, said this was used as a trotting song or lullabye.

Sung by Mrs. Janie Barnard Couch, Guntersville, 13 June 1947.

Rac - coon and the pos - sum down that hill a - fight - ing,

Old gray fox sit-ting on a fence kill-ing his-self a - laugh-ing.

Ride Away

Sung by Mrs. Laurie Cater Carleton, Grove Hill, 5 July 1947.

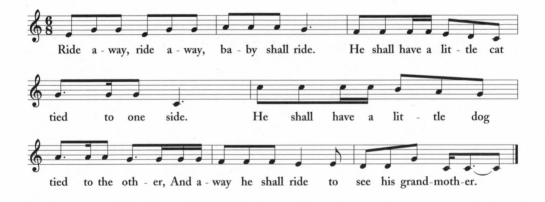

Ride a - way, ride a - way, ba - by shall ride. He shall have a lit - tle cat

tied to one side. He shall have a lit - tle dog

tied to the oth - er, And a - way he shall ride to see his grand-moth-er.

Go to Sleepy

This is the most frequently found lullabye in the southern United States. It may well have originated among blacks and been passed by mammies to generations of white children. Today it is equally well known among singers of both races. Miss Milner called her lines "The Little Ponies" and said they were all she could remember of a longer song. They are, in effect, the conclusion of "Go to Sleepy." For the first song in his collection of *American Folk Poetry*, Duncan Emrich chose a version of this collected by John A. Lomax from Aunt Flora Hampton of Livingston in 1937.

A

Sung by Ms. Mary Chapman, Grove Hill, 5 July 1947.

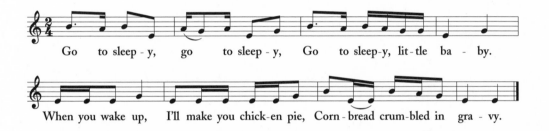

Go to sleep - y, go to sleep - y, Go to sleep-y, lit - tle ba - by.
When you wake up, I'll make you chick-en pie, Corn - bread crum-bled in gra - vy.

2 Go to sleepy, go to sleepy,
Go to sleepy, little baby.
When you wake up, I'll make you apple cake,
And buy you those pretty little horses.

B

Sung by Miss Josie Milner, Florence, 23 August 1945.

All the pretty little ponies,
White and gray and black and bay,
All the pretty little ponies,
You shall see someday, someday.

PART 3
SPIRITUALS

Of all the songs in this book, the spirituals are the most difficult to categorize. The songs least dependent upon their texts for their distinction, the spirituals were and are sung largely because their tunes are attractive as melodies and effective as stimulants of religious fervor. The literary interest of most of these religious songs is slight when compared, say, to that of the ballads. They pick up phrases from the Bible, from old hymns, and from revival sermons and weave them into a tapestry of sound whose power depends hardly at all upon its words. Certain concerns appear frequently: the trials of earthly life, the consolation of religion, the love of Jesus, the glory of heaven. Favorite stanzas achieve a holy promiscuity, lending their graces to many different songs.

The spirituals have been known as "slavery songs," and as "sorrow songs" because of that connotation, no matter how joyful their tunes and texts. Because of this, many blacks avoided singing these songs, at least in the presence of whites, for about fifty years after emancipation. Their public revival began with concert tours of singing groups from black colleges, notably Fisk University, to raise money for their institutions. And today spirituals are sung with fervor by both blacks and whites. They are not limited to church performance but are among the songs most favored to accompany labor.

Because many spirituals date back to the years of physical oppression of African Americans, some scholars like to examine their texts for veiled expressions of revolt. In doing so, they have probably exaggerated this element in the songs. Few would deny that a spiritual such as "Free at Last" is likely to have social as well as religious meaning. Much less certain is the scholar's interpretation of the heavenly footwear in "All God's Chillun Got Shoes" as the potential of the slave, restricted on earth but loosed in heaven. Generally, the oppression depicted in the spirituals is that of sin and of mortal hardships, oppression that weighs equally on all.

The first group of songs deals with the difficulties of living in this world, and opens with Job, the supreme example of patience and trust. Even for Christians of deep faith, temptations are strong and doubts are seductive, but they can be resisted with humbleness and persistence. Songs of forgiveness proclaim that "All My Sins Been Taken Away" and that the prodigal must realize the need for reconciliation. A number of fine spirituals deal with the personal love of Jesus and with the pleasures and consolation of religion in the desert of earthly life—the "Honey in the Rock." Themes of death and dying lend poignancy to many fine religious songs, from the frightened "Oh Death Is Awful," to the visionary "If Dyin' Was All," to the confident "Jesus Goin' to Make Up My Dyin' Bed." Beyond death, "I'm On My Way" to heaven, that "Wonderful City." The vision of entering heaven is most frequently equated with the Old Testament's of entering the promised land, though in one spiritual the Christian travels to glory on a celestial railroad. Several songs dwell on the vision of the apocalypse from the book of Revelation, and the collection concludes with spirituals of jubilation: "Free at Last," "Good News," "Hallelujah Amen."

Chapter 22
Worldly Woe

~

Ah, Job, Job

This spiritual reveals the singers' deep earthly compassion for the sorely afflicted Job. His strength is always seen as acceptance of God's will and faith in God's justness and power. Of particular interest here is the explicit identification of Job's afflictions with this song, which draws the spiritual to conclusion as his trials end with the defeat and incarceration of the devil. Other versions use this structure to move beyond the story of Job to those of diverse biblical figures and events. The choruses traditionally vary greatly in length, content, and the timing of their appearances.

Sung by Mr. Dock Reed and Miss Vera Hall, Livingston, 17 June 1947.

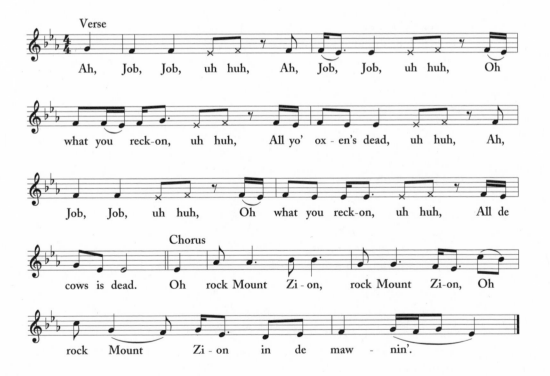

2 Ah, Job, Job, uh huh,
   Ah, Job, Job, uh huh,
   All your daughters dead, uh huh,
   Jes' listen at Job, uh huh,
   What Job said, uh huh,
   Oh blessed be, uh huh,
   The name of the Lord, uh huh.

3 Ah, Job, Job, uh huh,
   Ah, Job, Job, uh huh,
   Oh what you reckon, uh huh,
   The Lord giveth, uh huh,
   He taketh away, uh huh,
   Then blessed be, uh huh,
   The name of the Lord, uh huh.

   Chorus
   Oh rock Mount Zion, rock Mount Zion,
   Oh rock Mount Zion in de mawnin'.
   I wanta go to heaven, I wanta go to heaven,
   I wanta go to heaven in de mawnin'.

4 Ah, Job, Job, uh huh,
   Ah, Job, Job, uh huh,
   Oh what you reckon, uh huh,
   Job a strong man, uh huh,
   Was a strong man, uh huh,
   He prayed to God, uh huh,
   To stop this song, uh huh.

5 Ah, Job, Job, uh huh,
   Ah, Job, Job, uh huh,
   Oh what you reckon, uh huh,
   God done stop doin' it, uh huh,
   Right on the line, uh huh,
   An' the devil spouted, uh huh,
   An' is servin' time, uh huh.

   Chorus
   Swing low chariot, swing low chariot,
   Swing low chariot in de mawnin'.
   I wanta go to heaven, I wanta go to heaven,
   I wanta go to heaven in de mawnin'.

In-a My Heart

One of the most fervent of spirituals, "In-a My Heart" decries hypocrisy and prays for true Christian commitment, which resides not in external appearance and actions but in the deepest recesses of the soul, visible only to God. Other versions of this spiritual often bear the title "I Want to Live a Christian," the matter of the third stanza here.

Sung by Mr. Dock Reed and Miss Vera Hall, Livingston, 17 June 1947.

2 Lord, I wants to love everybody in my heart, in-a my heart,
   Lord, I wants to love everybody in my heart,
   Oh in-a my heart, in-a my heart, in my heart,
   Lord, I wants to love everybody in my heart.

3 Yes, I wants to live a Christian in my heart, in-a my heart,
   Yes, I wants to live a Christian in my heart,
   Oh in-a my heart, in-a my heart, in my heart,
   Yes, I wants to live a Christian in my heart.

4 Yes, I wants to love my brother in my heart, in-a my heart,
   Yes, I wants to love my brother in my heart,
   Oh in-a my heart, in-a my heart, in my heart,
   Yes, I wants to love my brother in my heart.

5 Yes, I wants to be like Jesus in my heart, in-a my heart,
   Yes, I wants to be like Jesus in my heart,
   Oh in-a my heart, in-a my heart, in my heart,
   Yes, I wants to be like Jesus in my heart.

6 Yes, I don' want to be like Judas in my heart, in-a my heart,
   Yes, I don' want to be like Judas in my heart,
   Oh in-a my heart, in-a my heart, in my heart,
   Yes, I don' want to be like Judas in my heart.

Two Wings

While the lyrics of this and the next song are clearly related, their tunes are quite distinct.

Sung by Mr. Dock Reed and Miss Vera Hall, Livingston, 17 June 1947.

Chorus

2 I wouldn't live a sinner;
   Tell you the reason why.

Sudden pain might strike me,
And I wouldn't be ready to die.

Chorus

Lord, I Want Two Wings

The singer repeated her single verse, substituting "Lord, I want two wings to veil my face" for the first line.

Sung by Ms. Ella Bell Hazley, Atmore, 15 July 1947.

Workin' on the Buildin'

According to St. Paul (1 Cor. 3:9–17), each Christian is called to build himself or herself as a temple of the Holy Spirit upon the foundation of Jesus Christ. Perhaps the rains in this song are earthly hardships, temptations, or sins. If so, the temptation to move might signify the desire to abandon the difficult effort to serve God, but it is a temptation always resisted and always followed by new resolution to "work on the buildin' for the Lord." At least two other spirituals, one of which has appeared in sacred harp songsters and was known to Mrs. Alma Robinson, sometimes carry the same title.

Sung by Miss Vera Hall, Livingston, 17 June 1947.

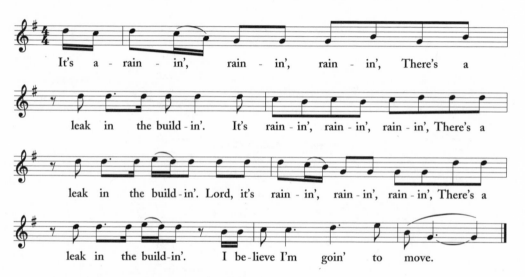

It's a - rain - in', rain - in', rain - in', There's a
leak in the build - in'. It's rain - in', rain - in', rain - in', There's a
leak in the build - in'. Lord, it's rain - in', rain - in', rain - in', There's a
leak in the build - in'. I be - lieve I'm goin' to move.

2 Gonna stop my way of talkin'
   And go work on the buildin'.
   Lord, stop my way of talkin',
   Gonna work on the buildin'.
   Lord, stop my way of talkin',
   Gonna work on the buildin',
   Work on the buildin' for the Lord.

3 Lord, it's rainin', rainin', rainin',
   There's a leak in the buildin'.
   Lord, it's rainin', rainin', rainin',
   There's a leak in the buildin'.
   It's rainin', rainin', rainin',
   There's a leak in the buildin'.
   I believe I'm have to move.

4 I'm gonna stop my ways of livin'
And go work on the buildin'.
Lord, stop my ways of livin'
And go work on the buildin'.
Lord, stop my ways of livin',
Go and work on the buildin',
Work on the buildin' for the Lord.

Nory

The question in this catechetical fragment is not sung, but is spoken in a high, intense voice. What seems foolish from a human perspective is not always seen to be so from a heavenly one.

Sung by Ms. Mattie Ford, Andalusia, 14 August 1946.

Some say No-ry was a fool-ish man, 'Cause No-ry built the ark on the high dry lan'.

Who built the ark? No - ry, No - ry, No-ry built the ark.

The Old Ark's Er-Movin'

This spiritual was one of the "hits" of the first tour of the Jubilee Singers of Fisk University in 1871.

Sung by Miss Vera Hall, Livingston, 17 June 1947.

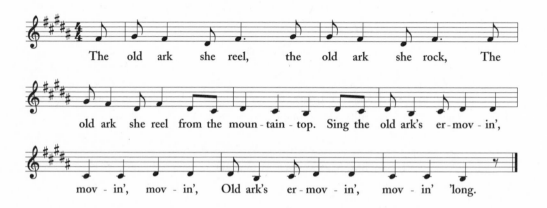

The old ark she reel, the old ark she rock, The old ark she reel from the moun-tain-top. Sing the old ark's er-mov-in', mov-in', mov-in', Old ark's er-mov-in', mov-in' 'long.

2 See that sister all dressed so fine?
   She ain' got Jesus on her min'.
   See that brother all dressed so gay?
   Death's gonna come for to carry him 'way.

3 See that sister there comin' on slow?
   She wants to go to heaven 'fore the heaven door close.
   Ain' but one thing on my min',
   My sister's gone to heaven an' a-left me behin'.

4 The old ark she reel, the old ark she rock,
   The old ark she reel from the mountaintop.
   Sing the old ark's er-movin', movin', movin',
   Old ark's er-movin', movin' 'long.

Scandalizin' My Name

This anti-backbiting spiritual is said to have originated in Alabama. Mrs. King's second verse substitutes "sister" for "brother," and her third uses "preacher."

Sung by Mrs. Irma Smith King, Selma, 15 August 1945.

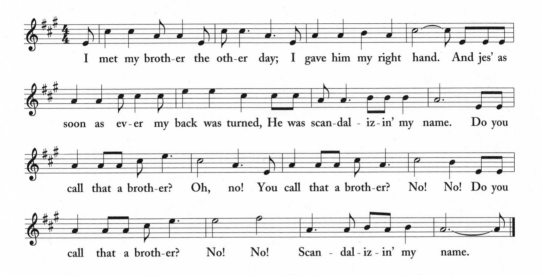

I met my broth-er the oth-er day; I gave him my right hand. And jes' as soon as ev-er my back was turned, He was scan-dal - iz-in' my name. Do you call that a broth-er? Oh, no! You call that a broth-er? No! No! Do you call that a broth-er? No! No! Scan - dal - iz - in' my name.

Low Is the Way

"He that humbleth himself shall be exalted" (Luke 14:11). Mrs. King sang additional verses, substituting "sister" and "preacher" for "brother."

Sung by Mrs. Irma Smith King, Selma, 15 August 1945.

Oh my broth - er, you must bow so low, so low, Oh my broth-er, you must bow so low, so low, For low is the way to that up - per bright world. Let the heav-en - ly light shine on me.

No Mo' Weepin' and Wailin'

In Kilby Prison, Arnold found an a cappella gospel quartet known as "The Famous Four" that sang this rapidly paced spiritual.

Sung by Messrs. Willie Calhoun, Big Charlie Small, Bud Campbell and
King Saul Chaney, Montgomery, August 1945.

Verse

There'll be no mo' weep-in' and wail-in', No mo' weep-in' and wail-in',

No mo' weep-in' and wail-in', I'm goin' home to live with God, my

Chorus

Lord. Soon I'll be done with the trou-bles of this world, well now,

Soon I'll be done with the trou-bles of this world, Soon I'll be done with the

trou-bles of this world, I'm goin' home to live with God, my Lord.

2 If you see my dear old mother,
   Will you please tell her this for me,
   When you saw me prayin'
   I was down on bended knee.

Chorus

3 If you see my dear old father,
   Will you shake his righteous hand;
   Tell him about my trouble,
   While travelin' through this land.

Chorus

Jesus Walked This Lonesome Valley

"This lonesome valley" is life, hedged about by pain and toil and terminated by a death that must be faced alone, beyond which lies the individual's final judgment, leading to heaven or hell. The image is probably derived from "the valley of the shadow of death" (Psalm 23:4). The singer and audience take comfort and encouragement from Jesus' having walked this valley and met human death out of love for all mankind.

Sung by Ms. Mildred Meadows, Tuscumbia, 9 June 1947.

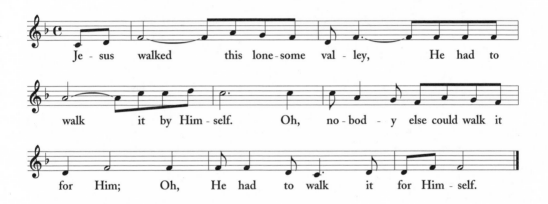

2　He had to go and stand His trial,
　　He had to stand it for Himself.
　　Oh, nobody else could stand it for Him;
　　Oh, He had to stand it for Himself.

3　I've got to walk this lonesome valley,
　　I've got to walk it by myself.
　　Oh, nobody else can walk it for me;
　　Oh, I've got to walk it by myself.

4　I must go and stand the judgment,
　　I've got to stand it for myself.
　　'Cause nobody else can stand it for me;
　　Oh, I've got to stand it for myself.

Tell All the World, John

The first two stanzas and, indeed, the sentiments of the whole song are shared with the folk-revival standard "All My Trials Soon Be Over."

Sung by Ms. Frances Thompson and Quartet, Pride Station, 2 August 1945.

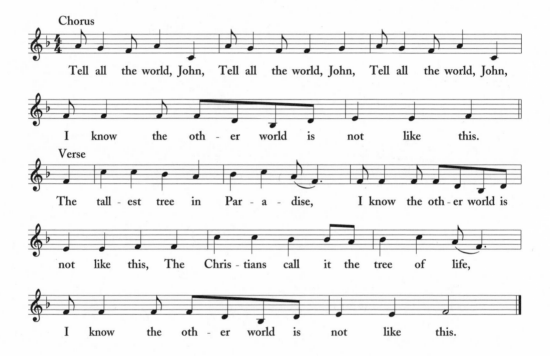

Chorus

2 Well, if religion was a thing that money could buy,
   I know the other world is not like this,
   The rich would live and the poor would die,
   I know the other world is not like this.

Chorus

3 Well, I've never been to heaven, but I've been told,
   I know the other world is not like this,
   The gates are pearl and the streets are gold,
   I know the other world is not like this.

Chorus

4 One of these mornings bright and fair,
I know the other world is not like this,
I'm goin' to meet my savior way up there,
I know the other world is not like this.

Chorus

If You Don't Want to Get in Trouble

Sung by Mr. Linton Berrien, Normal, 8 August 1945.

Verse

Well, I ask that li-ar to the mourn-ers' bench; See that liar be-gin to flinch. Well, I ask that liar the rea-son why. "The peo-ple in the church tell a lie like I."

Chorus

If you don't want to get in trou-ble, If you don't want to get in trou-ble, If you don't want to get in trou-ble, Just leave those liars a-lone.

2 Well, I ask that gambler to the mourners' bench;
See that gambler begin to flinch.
Well, I ask that gambler the reason why.
"The people in the church shoot a seven like I."

Chorus
If you don't want to get in trouble, (3)
Just leave those gamblers alone.

3   Well, I ask that drunkard to the mourners' bench;
    See that drunkard begin to flinch.
    Well, I ask that drunkard the reason why.
    "The people in the church kill a pint like I."

Chorus
If you don't want to get in trouble, (3)
Just leave those drunkards alone.

Sinner, Don't Let This Harvest Pass

Sung by Mr. Clarence L. Benton, Tuskegee, 21 July 1947.

2   There ain't but one thing I done wrong, (3)
    I stayed in the wilderness a day too long.

3   You can weep like a willow and mourn like a dove, (3)
    But you can't get to heaven without Christian love.

Chapter 23
Songs of Forgiveness

You Got to Clear the Line

The message here is that of Matthew 5:23–24: "Therefore if thou bring thy gift to the altar, and there rememberest that thy brother hath aught against thee; leave there thy gift before the altar, and go thy way; first be reconciled to thy brother, and then come and offer thy gift." The dominant image, however, seems to derive from the difficulty of placing a telephone call on a party line. Such telephone imagery was found frequently in American gospel songs of the 1920s and 1930s. The singer learned this spiritual from his mother, Mrs. Susie Fountain. The verse is sung to the same tune as the chorus.

Sung by the Reverend Mr. Alex Fountain, Florence, 9 June 1947.

1 If you have aught against your sister,
   Well go to her and her alone,
   And car' yo' gift before the altar.
   You got to clear the line before you call.

Chorus

2 If you have aught against your brother,
   Well go to him and him alone,
   And car' yo' gift before the altar.
   You got to clear the line before you call.

Chorus

3 If you have aught against your preacher,
   Well go to him and him alone,
   And car' yo' gift before the altar.
   You got to clear the line before you call.

Chorus

All My Sins Been Taken Away

One of the finest of black spirituals, this has found equal favor among whites. Almost every southern folk singer knows at least one or two verses set to the familiar tune, which also attracts stanzas from other songs. Ms. Priest's third stanza, for instance, comes from spirituals about Samson, who becomes like "a natural man" when his hair is cut. Making frequent appearances in this spiritual are Martha and Mary, mourning for their dead brother Lazarus (John 11), and the otherwise unidentified Mary with her holy chain. The story of Paul and Silas praying and singing in prison (Acts 16:25), which appears in several different spirituals, must surely hearten convicts and ex-convicts. It is particularly appropriate here, because its singer, the Reverend Mr. Winsor H. Swearingen, was chaplain of Kilby Prison. No song this well known can escape parody, and Mr. Mead's version sets the second and third stanzas, preferred by gang laborers, and the fifth stanza, a black children's rhyme, with two stanzas of a more conventional religious nature.

A

Sung by Ms. Mel Dora Priest, Gadsden, 28 August 1945.

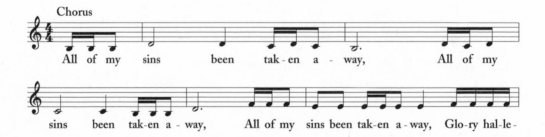

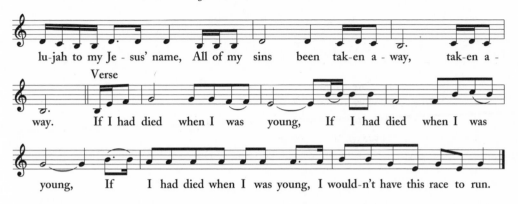

lu-jah to my Je - sus' name, All of my sins been tak-en a - way, tak-en a -

way. If I had died when I was young, If I had died when I was

young, If I had died when I was young, I would-n't have this race to run.

Chorus

2 Sister Mary wore three links of chain, (3)
  And every link was Jesus' name.

Chorus

3 You can shave my head just as clean as my hand, (3)
  I would not be a natural man.

Chorus

B

Sung by Ms. Mary Chapman, Grove Hill, 5 July 1947.

Mary weep and Marthie moan,
Mary weep and Marthie moan,
Them li'l' chillen ain't got no home,
Mary weep, Lord, Lord, and Marthie moan.

C

Sung by the Reverend Mr. Winsor H. Swearingen, Montgomery, August 1945.

1 Yonder comes John a-bending down,
  Yonder comes John a-bending down,
  Yonder comes John a-bending down,
  With a snow white robe and a sparklin' crown,
  All my sins been taken away, taken away.

2 Paul and Silas bound in jail, (3)
  One for to weep and one for to wail,
  All my sins been taken away, taken away.

D

Sung by Mr. Donald Mead, Russellville, 2 August 1945.

1 Sister Mary wore three links of chain,
   Sister Mary wore three links of chain,
   Sister Mary wore three links of chain,
   And every link was Jesus' name,
   All my sins been taken away, taken away.

2 Sally had a meat skin laid away, (3)
   To grease that wooden leg every day,
   All my sins been taken away, taken away.

3 I got a woman and a bulldog, too, (3)
   Oh, my woman don't love me but my bulldog do,
   All my sins been taken away, taken away.

4 If you'd been there when I come through, (3)
   Believe to my soul you'd have shouted too,
   All my sins been taken away, taken away.

5 I had an old mule and he wouldn't gee, (3)
   Hit him in the head with a single tree,
   All my sins been taken away, taken away.

I Believe I'll Go Back Home

The father embracing his prodigal son is always an effective image of God welcoming the sinner who has acknowledged his wrong and come back home.

Sung by Miss Vera Hall and Mr. Dock Reed, Livingston, 17 June 1947.

Chorus

I be-lieve I'll go back home, I be-lieve I'll go back home,

I be-lieve I'll go back home, An' ac-knowl-edge I done wrong.

Verse

When I was at home I was well sup-plied.

I done wrong for leav-ing; now I'm dis-sat-is-fied.

Chorus

2 My father saw me coming; he met me with a smile.
   He throwed his arms around me: "I permagine this my chil'."

Chorus

Chapter 24
The Love of Jesus

I Met Jesus in the Valley

"He that overcometh, the same shall be clothed in white raiment; and I will not blot out his name out of the book of life, but I will confess his name before my Father, and before his angels" (Rev. 3:5). Succeeding verses follow the pattern established by the first. Mrs. Robinson said of this song that her church congregation frequently "sang it till spirit got in all of 'em, then went into a shout." In a shout, the churchgoers would pray or sing aloud individually rather than in unison.

A

Sung by Mrs. Susie Fountain Robinson, Florence, 23 August 1945.

I met Je-sus in the val-ley, and He took my name,
I met Je-sus in the val-ley, and He took my name, I met Je-sus
in the val-ley, I met Je-sus in the val-ley,
I met Je-sus in the val-ley, and He took my name.

2 I told Jesus I had no mother, and He took my name.

3 I told Jesus I had no father, and He took my name.

4 I told Jesus I would serve Him, if He took my name.

5 I told Jesus I would trust Him, if He took my name.

6 I told Jesus I'd love my enemies, if He took my name.

B

Sung by Mr. Isaiah Holmes, Tuscumbia, 10 June 1947.

3 Jesus told me I'd have to live humble, if He taken my name.

4 I told Jesus I was willin' to risk it, if He taken my name.

5 Jesus told me the world would hate me, if He taken my name.

6 I told Jesus that 'ud be all right, if He taken my name.

He Knows

Mrs. Alma Robinson sang a more personal version of this by using "when I'm" in place of "who's" in Mr. Holmes's first three stanzas. Only one of her verses, included under B, was otherwise different from his.

A

Sung by Mr. Isaiah Holmes, Tuscumbia, 10 June 1947.

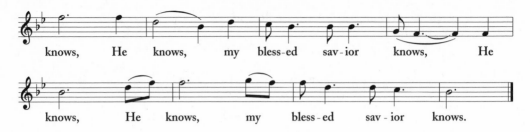

knows, He knows, my bless-ed sav-ior knows, He
knows, He knows, my bless-ed sav-ior knows.

2 He knows, He knows, my blessed savior knows,
   He knows, He knows, my blessed savior knows,
   He knows who's right and He knows who's wrong,
   My blessed savior knows,
   He knows who's right and He knows who's wrong,
   My blessed savior knows,
   He knows, He knows, my blessed savior knows,
   He knows, He knows, my blessed savior knows.

3 He knows, He knows, my blessed savior knows,
   He knows, He knows, my blessed savior knows,
   He knows who's weak and He knows who's strong,
   My blessed savior knows,
   He knows who's weak and He knows who's strong,
   My blessed savior knows,
   He knows, He knows, my blessed savior knows,
   He knows, He knows, my blessed savior knows.

4 My mother left me here and I'm shining bright and clear,
   My blessed savior knows,
   My mother left me here and I'm shining bright and clear,
   My blessed savior knows,
   He knows, He knows, my blessed savior knows,
   He knows, He knows, my blessed savior knows.

B

Sung by Mrs. Alma Robinson, Florence, 9 June 1947.

He knows, He knows, my blessed savior He knows,
He knows, He knows, my blessed savior He knows,
He knows when I'm sick and He knows when I'm well,
My blessed savor He knows,
He knows when I'm sick and He knows when I'm well,
My blessed savor He knows,
He knows, He knows, my blessed savior He knows,
He knows, He knows, my blessed savior He knows.

It's Jesus That Keeps Me Alive

Sung by Mrs. Rose Franklin Brown, Pritchard, 3 September 1945.

Verse

Well, He's all o-ver me and He keeps me a-live, Well, He's all o-ver me and He keeps me a-live, Well, He's all o-ver me and He keeps me a-live, Well, it's Je-sus that keeps me a-live.

Chorus

Well, it's Je-sus, it's Je-sus that keeps me a-live, Well, it's Je-sus, it's Je-sus that keeps me a-live, Well, it's Je-sus, it's Je-sus that keeps me a-live, Well, it's Je-sus that keeps me a-live.

2 And He feeds me when I'm hungry, and He keeps me alive, (3)
Well, it's Jesus that keeps me alive.

Chorus

3 And He clothes me when I'm naked, and He keeps me alive, (3)
Well, it's Jesus that keeps me alive.

Chorus

4 And He's all in my heart, and He keeps me alive, (3)
Well, it's Jesus that keeps me alive.

Chorus

Let's Go Down to the Water

Mrs. Brown told Byron Arnold: "Samuel Chapel is my church. I lead the singin' with a mouth organ. I jus' makes the cong'egation join in an' sing. That's what makes them cheer up." Indeed, this spiritual is full of the good cheer of the converted, baptized, and faithful Christian.

Sung by Mrs. Rose Franklin Brown, Pritchard, 3 September 1945.

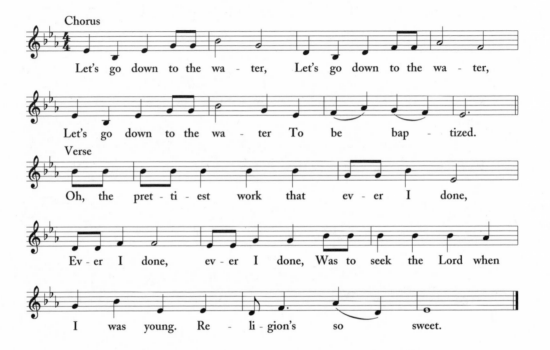

Chorus

2 I've gone to the water and been baptized,
Been baptized, been baptized,
I've gone to the water and been baptized.
Religion's so sweet.

Chorus

3 Oh, Satan's mad and I am glad,
I am glad, I am glad,
He missed the soul he thought he had.
Religion's so sweet.

Chorus

4 I done the work I had to do,
   Had to do, had to do,
   I been to the river and been baptized.
   Religion's so sweet.

Chorus
   Let's go down to Jordan,
   Let's go down to Jordan,
   Let's go down to Jordan,
   I been baptized.

I Got a Book

Mrs. Lambert said she learned this "moanin'" spiritual from the singing of cotton pickers as they worked.

Sung by Mrs. Corie Lambert, Mobile, 3 September 1945.

I got a book an' you got a book, An' I got a book an' a
Bi-ble too; I can read as well as you. Lord, Lord,
Lord, Lord, Lord, oh Lord, I think my Lord's might-y good and kind;
I'm so glad. I think my Lord's so good and kind;
I'm so glad. Took a-way the ba-by, lef' the
moth-er be-hind; I'm so glad, Lord, Lord, oh Lord.

Roun' the Wall

Mrs. Ernst told Byron Arnold: "I learned this from Aunt Liza Miller, who is now married to her third husband. When her second husband died, Aunt Liza came up to the big house asking for some black underwear, saying, 'Honey, when I mourns, I mourns deep.' As the spirit moves members of the congregation, they start a procession around the wall, chanting this song and making a little skipping hop twice to each line. When Aunt Liza really got religion she could jump two feet in the air in spite of her age and size. This song and dance might be derived from the Bible tale of the fall of the walls of Jericho." The religious ring dance was described by a writer in the *Nation*, 30 May 1867:

> But the benches are pushed back to the wall when the formal meeting is over, and old and young, men and women . . . all stand up in the middle of the floor, and when the "sperichil" is struck up begin first walking and by and by shuffling around, one after the other, in a ring. The foot is hardly taken from the floor, and the progression is mainly due to a jerking, hitching motion which agitates the entire shouter and soon brings out streams of perspiration. Sometimes they dance silently, sometimes as they shuffle they sing the chorus of the spiritual, and sometimes the song itself is also sung by the dancers. But more frequently a band, composed of some of the best singers and of tired shouters, stand at the side of the room to "base" the others, singing the body of the song and clapping their hands together or on their knees. Song and dance are alike extremely energetic, and often, when the shout lasts into the middle of the night, the monotonous thud, thud of the feet prevents sleep within half a mile of the praise house.

Sung by Mrs. Laurie Ernst, Mobile, 8 February 1946.

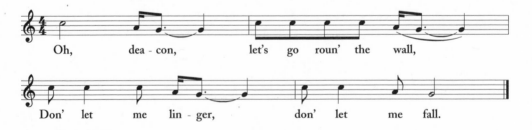

Oh, dea - con, let's go roun' the wall,

Don' let me lin - ger, don' let me fall.

2 Oh, preacher, etc.

3 Oh, brother, etc.

4 Oh, sister, etc.

5 Oh, father, etc.

6 Oh, mother, etc.

Drinkin' Wine

This delightful communion service song has been several times misidentified as a secular drinking song, probably from a college setting. Mrs. Jones, the wife of the minister of the Mount Triumph Baptist Church, said it was very old; she first heard it from her mother. Several collectors have, in fact, recovered "Drinkin' Wine" in secular settings, where it was used as a rhythmic work song. The spiritual can be expanded by adding more questioners.

Sung by Mrs. Theckle Jones, Atmore, 11 July 1947.

Chorus

2 If my father asks for me
  Tell him I'm gone to Galilee.
  You ought-a been back ten thousand years,
  Drinkin' wine.

Chorus

I Heard the Angels Singing

Of this song, Mrs. Robinson told Arnold: "My grandmother, who died in August 1943 at the age of eight-two, used to take me on her knee, look up to heaven, and hear the angels sing. It was her favorite song and is mine, too."

Sung by Mrs. Alma Robinson, Florence, 9 June 1947.

Chorus

One morn - ning soon, one morn - ing soon, One morn - ing soon,

I heard the an - gels sing-ing. Down on my knees, down on my knees,

Down on my knees, I heard the an - gels sing - ing. I be-

lieve, I be-lieve, I do be-lieve, I heard the an - gels sing-ing. My

soul King Je - sus will re-ceive, I heard the an - gels sing - ing.

Chorus
Couldn't keep from crying, couldn't keep from crying,
Couldn't keep from crying, when I heard the angels singing.
I just had to moan, I just had to moan,
I just had to moan, when I heard the angels singing.

2 Some of these mornings bright and fair,
I heard the angels singing,
Going to take my wings and try the air,
I heard the angels singing.

Chorus
One morning soon, one morning soon,
One morning soon, I heard the angels singing.

The Love Come Twinkling Down

The bright, magical, all-encompassing love of Christ for man revealed in this spiritual is best represented by his death, upon which singers sometimes comment in a line clearly akin to McCann's last: "the blood come trickling down." The song is continued by substituting "Brother," "Preacher," and so forth for "Auntie." On the record jacket, the singer's name is almost illegible, and the transcription of it here is by no means certainly correct.

Sung by Ms. Christine McCann, Montgomery, 1947.

On Your Bond

The idea here is that not even the most faithful individual has enough "collateral" to get into heaven unless Jesus "cosigns the note," pledging his redemptive sacrifice.

Sung by Mr. Isaiah Holmes, Tuscumbia, 10 June 1947.

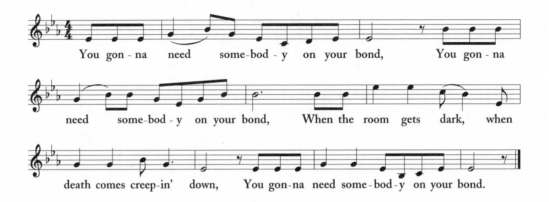

You gon-na need some-bod-y on your bond, You gon-na need some-bod-y on your bond, When the room gets dark, when death comes creep-in' down, You gon-na need some-bod-y on your bond.

2 Well, I got somebody on my bond,
   Well, I got somebody on my bond,
   When the room gets dark, when death comes creepin' down,
   Well, I got somebody on my bond.

3 Well, I got King Jesus on my bond,
   Well, I got King Jesus on my bond,
   When the room gets dark, when death comes creepin' down,
   Well, I got King Jesus on my bond.

4 You gonna need somebody on your bond,
   You gonna need somebody on your bond,
   When the room gets dark, when death comes creepin' down,
   You gonna need somebody on your bond.

I'm So Glad

Sung by Mr. Dock Reed, Livingston, 17 June 1947.

I'm so glad I got mah 'li-gion in time,
I'm so glad I got mah 'li-gion in time,
I'm so glad I got mah 'li-gion in time,
Oh mah Lawd, oh mah Lawd, What shall I do to be saved?

2 I heard a voice, never heard this voice before, (3)
  Oh mah Lawd, oh mah Lawd,
  What shall I do to be saved?

3 Call like Jesus, I never heard this voice before, (3)
  Oh mah Lawd, oh mah Lawd,
  What shall I do to be saved?

4 Death done been here, took my mother and gone, (3)
  Oh mah Lawd, oh mah Lawd,
  What shall I do to be saved?

5 Death done been here and lef' me a motherless chil', (3)
  Oh mah Lawd, oh mah Lawd,
  What shall I do to be saved?

6 Angel, angel, cleanin' up the chariot wheel, (3)
  Oh mah Lawd, oh mah Lawd,
  What shall I do to be saved?

7 Hush, hush, I heard them bell done ringin', (3)
  Oh mah Lawd, oh mah Lawd,
  What shall I do to be saved?

Honey in the Rock

The chosen of the Lord, for whom God has done much, will "suck honey out of the rock" in the desert (Deut. 32:13). Such care is provided only for those who admit their insufficiency and place complete and humble trust in the Lord. This gorgeous spiritual is extended by substituting new audiences for "mother." The singers addressed subsequent verses to "my father" and "my sister."

Sung by Miss Vera Hall and Mr. Dock Reed, Livingston, 16 June 1947.

Oh my moth-er, come and see What the Lord have done for
me. I am so hum - ble, nev-er gets tired, I am
walk-ing by my sav - ior's side. Oh hon-ey in the rock, oh hon-ey in the
rock, Oh it tastes like hon-ey in the rock. Go taste and
see, dear Lord 'tis good, And it tastes like hon-ey in the rock.

Chapter 25
Passing

⌒

Jesus Goin' to Make Up My Dyin' Bed

The title line of this spiritual brings home in striking fashion the comfort derived by the dying Christian from unshakable faith in Jesus. The B version's last stanza treats God's sending Ananias to the blinded and praying Saul to restore his sight and lead him to baptism. The name of that version's singer is barely legible on the field recording's sleeve, and its transcription here is a "best guess."

A

Sung by Miss Vera Hall and Mr. Dock Reed, Livingston, 16 or 17 June 1947.

Chorus

Well, don't you be un-eas-y, Well, don't you be un-eas-y,

Well, don't you be un-eas-y, Je-sus goin' to make up my dy-in' bed.

Verse

When you see me a-dy-in', I don't want no-bod-y to cry; But

all I want you to do for me Is to close my dy-in' eye.

Chorus
Well, I'll be sleepin' in Jesus, (3)
Jesus goin' to make up my dyin' bed.

2 When you see me dyin',
   Don't you weep and mourn;

All I want you to do for me,
Just give that bell a tone.

Chorus
Well, I'll be gone on over, (3)
Jesus goin' to make up my dyin' bed.

3 When you see me dyin',
Don't want you to sigh or moan;
Just go down to the Jordan,
Jesus will tell you I crossed.

Chorus
Well, I'll be gone over glory, (3)
Jesus goin' to make up my dyin' bed.

Chorus
Well, I'll be walkin' with Jesus, (3)
Jesus goin' to make up my dyin' bed.

Chorus
Well, don't you worry 'bout me, (3)
Jesus goin' to make up my dyin' bed.

B

Sung by Ms. Christine McCann, Montgomery, 1947.

Chorus
Jesus is a dyin' bed maker, now,
Jesus is a dyin' bed maker, now,
Jesus is a dyin' bed maker,
Jesus makin' up my dyin' bed.

1 When I get to heaven,
Somebody gwine-ta say I am lost,
But come on down to the Jordan,
An' my savior will tell you I crossed.

Chorus

2 When I get to heaven,
By God's right hand I'm gwine-ta stand;
I'm gwine-ta tell them jus' how you're treating me here
Whilst a-walkin' on bargoed land.

Chorus

3 Jesus said unto Ananias:
"Saw him comin' today,
An' I want you to lay your hands on him,
'Cause the Lord have heard him pray."

Chorus

Oh Death Is Awful

The negative and earthly view of death expressed here is very unusual in spirituals.

Sung by Miss Vera Hall and Mr. Dock Reed, Livingston, 17 June 1947.

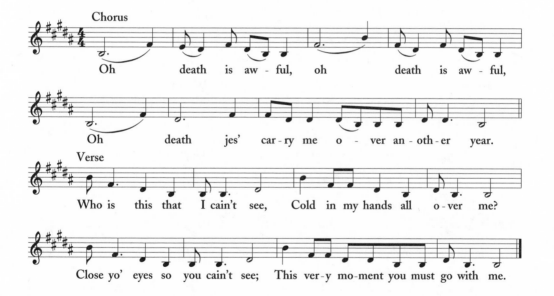

Chorus
Oh death have mercy, oh death have mercy,
Oh death jes' carry me over another year.

2 Fix yo' feet so you can't walk,
Lock yo' jaw so you can't talk.

Chorus
Oh death is easy, oh death is easy,
Oh death jes' carry me over another year.

3 This the way that death begin,
Close yo' eyes and stretch yo' limb.

Chorus
Oh Lord have mercy, oh Lord have mercy,
Oh death jes' carry me over another year.

4 I was a flower in mah bloom,
Make death cut me down so soon.

Chorus
Oh death is awful, oh death is awful,
Oh death jes' carry me over another year.

Bring God's Servant Home

Death in spirituals seems to be made "easy" not by any lack of immediate pain but by the singers' implicit comparison of the difficult life on this earth with the prospect of the rapturous life in heaven.

Sung by Mr. Dock Reed and Miss Vera Hall, Livingston, 17 June 1947.

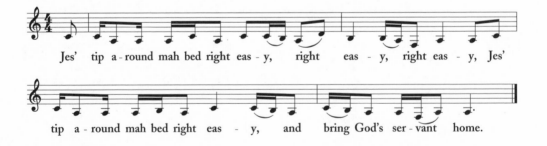

Jes' tip a-round mah bed right eas-y, right eas-y, right eas-y, Jes' tip a-round mah bed right eas-y, and bring God's ser-vant home.

2 Ah low down death right easy, right easy, right easy,
Ah low down death right easy, and bring God's servant home.

3 Jes' low down de chariot right easy, right easy, right easy,
  Jes' low down de chariot right easy, and bring God's servant home.

4 Jes' turn mah bed aroun' right easy, right easy, right easy,
  Jes' turn mah bed aroun' right easy, and bring God's servant home.

5 Jes' move mah pillow roun' right easy, right easy, right easy,
  Jes' move mah pillow roun' right easy, and bring God's servant home.

6 Jes' low down de chariot right easy, right easy, right easy,
  Jes' low down de chariot right easy, and bring God's servant home.

There's a Man Goin' 'Round Takin' Names

This census of mortality conducted by death personified usually has as the next-to-last line of each stanza: "And he filled my heart with pain." It is not immediately apparent why the deaths of relatives should put the singer's "heart to shame."

Sung by Mr. Sanford Bishop, Mobile, 30 August 1945.

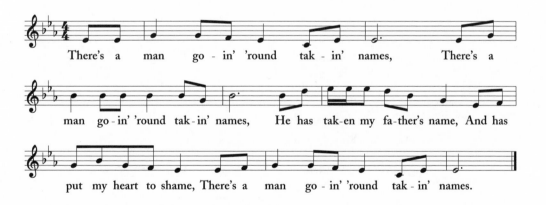

2 There's a man goin' 'round takin' names,
  There's a man goin' 'round takin' names,
  He has taken my sister's name,
  And has put my heart to shame,
  There's a man goin' 'round takin' names.

3 There's a man goin' 'round takin' names,
  There's a man goin' 'round takin' names,
  He has taken my brother's name,
  And has put my heart to shame,
  There's a man goin' 'round takin' names.

4 There's a man goin' 'round takin' names,
  There's a man goin' 'round takin' names,
  He has taken my mother's name,
  And has put my heart to shame,
  There's a man goin' 'round takin' names.

If Dyin' Was All

Nothing expresses more beautifully than this spiritual the idea that, for the true Christian, the judgment beyond this life is more important and frightening than the death leading to it.

Sung by Ms. Mozelle Longmire, Atmore, 17 July 1947.

2 After this, Lord, I gotta stand that test, (3)
Lord, I wouldn't mind dyin' if dyin' was all,
Wouldn't mind dyin', Lord, I've got to go by myself, (3)
Lord, I wouldn't mind dyin' if dyin' was all.

Tall Angel at the Bar

Arnold commented directly on a 1945 performance of this spiritual: "I was fascinated as Alma Robinson and Reverend Alex Fountain sang this 'ring shout.' It is reputed to be very old. The repartee of the two singers was remarkable. Each would hold the last note of his or her phrase while the other sang the next phrase. The song moved quite fast and never let up until they were out of breath." In 1947, when Arnold first brought his recording equipment to Florence, Mr. Fountain sang the lead and Mrs. Robinson and others sang the refrain, which becomes almost hypnotic through repetition. Of the spiritual, Fountain said: "This song was used in walking for a cake at a church social. We'd be sitting 'round the wall and the leader would start shuffling his feet and the men would get up and get their partners one by one, the couples lining up in a large circle. Up to now we would sing only 'Tall angel at the bar, well I wonder what's to matter.' When everybody was on the floor we'd go ahead with the rest of the piece, marching round and round. This isn't done any more. I can't remember how long ago I heard it the last time." The song is extended by repeating the first stanza and then continuing with other relatives: father, brother, sister, and so forth.

Sung by the Reverend Mr. Alex Fountain and others, Florence, 9 June 1947.

2 Tall angel at the bar,
Well my mother got to go.
Tall angel at the bar,
Well my mother got to go.

3 Tall angel at the bar,
  To the bar of God.
  Tall angel at the bar,
  To the bar of God.

4 Tall angel at the bar,
  She come stepping down the Jordan.
  Tall angel at the bar,
  She come stepping down the Jordan.

5 Tall angel at the bar,
  Well she stepping like the lightning.
  Tall angel at the bar,
  Well she stepping like the lightning.

6 Tall angel at the bar,
  Tall angel. [drawn out]
  Tall angel at the bar,
  Tall angel. [drawn out]

Chapter 26
Going to Heaven

I Hear the Train A-Comin'

It is pleasant to have the chariot and bands of angels swing low for the heaven-bound soul, but the best transportation to glory is still the gospel train with its earth-shaking power, its clarion bell and whistle, and its passengers drawn from every station of life. In other versions of this well-known spiritual, equally popular with blacks and whites, King Jesus is the "conductor" and the refrain forsakes Ms. Howard's serious Christian resolution for the familiar cheerful exhortation: "Get on board, little children, / Get on board, little children, / Get on board, little children, / There's room for many more."

Sung by Ms. Mollie Howard, Tuskegee, 11 August 1946.

Verse

I hear the train a-com-in', I hear it just at hand, I hear the wheels a-mov-in', And rum-blin' through the land; But when she makes her sta-tion blow, You'd bet-ter be read-y to go.

Chorus

Lord, I'm goin' to die with my staff in my hand, I'm goin' to die with this staff in my hand, I'm goin' to die with this staff in my hand. No mat-ter what they say, I'm goin' on my knees and pray. Lord, I'm goin' to die with my staff in my hand.

2 The train that runs to glory,
   It stops along the line;
   King Jesus is the captain,
   But still it makes the time;
   And if you want to stop the train,
   Just call on Jesus's name.

   Chorus

3 The fare is cheap and all can go;
   The rich and poor are there;
   No second class on board the train,
   No difference in the fare;
   If you want to stop the train,
   Just call on Jesus's name.

   Chorus

4 I hear the bell and whistle,
   She's comin' 'round the curve,
   Displayin' all steam and power,
   And strainin' every nerve;
   But when she makes a station blow,
   You'd better be ready to go.

   Chorus

Satan's a Liar

To the accompaniment of a ukulele, Mrs. Forman sang of Satan's powers in black magic and of heavenly actions and garb.

Sung by Mrs. C. L. Forman, Birmingham, 1947.

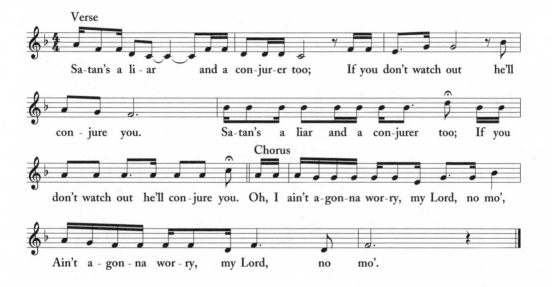

2 Going up to heaven on an angel's wings,
   And when I get there, oh how I'll sing.
   Going up to heaven on an angel's wings,
   And when I get there, oh how I'll sing.

   Chorus

3 When I get to heaven, gonna set me down,
   Gonna put on my wings and starry crown.
   When I get to heaven, gonna set me down,
   Gonna put on my wings and starry crown.

   Chorus

Room Enough

This and the next song celebrate the spaciousness of God's kingdom. Because none need fear exclusion, all should make plans for ultimate residence in heaven.

Sung by Ms. Mel Dora Priest, Gadsden, 28 August 1945.

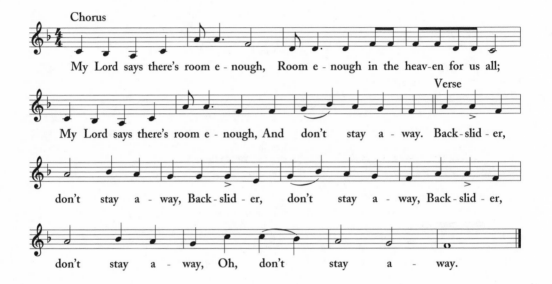

Chorus

2 If you run away, don't stay away,
   If you run away, don't stay away,
   If you run away, don't stay away,
   And don't stay away.

Chorus

3 Oh, sinner, don't stay away,
   Oh, sinner, don't stay away,
   Oh, sinner, don't stay away,
   And don't stay away.

Chorus

Plenty Good Room

Abraham's servant asked: "Is there room in thy father's house for us to lodge in?"
Rebekah replied: "We have both straw and provender enough, and room to lodge in"
(Gen. 24:23, 25).

Sung by Ms. Mel Dora Priest, Gadsden, 28 August 1945.

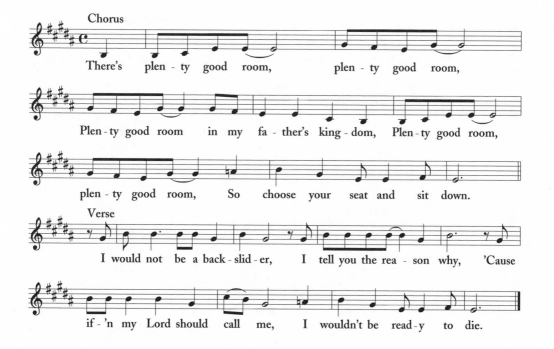

Chorus

2   I would not be a liar,
    I tell you the reason why,
    'Cause if'n my Lord should call me,
    I wouldn't be ready to die.

We Gonna Have a Good Time

Sung by Mrs. Alma Robinson, Florence, 1 August 1945.

Chorus

Way by and by, **way** by and by, We gon-na have a good time, way by and by.

Verse

Gon-na meet King Je-sus o-ver there, Gon-na meet King Je-sus o-ver there, We gon-na have a good time, way by and by.

Chorus

2 Gonna meet my mother over there, (2)
   We gonna have a good time, way by and by.

Chorus

3 Gonna meet my father over there, (2)
   We gonna have a good time, way by and by.

Chorus

4 Gonna shout, troubles over, over there, (2)
   We gonna have a good time, way by and by.

Chorus

5 Gonna shake glad hands over there, (2)
   We gonna have a good time, way by and by.

Chorus

6 Gonna take my seat and sit down, (2)
   We gonna have a good time, way by and by.

Chorus

Wonder Where Is Good Ol' Daniel

Versions of this song, usually titled "The Hebrew Children," appeared in sacred harp songbooks, including the *Southern Harmony* and the *Original Sacred Harp*. Although the spiritual has found favor with both white and black singers, the slaves and their descendants were surely more moved by its insistence on the inevitability of divine deliverance for the faithful. Mrs. Robinson said: "My husband's mother used to sit up and sing and hum this old song. She was sick a long time, rocking, singing, and humming." The chorus is sung to the same tune as the verse.

Sung by Mrs. Alma Robinson, Florence, 23 August 1945.

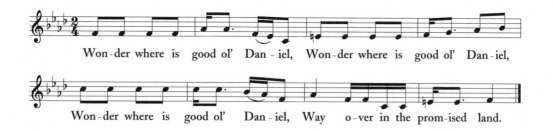

Won-der where is   good ol' Dan-iel, Won-der where is   good ol' Dan-iel,

Won-der where is   good ol'   Dan-iel, Way   o-ver in the prom-ised land.

Chorus
Bye and bye we goin' to meet him, (3)
Way over in the promised land.

2 Wonder where's them Hebrew children, (3)
Way over in the promised land.

Chorus
Bye and bye we goin' to meet them, (3)
Way over in the promised land.

3 They come through the fiery furnace, (3)
Way over in the promised land.

Chorus
Bye and bye we goin' to meet them, (3)
Way over in the promised land.

4 Wonder where is doubtin' Thomas, (3)
Way over in the promised land.

Chorus
Bye and bye we goin' to meet him, (3)
Way over in the promised land.

5 Wonder where is sinkin' Peter, (3)
Way over in the promised land.

Chorus
Bye and bye we goin' to meet him, (3)
Way over in the promised land.

I'm On My Way

Sung by Mrs. Alma Robinson, Florence, 1 August 1945.

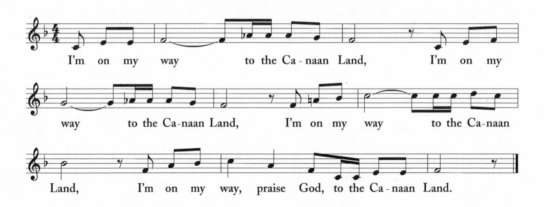

I'm on my way to the Ca-naan Land, I'm on my

way to the Ca-naan Land, I'm on my way to the Ca-naan

Land, I'm on my way, praise God, to the Ca-naan Land.

2 If you don't go, don't you hinder me, (3)
I'm on my way, praise God, to the Canaan Land.

3 My mother's gone to the Canaan Land, (3)
I'm on my way, praise God, to the Canaan Land.

4 My father's gone to the Canaan Land, (3)
I'm on my way, praise God, to the Canaan Land.

Beulah's Land

Ms. Ford sang a second verse in which "a baby" was substituted for "a mother." Similar songs run through long lists of various relatives. Some versions of this spiritual carry the title "Do Lord, Remember Me." The phrase "outshines the sun" is often used in other songs to describe the appearance of Jesus upon the Second Coming.

Sung by Ms. Mattie Ford, Andalusia, 14 August 1946.

I Am Going Home

The third line is frequently found as "If you get there before I do."

Sung by Ms. Theckle Jones, Atmore, 11 July 1947.

I am go - ing home, I am go - ing home, I am
go - ing home to die no more. He'll help you be there
be - fore I do. Pray tell my friends I am com - ing too.

Settin' Down

Sung by Mrs. Jennie Chandler, Guntersville, 13 June 1947.

Set-tin' down, set-tin' down, By the side of the Lamb,
the Lamb, I'm gwine tell my Lord,
I'm gwine tell my Lord, I nev - er heard no-bod - y pray,
way down yon - der, I nev - er heard no-bod - y pray,
no-bod - y pray, I nev - er heard no-bod - y pray.

Don't Call the Roll

Sung by Ms. Frances Thompson, Pride Station, 2 August 1945.

Chorus

2 Oh, please, please, please, my Father,
   Don't call the roll till I get there.

Chorus

3 If it's raining, Lord, I'm coming anyhow,
   Don't call the roll till I get there.

Chorus

4 Well, if I go blind I'll feel my way there,
   Don't call the roll till I get there.

Chorus

Wonderful City

This spiritual celebrates glorious heaven, the celestial New Jerusalem as seen by John in the book of Revelation. It is sometimes called "Twelve Gates to the City."

Sung by Ms. Annie Dixon, Dog River, 8 July 1947.

Chorus

2 You go to the east,
   I go to the west,
   You go to the north,
   I go to the south,
   That makes the twelve gates to the city,
   Hallelu, hallelu.

Chorus

3 You go to the north,
   I go to the south,
   You go to the west,
   I go to the east,
   That makes the twelve gates to the city,
   Hallelu, hallelu.

Chorus

Chapter 27
The Apocalypse

Ezekiel Saw a Wheel

This well-known spiritual is derived from the book of the Prophet Ezekiel: "The appearance of the wheels . . . and their work was as it were a wheel in the middle of a wheel" (1:16). The presence of "my mother" in the wheel indicates that the vision is of heaven; it may also be of the apocalypse. This song was a favorite on the 1871 tour of the Fisk University Jubilee Singers.

Sung by Mrs. Sarah Carter, Carlosville, 19 July 1947.

E - zek-iel saw a wheel, a wheel, Way up in the mid-dle of the air. E-

zek-iel saw a wheel, a wheel, Way up in the mid-dle of the air.

2 My mother was in that wheel, a wheel,
   Way up in the middle of the air.
   My mother was in that wheel, a wheel,
   Way up in the middle of the air.

3 The big wheel run by faith, a wheel,
   Way up in the middle of the air.
   The big wheel run by faith, a wheel,
   Way up in the middle of the air.

4 The little run by the grace of God,
   Way up in the middle of the air.
   The little run by the grace of God,
   Way up in the middle of the air.

Go Chain the Lion Down

The striking image of the title has been derived traditionally from the story of the deliverance of Daniel in the den of lions (Dan. 6), but it also takes coloring from the angel's binding of "the dragon . . . which is the Devil" with "a great chain" (Rev. 20). To "wag" is to move along or travel. The informant said that the song was expanded by substituting "mother, sister, brother, etc." for "father" and that this spiritual was often used in the black community as a lullaby. Unfortunately, the information Arnold provided for this informant is uncharacteristically incomplete.

Sung by Sayre, Montgomery, between 2 and 10 August 1946.

Midnight Cry

Based directly on the parable of the wise and foolish virgins (Matt. 25:1–13), this song, usually in longer versions, was printed in many shape-note songbooks, including *The Original Sacred Harp, Southern Harmony,* and *The Social Harp.*

Sung by Miss Callie Craven, Gadsden, 27 July 1945.

When that mid-night cry be-gan, Oh, what lam-en - ta - tion,

Thou-sands sleep-ing in their sins, Ne-glect-ing their sal - va - tion.

For the bride-groom is at hand; he will kind-ly treat them.

Sure - ly all the wait-ing band Will now go forth to greet Him.

Indian Song

Like most of its singers, Mrs. Couch believed this song to be the folk property of American Indians. Specifically, she associated it with an Indian named Parch Corn, a friend of her great-grandfather. Scholars, however, disagree about the song's origins. Some hold with the Indian theory, while others believe it to be a black spiritual, and still others see it as an adaptation of the church hymn "Am I a Soldier of the Cross?" In any case, its imagery derives from the sixth chapter of the book of Revelation, which is also the basis for the frequently found spiritual "Oh, Sinner Man." In 1945 Mrs. Couch gave Arnold directions for singing this piece: "When you sing this song speak the words 'blood, hmm, wah,' 'God, hmm, wah,' and the last 'wah' and 'soul' in a low tone of voice. And you must nod your head on each 'wah' like Parch Corn did." In fact, Arnold's later recording of Couch reveals that the piece is closer to a chant than to a song.

Sung by Mrs. Janie Barnard Couch, Guntersville, 13 June 1947.

Oh sin-ner, what you do that day When the moon goes down in blood? hmm, wah. You hide your-self on the moun-tain-top To keep your face from God. hmm, wah. Talk with Je-sus, hal - le, hal - le - lu - jah, Hmm, hmm, hmm, wah, way o-ver in my soul.

Run to the Rock

Sung by Ms. Ella Bell Hazely, Atmore, 11 July 1947.

Run to the rock, run to the rock When the world's on fire; Run to the rock, run to the rock, Run to the rock when Je-sus calls.

2 You can't hide, you can't hide
When the world's on fire;
You can't hide, you can't hide,
You can't hide when Jesus calls.

3 I'm goin' home, I'm goin' home
When the world's on fire;
I'm goin' home, I'm goin' home,
I'm goin' home when Jesus calls.

One of These Days

One of the most militant of spirituals, this song was often appropriated by the Wobblies, members of the Industrial Workers of the World. These violent unionists, who wrecked jails and defied laws and governments they considered corrupt, were particularly fond of the apocalyptic stanza about God's setting the world on fire.

A

Sung by Ms. Mildred Meadows, Tuscumbia, 2 August 1945.

God's goin' to bring your sins be-fore you, hal-le-lu-jah,
God's goin' to bring your sins be-fore you One of these days, hal-le-lu-jah.
God's goin' to bring your sins be-fore you, God's
goin' to bring your sins be-fore you One of these days.

2 God's goin' to set this world on fire, hallelujah,
God's goin' to set this world on fire
One of these days, hallelujah.
God's goin' to set this world on fire,
God's goin' to set this world on fire
One of these days.

3 I'm goin' to sit at the welcome table, hallelujah, etc.

4 I'm goin' to tell God how you treat me, hallelujah, etc.

5 God's goin' to bring your sins before you, hallelujah, etc.

B

Arnold's note: "From Kilby Prison—Don't know who gave it to me." August 1945.

1 I'm goin' to tell God all my trouble, hallelujah,
I'm goin' to tell God all my trouble
One of these days, hallelujah.
I'm goin' to tell God all my trouble,
I'm goin' to tell God all my trouble
One of these days.

2 I'm goin' to drink at the Christian fountain, hallelujah, etc.

Chapter 28
Jubilation

∽

Oh Mary Don't You Weep

Weeping Mary, a familiar figure in spirituals, is consoled that the promise of heaven more than compensates for earthly hardships and that even on earth the evil do not always prosper: "Pharaoh's army got drownded." That last aspect has made this spiritual particularly attractive to protest and unionist singers. Found in many black spirituals, both the "kadige" (carriage) and the train symbolize means of escape, either from slavery or from the trials of existence. Many versions of the chorus, less interesting than Mrs. Montgomery's, merely repeat the first line for the second and shorten the last line by deleting the second command.

Sung by Mrs. Adele Harrison Montgomery, Tuscaloosa, 11 September 1945.

Chorus

Oh Mary don't you weep, don't you moan, Here comes a ka-dige to carry us home. Pharaoh's army got drownded, Oh Mary don't you weep, don't you moan.

Verse

Some of these here mornings 'bout nine o'clock, This here old world going to reel and rock. Pharaoh's army got drownded, Oh Mary don't you weep, don't you moan.

Chorus

2 If my mother wants to come with me,
    Tell her, get on train and follow me.
    Pharoah's army got drownded,
    Oh Mary don't you weep, don't you moan.

Chorus

3 If my father wants to come with me,
    Tell him, get on train and follow me.
    Pharoah's army get drownded,
    Oh Mary don't you weep, don't you moan.

Chorus

4 If my sister wants to come with me,
    Tell her, get on train and follow me.
    Pharoah's army got drownded,
    Oh Mary don't you weep, don't you moan.

Chorus

Wilderness

Spirituals about the wilderness seem fairly evenly divided between those that urge us to enter it if we would find the Lord and those that urge us to leave it if we would be saved. In the latter songs, such as Ms. Ison's, it clearly represents the world of sin and unbelief. A version of this spiritual was used as a marching song by black Union troops and was picked up from them by their white comrades-in-arms. It must have had a special poignancy for those serving under Grant who met Lee's army in 1864 in that awful bloody tangle in Virginia known as the Wilderness.

Sung by Ms. Frances Ison, Tuscaloosa, 18 March 1946.

And I clap glad hands when I come out the wil-der-ness, Come out the wil-der-ness, come out the wil-der-ness, I clap glad hands when I come out the wil-der-ness, Lean-in' on my Lord, I'm lean-in' on the Lord, I'm lean-in' on the Lord, who died on Cal-va-ry.

2 Oh my hands look new, when I come out the wilderness,
Come out the wilderness, come out the wilderness,
My hands look new, when I come out the wilderness,
Leanin' on my Lord, I'm leanin' on the Lord,
I'm leanin' on the Lord, who died on Calvary.

3 And I'll shout and I'll shout, when I come out the wilderness,
Come out the wilderness, come out the wilderness,
I'll shout and I'll shout, when I come out the wilderness,
Leanin' on my Lord, I'm leanin' on the Lord,
I'm leanin' on the Lord, who died on Calvary.

Free at Last

Perhaps one reason for the popularity of this spiritual lies in the fact that its chorus can mean so many things: the freedom of an escaped or emancipated slave, the freedom from sin and worry experienced by a newly devoted Christian, the freedom from the trials of this world offered by death, the freedom from bigotry and racial prejudice sought in the civil rights movement. Dr. Martin Luther King Jr. used the chorus for the vibrant conclusion of his most famous speech: "I have a dream" that one day "black men and white men, Jews and Gentiles, Protestants and Catholics, will be able to join hands and sing in the words of that old Negro spiritual, 'Free at last! Free at last! Thank God almighty, we are free at last!'"

Sung by Mr. Dock Reed and Miss Vera Hall, Livingston, 17 June 1947.

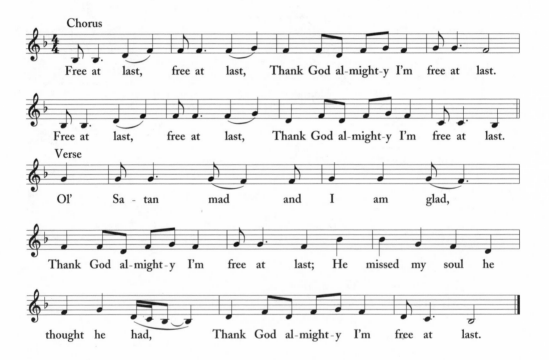

Chorus

2 You can talk about me as much as you please,
  Thank God almighty I'm free at last;
  The more you talk I bend my knees,
  Thank God almighty I'm free at last.

  Chorus

John Done Saw That Number

John the Divine, apostle and author of the book of Revelation, merges here with John the Baptist. The description of the latter is almost word for word from Matthew 3:4, allowing for the variation of "about his loins" to "around his line." The position of "though" in the spiritual's last line is occupied by "'less" in several other versions.

Sung by Mr. Dock Reed and Miss Vera Hall, Livingston, 17 June 1947.

Good News

This is one of only a handful of spirituals treating the birth of Jesus. Miss Hall may have sung a longer version for Arnold, but his field recording is lost and only these words are included with the transcribed tune in his manuscript notebook.

Sung by Miss Vera Hall, Livingston, 16 or 17 June 1947.

Good news, good news, An-gels done brought the ti-dings down. Good

news, good news, I'm hunt-ing for the Lord.

One dark night in De-cem-ber, My good Lord here was born. The

bright light shone from heav-en, From Beth-le-hem's sta-ble door. Good

news, good news, An-gels done brought the ti-dings down. Good

news, good news, I'm hunt-ing for the Lord.

All God's Chillun Got Shoes

The celestial possessions in this spiritual may derive from images in the book of Revelation, but they have passed completely into the popular imagination. Sung in complete seriousness, as it is by Mrs. Jones, "All God's Chillun" provides an effective contrast of the grinding poverty of earth with the infinite luxury of heaven. Sung in a different manner, however, its devout simplicity can be made to seem ludicrous, and, in this guise, it was a favorite of many college glee clubs and was featured once in Ziegfield's Follies. As I noted in the introduction to this section, this piece figures in the controversy about the secular or sacred implications of black religious song. White singers raised it to new heights of popularity during the Great Depression as a comic rejoinder to the tactless public suggestion by FDR's secretary of labor that American shoe manufacturers should concentrate their marketing efforts on the South, because so many of its people went barefoot. There is knowing ironic humor in the observation that not all those who talk about salvation are likely to achieve it. Other versions add harps, wings, and songs to the list of heavenly possessions.

Sung by Mrs. Theckle Jones, Atmore, 11 July 1947.

2 You got a crown, I got a crown, all God's chillun got crowns.
  When I get to heaven gonna try on my crown;
  Goin'-ta shout all over God's heaven, heaven, heaven.
  Everybody talkin' 'bout heaven ain't goin' there, heaven, heaven,
  Goin'-ta shout all over God's heaven.

3 You got a robe, I got a robe, all God's chillun got robes.
  When I get to heaven gonna try on my robe;
  Goin'-ta shout all over God's heaven, heaven, heaven.
  Everybody talkin' 'bout heaven ain't goin' there, heaven, heaven,
  Goin'-ta shout all over God's heaven.

I'll Be Waiting Up There

The cheerful confidence of this spiritual made it the perfect basis of the civil rights movement song that begins: "If you miss me at the back of the bus, / Can't find me nowhere, / Come on up to the front of the bus, / 'Cause I'll be riding up there."

Sung by Mrs. Theckle Jones, Atmore, 11 July 1947.

If you miss me way down here, You can't find me no - where,
Come on up to bright glo - ry; I'll be wait-ing up there.
I'll be wait-ing up there, I'll be wait-ing up there,
Come on up to bright glo - ry, I'll be wait-ing up there.

Hallelujah Amen

Blowing the trumpet and being helped by Christ appear also in the spiritual "Let Us Cheer the Weary Traveller," but I have not found the speaker chosen as watchman in versions of that song. The late Robert Nicolosi suggested this for a concluding song, and I quite agree with his choice.

Sung by Mrs. C. L. Benton, Tuskegee, 11 August 1946.

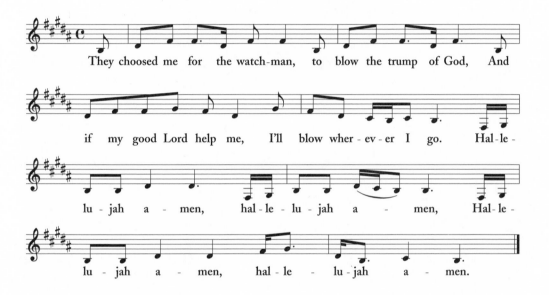

They choosed me for the watch-man, to blow the trump of God, And if my good Lord help me, I'll blow wher-ev-er I go. Hal-le-lu-jah a-men, hal-le-lu-jah a-men, Hal-le-lu-jah a-men, hal-le-lu-jah a-men.

Janie Barnard Couch

While I was a guest in the Couch home in Guntersville some years ago, the matter of preserving the folksongs in Alabama was discussed. The inspiration of that evening really started this project. Janie Barnard Couch has been indefatigable in making contacts with other singers and completing ballads, which she remembered only in part, from relatives.

May I add that she cures the best ham and bakes the best biscuit in North Alabama.

"My grandfather, Robert W. Barnard, was born in 1833 in the western part of Marshall County. It was he who built the old log house that enters so vividly into the picture when the search for the folksongs is made. The house had three large rooms with a dogtrot between, and a long porch extending from the dogtrot to the kitchen wing. This house was one of the favorite gathering places for the young people of the valley. I've heard many of the old residents tell of gathering about two o'clock in the afternoon and singing and dancing to the old-time fiddler's music until the wee hours of the morning. In this home Bill Gross also lived for about twelve years as hired man and member of the family as was the rule in those days.

"Great-grandfather, Joseph B. Barnard, must have come to this territory about the time of the War of 1812, for he was here before the Indians were moved, and was a friend and associate of Parch Corn, for whom the Cove was named. Parch Corn had so many friends among the white settlers he would not move with the Indians, so was allowed to stay.

"My mother, Martha Frances Morris, came when a small child, with her parents from Buena Vista, Georgia. It was through my grandmother Morris that the heritage of folksongs has come to our family. Her wonderful memory and rich contralto voice preserved by far the major portion. My memories of her singing are especially sweet since I am the oldest of a family of nine girls and heard her singing to all that succession of babies as well as about her work.

"As would be expected, my parents had to work very hard and the children along with them. My father farmed and taught school. His family have been outstanding in the history of the county as leaders in education, many of them being teachers and doctors. I began teaching at the age of eighteen and continued until I was married to Dr. E. H. Couch. His family were also pioneers of Marshall County."

Callie Craven

Miss Callie Craven was the first singer I visited in making this collection. My original appointment with her had to be postponed a day because she had one of her heart attacks. On account of her frail health, she could sing for only a short time without tiring. Consequently I made several enjoyable visits to hear her. She was very proud to know that her songs would be in a book. When we were talking about publishing the songs, she asked that hers be kept in a group and called "Callie's Songs."

When I went back to Gadsden in 1946 on my second folksong trip, I found that Miss Callie had passed away on July 1 at the age of seventy-five. The following information about her was given me by Mrs. C. H. Ham, who was Verna Duke, one of Miss Callie's girls.

"Callie Craven was born near Blue Mountain, outside Anniston, Alabama. She learned these songs from her mother, who came from Charleston, South Carolina. Her father was killed when she was quite young, leaving her mother with four little girls. These children had to go to work at an early age, so Callie never learned to read and write. In 1889 at Grandmother Easterwood's funeral my father, Mr. B. W. Duke, heard of this destitute family needing a home. Papa and Mama went by Wilkesons and moved the whole family to a house on our farm. One sister helped with the chores, another did the washing, and Papa paid them. When the girls grew up three of them left, but Callie stayed on and became just like a member of our family.

"She helped raise the six of us Duke children. My father kept up the old home in the country for a long time after our family moved to town. When my mother had a stroke, Callie came in to take care of her and stayed with us for the rest of her life.

"Callie was a tiny little lady weighing only ninety-six pounds. She had a manner about her that was at once sweet, charming, and always happy. Her life was a life of doing things for other people. Her singing was the joy of her life. She loved to sing the old songs she knew for company, to rock the children to sleep by, and at entertainments. We Duke children, and later—when we were grown and married—our children too were always begging her to sing for us, which always made her happy."

Myrtle Love Hester

I met Myrtle Love Hester at the Florence State Teachers College just before she graduated in 1945. Her hearty cordiality and jovial disposition kept me in laughter most of the time I worked with her. She said of herself, "I am a great woman only in size." When I asked if I could take a snapshot she gave me a photograph, saying, "Snapshots just aren't big enough to get me all in!" She gave me the following account of the background of her songs. In it she neglected to say that she is married and has raised a family.

"My father, Reverend Samuel R. Love, was born in Marshall County, Alabama, October 8, 1876. His parents were English and Irish. It must have been from the Irish strain that he inherited his keen wit and fine sense of humor. These characteristics certainly proved very valuable to him; for as he grew older the burden of the care and responsibility of feeding, rearing, and educating a family of ten husky youngsters on the salary of a Baptist preacher must have lain heavily upon his shoulders.

"He had to face many disappointments in life. There were six girls before the long-hoped-for son arrived. I was first in this line of disappointments. My father used to say when looking around the dinner table at his eight little girls that he guessed the devil owed him a debt and would pay it off in sons-in-law.

"My mother was quite an industrious person who could always find enough tasks around the house to keep us all busy, including father. His first task each morning was tending to the baby while she cooked breakfast. This he would do by trotting or rocking the baby and singing old love songs. These, however, proved to be far more entertaining to us older youngsters than soothing to the baby.

"There were other times when we heard old-fashioned love songs and 'ballets,' as she called them, from Grandma Love. Regularly every other year for many years she would come and stay two weeks with us to take care of Mama and the newest baby. I used to think that the stork brought Grandma, too. After her work for the day was done and while we sat around the fire at night we begged for her songs. These she sang in a clear, sweet voice for she was quite a popular 'top line' or treble singer at the all-day 'fa sol la' singings with dinner on the ground, that the people of her community enjoyed throughout the summertime. Sometimes she and father would sing together and some of us other children would join in. Since there were no radios and only one or two phonographs in the entire community, hymn and ballad singing was quite a popular form of entertainment for young and old alike.

"Through the years of memories nothing seems sweeter to me than the stories of brokenhearted or lovesick lovers that she brought to us over and over again in her ballads with quaint words and melodies."

Lena Hill

While in Florence, Alabama, I heard that one of the Red Cross workers was going to the country to do some casework. My friends said that it was in a district where I should be able to find some folksongs; so I went along. I was taken to Lexington and at the school there met Aline Hill, who knew a version of "Barbara Allen." She said that her grandmother knew a great many of the "old timey" songs. When the Red Cross worker picked me up I asked if she had time to run out to the Hills'.

Mrs. Hill was busily engaged in shelling peas when we arrived. When I stated the purpose of my visit she said that she had not sung for five years, since the death of her daughter. She told me that I was welcome to some ballads she had written down as a girl if I would like to see them. She and her girlfriend, Maudie King, used to write down the ballads as they heard them sung and then exchange with each other. They were stored in a box on top of the wardrobe.

As we were looking over these yellowed pages I asked her if she could remember the tune of one, "Lovely Willie," and then she started to sing. Her husband said he had not heard her sing as pretty as that since the days they were courting. After singing several songs she said it made her think of her boy in France, and as the Red Cross worker was impatient to get back to town we left.

On subsequent trips Mrs. Hill proudly showed me the trophies her son had sent home from Germany and gave me a great many more songs and the following sketch of her life:

"My father's name was James J. McGee. He was born in Lauderdale County, Alabama, October 11, 1851. His parents were Irish. He was a farmer of those good old days. He worked on the canal and on the Tennessee River. In early life he married Miss Katie King, and they lived a happy life together. My father was a Baptist of that time and a song leader in his church. He was a lover of good sacred songs. He loved to sing love songs and heart ballads. My mother was a mother of good faith and loved to worship God. To their family there were born six children, two girls and four boys, four of us still living, two sisters and two brothers. We are all very happy that we are still living.

"I was born on March 4, 1884. I am sixty-two years old. I stayed with my father and mother until I was twenty-two years old; then I was married to Mr. Thomas C. Hill, and to this family there were born eight children, four boys and four girls, seven still living, three sisters and four brothers.

"My husband and I are farmers. We try to make an honest living for us and our children. I would sing those old love songs and heart ballads to my children, and sure did love to sing them, and still love to sing them. I listen to them over my radio and like to hear them very much."

Mae Erskine Irvine

When I met Mae Erskine Irvine she was most enthusiastic about the folksong project and the preservation of the songs she knew. She sang with great ease and distinctness. I spent a jolly afternoon with her and her friends in the delightful home on the outskirts of Florence, an old town on the Tennessee River.

As to the background of her songs she said:

"My brother and I were born and reared in the home of our grandparents, Dr. and Mrs. Albert Russell Erskine, of Huntsville, Alabama. The songs I gave you were sung to us by our grandfather.

"When he came home for the night, we would run to meet him and put our arms around his knees and walk that way with him into their bedroom. Then he would take one on each knee, 'trot us,' and sing the old songs. He had a good bass voice and loved music and loved to sing.

"These old songs have always been dear to me so I sang them to my children and grandchildren. They bring back sweet memories of the grandparents whom I loved so dearly."

Mary Wallace Kirk

"My home is named 'Locust Hill' and I am the fourth generation of my family who has lived here. My dalmation dog is named 'Page.' I have had some verses published in various magazines.

"I won the loving cup given by the Alabama Poetry Society in 1937. My etchings have been rather widely exhibited, but this is my first effort at making music. I really cannot sing, even if I am a graduate of Agnes Scott College, Phi Beta Kappa, and a trustee of that institution.

"The nurses who sang me 'Let's Go Down to Jordan,' 'I Wish I Was in Tennessee,' etc., were named Ida Johnson and Fanny Keller. I remember the real old mammy of my mother's younger brothers and sisters who lived with us until her death. She was a wonderful character and looked after us and bossed us all up to the last. She was named Sarah Dixon, but we called her 'Ghee.' Whenever her advice was asked on any questions of conduct of doubtful propriety she always replied, 'Your grandmother would never have done it.'

"Isaiah Holmes worked for us as gardener since I was a child. He feels a great proprietorship in me. He always gives me minute instructions about taking care of myself on trips because I am 'away from home and in strange cities.' He greatly appreciated your donation to his church and has asked me to tell you that he 'thanks you in Christ's name and hopes to meet you by and by in the sweet fields.'"

Mary Wallace Kirk's beautiful big dog met me at the gate and escorted me up the boxwood bordered walk to the low, rambling home. It was in the front parlor sitting on a rosewood love seat with Page at his mistress's feet that I took down the songs she remembered.

Corie Lambert

I called on Corie Lambert one Sunday evening at her home to make an appointment for the next day. As we were talking about folksongs she asked if I knew this one and started singing; so I took down several of her songs that evening. When I returned the next morning she said that she had not been able to sleep for trying to recall all of the verses of some of her songs which she had not sung in a long time. She had all of these verses neatly written out and sang them in a clear voice that was accurate and true. She is now singing to her grandchildren as her Grandmother Jolly sang to her. She gave me the following background for the songs she remembered:

"I was born on a cotton plantation near Stylesboro, Georgia, not far from Savannah. I remember that from the house as far as you could see were cotton fields. My mother and grandmother were born in the same old plantation home. We went back when I was eleven and some of the old slave houses were still standing. I've often heard Mother say that Grandmother Elizabeth Jolly was part French. Lots of French people settled around Savannah.

"Mother has often told me how when Grandmother was a girl the Northern army came through on that march, drove off all the cattle, and burned the cotton. The slaves buried the hams back of the garden to keep the Yankees from getting them. The jewelry and silver were buried under the house near the fireplace. I never knew if Mother's old brooch and earrings were among that buried jewelry. When I read *Gone With the Wind* it was the same experience Grandmother Jolly had gone through. The setting of the book is about twenty miles from Grandmother's plantation.

"I also remember Mother telling how, when she was a little girl, they went down to

Aunt Cheenie's cabin. Aunt Cheenie had been a slave and cooked ash cakes and briar-leaf greens in the fireplace to show the children that was all they had to eat during the war.

"Not any of the plantation passed down to Grandmother Jolly's children because after her death Grandfather married again and those children got everything.

"Father was a sawmill man. My father and mother came to Alabama when I was six months old. We didn't stay in one place for very long but moved around a lot wherever there were large tracts of timber. Dad's people were Irish and Dutch. His father, John L. Burnett, was pure Irish and is still living. He will be eighty-one soon."

Mildred Meadows

Mildred E. Meadows possesses a remarkable contralto voice of great sympathy. She sang her spirituals in such a low key that I had to write them an octave higher.

"I was born in Whitehall, Alabama, a strictly rural section of Lowndes County. I received a B.S. degree in Home Economics from Tuskegee Institute, Alabama, in 1937 and have served as Home Demonstration Agent in Colbert County since 1939.

"While at Tuskegee Institute, I became associated with the Tuskegee Choir and accompanied it to New York City both in 1933, when we sang at the opening of Radio City, and in May 1946, at the unveiling ceremonies of Booker T. Washington's bust in New York University's Hall of Fame.

"The songs I sang for you were some of my mother's favorites, and I learned them from her as she sang while doing the chores around home. I remember you asked me why she sang so many songs about death. It seems to me that she was relieved of anything that oppressed her whenever she sang these songs."

"It was always my ultimate objective to sing also, and my first opportunity came when I was five years old. It happened that we were having 'prayer meeting' at our church and the minister asked that someone lead a hymn. Glad of the opportunity to lead a song, I began with a little song I had learned, 'Go Tell Aunt Tabby Her Old Gray Goose Is Dead,' etc. No one laughed, but joined in the singing instead. I think of that little incident each time I am asked to lead a song of any sort."

Elizabeth Henshaw Pillans

Elizabeth Henshaw Pillans was a native of Claiborne, Alabama, and was the daughter of Rufus C. Torrey and Elizabeth Henshaw Torrey. She was married to Mr. Pillans at Claiborne on April 21, 1875, and had lived in Mobile since that time. I met her when she was ninety-one years of age. Her mind was active and alert. She was a sweet, fragile-looking lady whose singing voice, although a little weak, was still vibrant and accurate. After singing the first three songs, she became tired; her daughter, Laura Pillans, gave me the remainder with some prompting from her mother. I enjoyed my hour with her very much. She made a picture as she sat in her antique chair in the drawing room of the beautiful old home on Government Street. She died on August 30, 1946. Laura Pillans gave me the following interesting account of her mother's recollections.

"There was an incident she was fond of relating about something the Negroes did after the war ended. My mother's mother (Elizabeth Henshaw) lived in Virginia. When she married Judge Torrey and came to live in Alabama her father gave her a number of slaves. They had always raised tobacco in Virginia, but had to raise cotton in Alabama. They were put on a plantation a little way up the river from Claiborne where the family lived. When the war ended and they were freed, they went back to what they knew best and planted tobacco, built the slats to shade it, raised it, dried it, and cured it and so forth, and put it on a barge and sent it down the river to my grandmother with a note saying they wanted their 'Dear Mistis' to sell it, that they knew the war had left her with very little, so they raised this crop for her to help her out.

"The family lived in a large old home with wide hall and large rooms, near their plantation in Claiborne. Mama had a little colored maid of her own and the four children had a mammy who acted as nurse and mentor. She taught them most of the old songs Mama remembered and told them many tales. My mother was ten in the last year of the war, and had very vivid recollections of the arrival of the Northern troops. First the Confederate soldiers in retreat came along the road near them. Her parents gave the Confederates all of their horses except a small white Shetland pony. Then came the Union forces, composed chiefly of hired Hessians (which may explain some of their behavior). They did not burn my mother's home because it was so well adapted for use as a hospital. The family was allowed to use two rooms, and all the rest was full of cots for the sick and wounded, of both sides, Union and Confederate. My grandmother helped with the nursing. The men were wantonly destructive and took possession of everything, but a description of their actions is not what you want. As a child she was taught petit point, to embroider, and to play the piano, as were all little girls then. But after the war she and her older brother were taken by coach to Virginia, then by train to Massachusetts where she went to school near Boston for several years. Her brother was sent to Harvard. Her father, Judge Rufus C. Torrey, came to Alabama from Massachusetts for his health when he was a young man, hence sent his children there to be educated.

"She used to tell of how her mammy would sing them to sleep with the old songs.

"I realize that I have given you little of the color or flavor of her life as a child, whence came the old songs; however, she said so little about that and so much and often about the experiences at the close of the war, in Massachusetts, etc. She loved to tell of the Negroes' loyalty to her parents. She said old Uncle Ben buried the family silver and refused to betray its location to the Yankees. They loved their house servants and were loved by them."

Pansy Richardson

"I was born at 1055 State Street in Mobile, Alabama. This street ended just above our home, and there being no traffic in the last block of a dead-end street, the result was a lovely grassy court that was known locally as 'The Lane.'

"There were just a few very old homes in this block, all occupied by the descendants of the builders of the houses.

"Each of 'The Lane' families had at least one old Negro servant. The two I remember most were our Aunt Emma and the old yard man from next door, Uncle John. Both had been slaves. I'm sure some of the songs were learned from these two old Negroes, as I loved them both dearly and spent most of my time with them. Uncle John was too old to do any work, his hair was as white as snow, and he sat all day on a wooden box at the back gate. Every afternoon when I came home from kindergarten I entertained him with the songs and folk dances I had learned there. He used to slap his hands to make the rhythm for my dance steps, and I still remember his wrinkled, kind old face beaming with smiles.

"Both Uncle John and Aunt Emma called me 'Miss Tansy.' I don't know why the 'T' was substituted for the 'P' unless it was easier to pronounce in their soft, slow drawl.

"The first real sadness in my life was when Uncle John's real 'Marster' called him home. He just went to sleep one night in his little room in the old barn and didn't awaken again on this earth.

"Where we acquired Aunt Emma has never been clear to me. All slaves on both sides of my mother's and father's family were freed at the end of the Civil War, but Aunt Emma just seemed to have always been around and was as much a member of the family as any of us. She occupied a small room off the kitchen, and she kept this room immaculate. Her bed with its enormous feather mattress and loud patchwork quilt was the most comfortable bed in the world. I *know*, for I've slept in it many times—yes, with Aunt Emma, too.

"One of my earliest memories is of sitting by the ironing board while Aunt Emma did the family ironing with huge flatirons which she heated on a charcoal furnace. She entertained me with her own original chants. This one was my favorite:

AUNT EMMA: Little gal, little gal!
PANSY: Yes, Ma'am.
AUNT EMMA: Did you feed my pony?
PANSY: Yes, Ma'am.
AUNT EMMA: Did the pony eat?
PANSY: Yes, Ma'am.
AUNT EMMA: Did the pony die?
PANSY: Yes, Ma'am.
AUNT EMMA: Did the buzzards come?
PANSY: Yes, Ma'am.
AUNT EMMA: How'd dey do?

At this point I rose from my chair and circled the room with my arms flapping like a buzzard's wings.

"Where the party games and songs originated, I am not sure, but from my earliest memory my three sisters and I with the girls of the other families of 'The Lane' gathered just before dusk and played and sang these songs out on the grassy court which was shaded by the largest sycamore tree I ever saw. No boys ever participated in these games, as our parents wouldn't allow us to enter into any games with boys, only at parties. The result of this was that we were so self-conscious at parties that they were miserable affairs. Girls in those days didn't play baseball or any 'unladylike' games.

"Of our group that played the old beloved games, only one other than myself remained in Mobile. The others are widely scattered. If they should read this book they will know it is of them that I write, and I'm sure they cherish these memories just as I do.

"'The Lane' is no longer there. The street was cut through and a section for colored was developed. Our old home was destroyed years ago by fire, and only one of the old homes remains looking out on the old sycamore, which has withstood tropical storms and lightning."

I learned of Pansy Richardson's play-party songs through references I found in the State Archives, Montgomery, Alabama. I spent a most delightful afternoon with her as she recalled the happy scenes of her childhood and sang these well-remembered songs to me.

Alma Robinson

Alma Robinson was born in Uniontown. A graduate of State Teachers College, Montgomery, she directs the band and teaches in the Burrell High School, Florence, Alabama. She has a class of private piano pupils and is organist and director of the choir at the Saint Mark's Baptist Church. She has been an organist for twenty-five years. She started playing when she was nine years old. Her mother died when Alma was six, and the family moved to Florence, where she still lives.

She was most interested in this folksong project and spent much time looking up other contacts for me. It was through her that I met Mildred Meadows and the Reverends William Craig and Alex Fountain. I spent one Sunday evening in the services at Saint Mark's, enjoying the singing immensely.

Ruby Pickens Tartt

Ruby Pickens Tartt has done more for the cause of folk music in the state of Alabama than any other individual. She is nationally known through references to her and to her work in Sumter County in books by such well-known authorities on folklore as Elie Siegmeister and the Lomaxes of the Library of Congress. They speak in glowing terms of her work among the blacks in Sumter County and of her hospitality. I can personally verify all the wonderful things they have said about her.

I met Mrs. Tartt while I was working in the Works Progress Administration (WPA) files of folk music in the State Archives in Montgomery. She had come over to the capitol to see if by chance copies of any of the hundreds of black folksongs that she had been collecting all her life were filed in the archives. She had sent them in, both words and music, during the WPA Federal Writers' project. We had a most enjoyable visit. She invited me to come to Livingston as soon as she returned from a health resort in North Carolina. The previous spring a hurricane had blown her house down, destroying all of her records and pinning her beneath the debris. She looked frail but had since regained her health.

Everywhere that I went with Mrs. Tartt in Sumter County she was affectionately called "Miss Ruby" by her numerous black friends. They respected and admired her and seemed delighted to do anything she asked, even if it meant dropping the work at hand to come in and sing for me.

She knew her people. When we went to the county road farm, where prisoners are housed who work on the roads, there was one black man who said he knew a song. She said she did not recognize him as a Sumter County black, and he admitted that he was not.

Mrs. Tartt heard of a black church that needed a new stove. She told the congregation that she would raise the money for it among her white friends if they would promise to continue singing the old-time spirituals. This they have done. Vera Hall and Doc Reed were the two best singers I heard. Their repertoire seemed unlimited. The encouragement of Mrs. Tartt is entirely responsible for the continuance of the remarkable folk singing among the blacks around Livingston and in Sumter County, Alabama.

Appendix B: Selected Song References

Collections have been selected for reference here because they are widely accessible, because they represent Alabama and its border states, or because they contain particularly interesting song versions. Additional references will be found in many of these works. The books by Coffin and Renwick and by Laws are bibliographic guides to ballads rather than collections of songs. References to Cohen's abridgment of Randolph's Ozark collection are included parenthetically in the Randolph entries. Cohen updates Randolph's references, and his bibliographic and discographic material is excellent. Each entry contains a compiler's name, volume number (if any), and page number. Titles, publication data, and reference codes are included in the list of works cited.

The Miller's Daughter (p. 3): Belden 66, Bronson II 448, Brown I 56, II 143, & IV 76, Burton I 85, Child II 346, Coffin 91, 243, Cox 115, Davis 360, Hudson 111, McNeil 86, Moore 74, Morris 295, Randolph I 143 (Cohen 45), Sandburg 72, Scarborough 35, 284, Sharp I 208.

Pretty Mohea (p. 5): Belden 143, Brown II 340 & IV 195, Burton II 39, 55, Cox 372, Hudson 162, Laws N 224, Moore 192, Morris 356, Randolph I 280 (Cohen 484).

Katie Dear (p. 6): Belden 118, Brown II 255 & IV 147, Burton II 91, Cox 348, Emrich 83, Hudson 161, Laws B 182, McNeil 72, Moore 196, Morris 362, Randolph I 244 (Cohen 83), Sharp I 358.

Last Night I Dreamed of My True Love (p. 7): Belden 168, Brown II 284 & IV 157, Laws B 186, McNeil 74, Moore 209, Randolph I 413, Sandburg 149, Sharp II 17.

Jack the Sailor (p. 9): Belden 171, Brown II 314 & IV 182, Cox 330, Emrich 165, Hudson 147, Laws B 205, Lomax 164, Moore 185, Morris 353, Randolph I 215 (Cohen 92), Sharp I 385.

Oh Johnny (p. 11): Belden 177, Brown II 317 & IV 184, Burton II 10, 50, Laws B 241, Randolph I 224 (Cohen 94), Sharp II 111.

A Fair Damsel (p. 13): Belden 148, Brown II 304 & IV 169, Burton I 80 & II 7, 89, Cox 316, Emrich 152, Hudson 150, Laws B 224, McNeil 80, Moore 187, Morris 346, Randolph I 258 (Cohen 97), Sandburg 68, Sharp II 70.

Billy Came Over the Main White Ocean (p. 15): Belden 5, Bronson I 39, Brown II 15 & IV 4, Child I 22, Coffin 25, 211, Cox 3, 521, Davis 62, Hudson 61, Lomax 18, Moore 12, Morris 237, Randolph I 41 (Cohen 16), Sandburg 60, Scarborough 43, Sharp I 5.

Love Henry (p. 18): Belden 34, Bronson II 60, Brown II 67 & IV 29, Child II 142,

Coffin 66, 230, Cox 42, Davis 182, Emrich 280, Hudson 77, Moore 47, Morris 263, Randolph I 90 (Cohen 28), Sandburg 64, Sharp I 101.

The Brown Girl (p. 19): Belden 37, Bronson II 88, Brown II 69 & IV 30, Burton I 25, Child II 179, Coffin 68, 231, Cox 45, Davis 191, Emrich 281, Hudson 78, McNeil 137, Moore 51, Morris 265, Randolph I 93 (Cohen 31), Sandburg 156, Sharp I 115.

Barbara Allen (p. 22): Belden 60, Bronson II 321, Brown II 111 & IV 57, Burton I 7, 39, 41, 51, 57, 74, 85 & II 28, Child II 276, Coffin 82, 239, Cox 96, 523, Davis 302, Hudson 95, Lomax 183, McNeil 102, Moore 68, Morris 283, Randolph I 126 (Cohen 41), Sandburg 57, Scarborough 59, Sharp I 191.

Rosella (p. 26): Belden 324, Brown II 578 & IV 289, Burton I 78, Cox 197, Emrich 679, Hudson 185, Laws N 184, Lomax 93, Morris 76, Randolph II 44 (Cohen 158).

True Lovers Part (p. 27): Belden 123, Brown II 258 & IV 149, Cox 350, Emrich 75, Hudson 188, Laws N 217, Morris 80, Randolph II 53 (Cohen 161), Sharp II 229.

Johnson City (p. 29): Belden 201, Brown II 271 & IV 155, Burton II 59, Cox 430, 530, Emrich 132, Hudson 160, Laws B 260, Morris 334, Randolph I 226, Sandburg 324, Sharp II 76.

Lord Lovel (p. 31): Belden 52, Bronson II 189, Brown II 84 & IV 43, Child II 204, Coffin 72, 233, Cox 78, Davis 240, Emrich 286, Hudson 90, Lomax 401, McNeil 93, Moore 56, Morris 273, Randolph I 112 (Cohen 34), Sandburg 70, Scarborough 55, Sharp I 146.

Sailor Shantey (p. 33): Belden 186, Brown II 323 & IV 187, Browne 120, Burton II 61, Cox 353, Laws B 146, Moore 174, Randolph I 296 (Cohen 68), Sharp II 84.

Fair Lady Bright (p. 34): Belden 164, Brown II 293 & IV 162, Cox 342, 529, Emrich 80, Laws B 181, Lomax 195, McNeil 70, Moore 197, Morris 343, Randolph I 346 (Cohen 81), Sharp II 103.

Winter's Night (p. 35): Belden 480, Brown III 299 & V 181, Cox 413, Davis 476, Moore 58, Morris 278, Randolph I 115, Sharp II 113.

The Rich Irish Lady (p. 37): Belden 111, Brown II 299 & IV 166, Burton I 34, Coffin 159, 281, Cox 366, Emrich 133, Hudson 128, Laws B 252, McConathy 158, Moore 139, Morris 330, Randolph I 205 (Cohen 104), Sharp I 295.

Robin Gray (p. 38): Smith 541.

Logan O. Bucken (p. 40): Hudson 171, McConathy 216.

Joe Bowers (p. 41): Belden 341, Brown II 607 & IV 295, Cox 234, 527, Emrich 565, Hudson 197, Laws N 139, Lomax 336, Moore 323, Randolph II 191 (Cohen 190).

Jack and Joe (p. 42): Brown II 635 & IV 307, McNeil 116, Morris 64, Randolph IV 336.

That Little Black Mustache (p. 44): Brown II 479 & IV 260, Browne 184, Morris 142, Randolph III 128.

It Rained, It Mist (p. 47): Belden 69, Bronson III 72, Brown II 155 & IV 82, Burton I 1, Child III 233, Coffin 107, 248, Cox 120, Davis 400, Hudson 116, Lomax 511, Moore 89, Morris 302, Randolph I 148 (Cohen 47), Scarborough 53, Sharp I 222.

Three Babes (p. 49): Belden 55, Bronson II 246, Brown II 95 & IV 48, Child II 238, Coffin 77, 236, Cox 88, Emrich 291, Davis 279, Hudson 93, Lomax 185, Moore 61, Morris 279, Randolph I 122 (Cohen 39), Sharp I 150.

The Orphan Girl (p. 52): Belden 277, Brown II 388 & IV 216, Burton I 6, 18 & II 89, Cox 446, Emrich 772, Morris 119, Randolph IV 194, Sandburg 316.

Put My Little Shoes Away (p. 54): Randolph IV 178 (Cohen 463).

The Blind Child's Prayer (p. 55): Belden 275,

Brown II 392 & IV 218, Burton I 5, 15, 61 & II 81, Morris 117, Randolph IV 191 (Cohen 472).

The Romish Lady (p. 59): Belden 450, Brown II 212 & IV 132, Hudson 137, Laws B 288, Moore 236, Morris 388, Randolph IV 32.

The Letter Edged in Black (p. 60): Randolph IV 162 (Cohen 475).

Little Dove (p. 62): Belden 486, Brown III 359 & V 217, Randolph IV 39, Sharp II 197.

Drunkard's Song (p. 64): Belden 468, Brown III 44 & V 24, Cox 403, Randolph II 392, Sandburg 104.

Ragged Pat (p. 66): Randolph II 417.

Charles Guiteau (p. 68): Belden 412, Brown II 572 & IV 288, Emrich 460, Hudson 238, Laws N 176, McNeil 58, Morris 72, Randolph II 29.

Little Mary Phagan (p. 69): Brown II 598 & IV 295, Laws N 196, Morris 81.

Stagalee (p. 71): Courlander I 178, Johnson R 194, Laws N 240, Lomax 571, Odum I 196, Odum II 245, Scarborough 92.

Boston City (p. 73): Brown II 554 & IV 281, Cox 296, Emrich 712, Laws B 175, Morris 387, Randolph II 37, Spaeth 177.

The Blue-Tail Fly (p. 76): Brown III 496, Laws N 243, Lomax 505, Scarborough 201.

Springfield Mountain (p. 77): Belden 299, Brown II 489 & IV 265, Cox 292, Emrich 150, Hudson 184, Laws N 213, Lomax 13, 403, Moore 378, Morris 112, Randolph III 167, Sharp II 166.

Billy Grimes (p. 79): Belden 251, Brown II 466 & IV 248, Hudson 281, Morris 144, Sharp II 248.

The Old Man Lived in the West (p. 82): Belden 92, Bronson IV 143, Brown II 185 & IV 113, Burton I 56, Child V 104, Coffin 146, 274, Cox 159, Davis 497, Hudson 123, Lomax 167, Moore 124, Morris 322, Randolph I 187, Sharp I 271.

Father Grumble (p. 84): Belden 225, Brown II 445, Cox 455, Emrich 219, Hudson 175,

Laws B 273, Lomax 26, Moore 246, Randolph I 318 (Cohen 124), Sharp II 265.

The Frog He Would A-Courting Ride (p. 86): Belden 494, Brown III 154 & V 85, Cox 470, 531, Emrich 21, Hudson 282, McConathy 162, Moore 251, Morris 407, Randolph I 402 (Cohen 139), Sandburg 143, Scarborough 46, Sharp II 312, 320.

The Fox (p. 90): Brown III 178 & V 107, Cox 474, 531, Moore 261, Randolph I 386 (Cohen 135), Sharp II 332.

Old Abe's Elected (p. 97): Randolph II 317.

In the Year '61 (p. 98): Brown II 529, III 444, & V 252, Emrich 447.

The Year of Jubilo (p. 99): Brown II 541 & IV 275, Dennison 203, Randolph II 290.

The Soldier's Fare (p. 101): Hudson 257.

Tombigbee River (p. 104): Brown III 318, Browne 107, Randolph IV 302.

Rosalee (p. 106): Randolph IV 172.

Come, My Love, Come (p. 108): Brown III 491 & V 272.

Another Man Done Gone (p. 109): Courlander II 108, Lomax 539 (Hall with Rich Amerson).

Lining Track (p. 112): Cohen 646, Emrich 650, Lomax 545, Odum I 262.

Laying Rails (p. 114): Emrich 648.

Tamping Ties (p. 116): Cohen 647, Emrich 649, Odum II 90.

Old Smoky (p. 118): Belden 473, Brown III 287 & V 170, Burton I 50, Emrich 117, Lomax 221, Morris 134, Sharp II 123.

Long Ways from Home (p. 119): Belden 487, Randolph I 271.

A-Walking, A-Talking (p. 120): Brown III 271 & V 154, Cox 425, Emrich 118, Hudson 166, Lomax 217, Morris 364, Randolph I 237 (Cohen 117), Sharp II 177.

Pretty Mollie (p. 123): Cox 433.

Bertha (p. 124): Randolph I 255.

Lonesome Dove (p. 125): Belden 484, Brown III 301 & V 181, Browne 122, Burton I

106, Emrich 96, Hudson 170, Morris 278, Sharp II 113.

Paper of Pins (p. 126): Belden 507, Brown III 6, 9 & V 3, 5, Emrich 35, Hudson 276, Moore 256, Morris 422, Randolph III 40 (Cohen 293), Sharp II 45.

I'll Have No Drunkard to Please (p. 128): Brown III 10 & V 6, Burton I 98, Hudson 167, Lomax 210, Randolph III 53, Sharp II 249.

Courting Song (p. 130): Belden 265, Brown I 123 & III 16, Cox 465, Emrich 203, 207, Lomax 28, Moore 215, Morris 378, Randolph III 55 (Cohen 295), Sandburg 71, Sharp II 279.

La La Trudum (p. 131): Belden 266, Hudson 280, Moore 383, Randolph III 77 (Cohen 299), Sharp II 159.

Old Shiboots and Leggins (p. 133): Belden 264, Brown III 17 & V 9, Cox 489, Emrich 198, Moore 253, Morris 376, Randolph I 291 (Cohen 129), Sharp II 93.

Niggljy Naggljy (p. 136): Randolph III 190.

I Wish I Was Single Again (p. 137): Belden 437, Brown III 37 & V 21, Burton II 13, Emrich 187, Moore 382, Morris 154, Randolph III 66 (Cohen 329), Sandburg 47.

I Wish I Were a Single Girl Again (p. 138): Belden 437, Brown III 54 & V 28, Burton II 12, Emrich 183, Lomax 166, Morris 155, Odum II 163, Randolph III 69, Sharp II 32, Spaeth 26.

All for the Men (p. 140): Brown III 20 & V 10, Emrich 188.

Rosen the Beau (p. 142): Belden 255, Brown III 61 & V 32, Browne 404, Hudson 203, Randolph IV 371 (Cohen 386), Spaeth 40.

Till I Die (p. 143): White 145, 287.

Hesitatin' Whiskey (p. 145): Handy 60.

Fifty Cents (p. 148): Browne 362, Gilbert 121, Randolph III 250.

Hard Times (p. 150): Belden 433, Brown III 385, 419 & V 231, Cox 511, Emrich 767, Hudson 215, Lomax 438.

The Watermelon Song (p. 151): Brown III 539 & V 309.

Work Song (p. 152): Spaeth 245.

Bible Tales (p. 154): Brown III 399 & V 238.

Boil Them Cabbage Down (p. 156): Botkin 117, 145, Brown III 143, 206, 353, 519 & V 79, 119, 213, 290, Emrich 62, Lomax 506, Parrish 121, Randolph III 324 (Cohen 399), Scarborough 124, 168.

Cindy (p. 158): Brown III 482 & V 267, Lomax 233, Randolph III 376.

Melinda (p. 160): Botkin 126, 318, Browne 218, Randolph III 183.

Buckeye Rabbit (p. 161): Brown III 208, 487, 528 & V 122, 270, 301, Burton I 105, Odum II 110, Randolph II 360, Scarborough 166.

Walk Tom Walker (p. 162): Brown III 402, Dennison 143, Scarborough 178, 182.

Lank Dank (p. 163): Belden 270, Lomax 142, Morris 393, Sharp II 324.

Carve Dat Possum (p. 164): Johnson R 149, Odum I 240, Randolph II 357 (Cohen 237).

Run, Nigger, Run (p. 165): Botkin 299, Brown I 203, III 210, 508, 531, 565, & V 282, 303, Browne 447, Morris 25, Randolph II 338 (Cohen 225), Scarborough 12, 23, White 168.

The Jaybird Song (p. 166): Brown III 201, 509, 538, 541 & V 307, 311, Randolph II 362, 388 (Cohen 239), Scarborough 156, 163, Sharp II 353, Spaeth 92, 123, White 175.

We Whooped and We Hollered (p. 168): Belden 246, Brown II 460, Cox 478, 532, Lomax 12, Moore 249, Randolph I 328, Scarborough 57.

Hog Drovers (p. 170): Botkin 205, Brown I 94 & III 101, Emrich 48, Hudson 296, Lomax 399, Randolph III 367.

Little Gentleman from the Spring (p. 171): Brown I 93, Randolph III 360 (Cohen 406).

Here Comes Someone A-Roving (p. 172): Botkin 328, Brown I 89.

Come Over the Heather (p. 173): Botkin 67, 345, Brown I 104, III 100, & V 50, Emrich 39, Randolph III 297 (Cohen 397), Sandburg 161, Sharp II 375.

Acorns Grow on White Oak Trees (p. 174): Botkin 164, Brown III 110 & V 55, Hudson 301, Morris 205, Randolph III 309, Scarborough 105.

Green Gravel (p. 176): Brown I 56, Morris 219, Randolph III 322.

Riggety Jig (p. 177): Botkin 298, Brown I 128, Randolph III 51.

Little Sally Walker (p. 179): Brown I 130, Hudson 290, Morris 215.

The Little White Daisies (p. 181): Morris 209.

Old Pompey (p. 182): Belden 509, Brown I 46, Emrich 19, Hudson 284, Moore 255, Morris 425, Randolph III 381 (Cohen 411), Scarborough 136, Sharp II 370.

Miss Jennie O. Jones (p. 183): Brown I 44, Morris 210.

Jenny Jane (p. 186): Brown III 102 & V 51, Browne 416, Emrich 23, Randolph III 208.

Bullfrog Jumped (p. 190): Brown III 222 & V 129, Scarborough 198, Sharp II 320.

The Black Cat (p. 191): Brown III 195 & V 113.

Short'nin' Bread (p. 193): Brown III 535 & V 305, Johnson R 163, Lomax 504, Randolph II 328, Scarborough 149, White 193.

Alabama Coon (p. 198): Brown III 151 & V 83, Scarborough 146, White 397.

Bones (p. 199): Brown I 183, III 152, & V 84, Emrich 6, Randolph II 345, Scarborough 148.

Come, Butter, Come (p. 199): Brown I 18, Scarborough 215, 287.

Go to Sleepy (p. 201): Brown III 150 & V 82, Emrich 3, Sandburg 454, Scarborough 145, Sharp II 341.

Ah, Job, Job (p. 205): Courlander II 53.

In-a My Heart (p. 207): Johnson II 72, Work 76.

Two Wings (p. 208): Johnson R 31.

Lord, I Want Two Wings (p. 209): Grissom 80, Kennedy 121.

Workin' on the Buildin' (p. 210): Odum I 72, Work 97.

Nory (p. 211): Courlander II 44, Johnson R 92, Odum II 191, Scarborough 222, White 99.

The Old Ark's Er-Movin' (p. 212): Johnson II 25, Lomax 475, Scarborough 28, Work 175.

Scandalizin' My Name (p. 213): Dennison 1.

Jesus Walked This Lonesome Valley (p. 215): Grissom 2, Parrish 196, Sandburg 486, Work 108.

Tell All the World, John (p. 216): Brown III 676 & V 399, Johnson II 110, 140, Johnson R 50, Odum I 123, White 101, Work 58.

If You Don't Want to Get in Trouble (p. 217): Odum II 168.

Sinner, Don't Let This Harvest Pass (p. 218): Johnson II 50, Parrish 250, White 92, 273.

All My Sins Been Taken Away (p. 220): Brown III 600 & V 340, Lomax 486, Morris 168, Odum I 60, Sandburg 474, White 60, 229, 268, 271, Work 158.

I Believe I'll Go Back Home (p. 223): Grissom 36.

Roun' the Wall (p. 230): Kennedy 131, Parrish 137, White 98.

Drinkin' Wine (p. 231): Brown III 78, Odum I 136, Parrish 249.

I Heard the Angels Singing (p. 232): Odum I 105, 106, 140, Parrish 140.

The Love Come Twinkling Down (p. 233): Kennedy 119, Tillman 42.

I'm So Glad (p. 235): Johnson R 46, Parrish 148, White 78, Work 162.

Jesus Goin' to Make Up My Dyin' Bed (p. 237): Grissom 4, Odum II 197, Parrish 178, Work 112.

Oh Death Is Awful (p. 239): Courlander I 50, Emrich 399.

Bring God's Servant Home (p. 240): Kennedy 60.

There's a Man Goin' 'Round Takin' Names (p. 241): Randolph IV 38, Sandburg 447.

If Dyin' Was All (p. 242): Parrish 243, Work 228.

Tall Angel at the Bar (p. 243): Kennedy 7, Work 134.

I Hear the Train A-Comin' (p. 245): Cohen 619, Johnson I 126, Odum I 113 & II 202, Scarborough 253, White 64.

Satan's a Liar (p. 247): Brown III 661 & V 387, Odum I 39, Sandburg 250, Work 71.

Room Enough (p. 248): Work 207.

Plenty Good Room (p. 249): Grissom 18, Work 188, 216.

We Gonna Have a Good Time (p. 250): Odum II 203.

Wonder Where Is Good Ol' Daniel (p. 251): Brown III 678, Sandburg 92, Tillman 17, White 429.

I'm On My Way (p. 252): White 114, 118.

Beulah's Land (p. 253): Grissom 94, Odum I 109, Tillman 31.

Settin' Down (p. 254): Johnson I 89, Lomax 473, Work 58, 72.

Ezekiel Saw a Wheel (p. 257): Courlander II 52, Johnson II 144, Sandburg 488, Work 148.

Go Chain the Lion Down (p. 258): Tillman 14.

Indian Song (p. 259): Brown III 637 & V 372, Morris 169.

One of These Days (p. 261): Brown III 574, 636 & V 329, 371, Grissom 20, Odum II 202, Sandburg 478, Work 166.

Oh Mary Don't You Weep (p. 263): Brown III 602 & V 341, Johnson R 62, Odum II 190, Sandburg 476, Tillman 6, White 58, Work 176.

Wilderness (p. 265): Work 185.

Free at Last (p. 266): Courlander I 46 (Hall and Reed), Johnson II 158, 178, Kennedy 38, Tillman 48, Work 197.

John Done Saw That Number (p. 267): Courlander II 61, Grissom 38.

All God's Chillun Got Shoes (p. 269): Brown III 607 & V 345, Courlander II 67, Johnson I 71, Kennedy 154, Odum I 97, White 69.

I'll Be Waiting Up There (p. 270): Courlander I 53, Tillman 54.

Hallelujah Amen (p. 271): Johnson I 184, Work 190.

Works Cited

Arnold, Byron. *Folksongs of Alabama.* University: University of Alabama Press, 1950.

Belden, Henry M. *Ballads and Songs Collected by the Missouri Folk-Lore Society.* 2nd ed. 1955; rpt. Columbia: University of Missouri Press, 1973.

Botkin, Benjamin A. *The American Play-Party Song.* University of Nebraska diss. Lincoln, 1937.

Bronson, Bertrand H. *The Traditional Tunes of the Child Ballads.* 4 vols. Princeton: Princeton University Press, 1959–72.

Brown, Frank C. *The Frank C. Brown Collection of North Carolina Folklore.* 7 vols. Durham: Duke University Press, 1952–64. Vol. I, *Games and Rhymes,* etc., ed. Paul G. Brewster et al. (1952); Vol. II, *Folk Ballads from North Carolina,* ed. Henry M. Belden and Arthur Palmer Hudson (1952); Vol. III, *Folk Songs from North Carolina,* ed. Belden and Hudson (1952); Vol. IV, *The Music of the Ballads,* ed. Jan Philip Schinhan (1957); Vol. V, *The Music of the Folk Songs,* ed. Schinhan (1962).

Browne, Ray B. *The Alabama Folk Lyric.* Bowling Green, Ohio: Bowling Green University Popular Press, 1979.

Burton, Thomas G., and Ambrose N. Manning. *East Tennessee State University Collection of Folklore: Folksongs.* 2 vols. Johnson City: East Tennessee State University, 1967, 1969.

Child, Francis James. *The English and Scottish Popular Ballads.* 5 vols. Boston: Houghton, 1882–98.

Coffin, Tristram Potter. *The British Traditional Ballad in North America.* Rev. and enl. by Roger deV. Renwick. Austin: University of Texas Press, 1977.

Cohen, Norm. *Long Steel Rail: The Railroad in American Folksong.* Urbana: University of Illinois Press, 1981.

———. *Ozark Folksongs,* by Vance Randolph, edited and abridged. Urbana: University of Illinois Press, 1982. (References to this work appear in parentheses after references to the original Randolph volume.)

Courlander, Harold. *Negro Folk Music, U.S.A.* New York: Columbia University Press, 1963. (Courlander II)

———. *Negro Folk Songs from Alabama.* 2nd ed. New York: Oak, 1963. (Courlander I)

Cox, John Harrington. *Folk-Songs of the South.* Cambridge: Harvard University Press, 1925.

Davis, Arthur Kyle, Jr. *Traditional Ballads of Virginia.* Cambridge: Harvard University Press, 1929.

Dennison, Sam. *Scandalize My Name: Black Imagery in American Popular Music.* New York: Garland, 1982.

Emrich, Duncan. *American Folk Poetry: An Anthology.* Boston: Little, Brown, 1974.

Gilbert, Douglas. *Lost Chords: The Diverting Story of American Popular Songs.* Garden City, N.Y.: Doubleday, 1942.

Grissom, Mary Allen. *The Negro Sings a New Heaven.* Chapel Hill: University of North Carolina Press, 1930.

Handy, W. C. *Blues: An Anthology*. New York: Boni, 1926.

Hudson, Arthur Palmer. *Folk-Songs of Mississippi and Their Background*. Chapel Hill: University of North Carolina Press, 1936.

Johnson, James Weldon. *The Book of American Negro Spirituals*. New York: Viking, 1929. (Johnson I)

———. *The Second Book of Negro Spirituals*. New York: Viking, 1933. (Johnson II)

Johnson, John Rosamond. *Rolling Along in Song: A Chronological Survey of American Negro Music*. New York: Viking, 1937. (Johnson R)

Kennedy, R. Emmet. *Mellows: A Chronicle of Unknown Singers*. New York: Boni, 1925.

Laws, G. Malcolm, Jr. *American Balladry from British Broadsides*. Philadelphia: American Folklore Society, 1957. (Laws B)

———. *Native American Balladry*. Philadelphia: American Folklore Society, 1950. (Laws N)

Lomax, Alan. *The Folk Songs of North America*. Garden City, N.Y.: Doubleday, 1960.

McConathy, Osbourne, John W. Beattie, and Russell V. Morgan. *Music Highways and Byways*. New York: Silver Burdett, 1936.

McNeil, W. K. *Southern Folk Ballads*. Little Rock, Ark.: August House, 1987.

Moore, Ethel, and Chauncy O. Moore. *Ballads and Folk Songs of the Southwest*. Norman: University of Oklahoma Press, 1964.

Morris, Alton C. *Folksongs of Florida*. Gainesville: University of Florida Press, 1950.

Odum, Howard W., and Guy B. Johnson. *The Negro and His Songs*. Chapel Hill: University of North Carolina Press, 1925. (Odum I)

———. *Negro Workaday Songs*. Chapel Hill: University of North Carolina Press, 1926. (Odum II)

Parrish, Lydia. *Slave Songs of the Georgia Sea Islands*. New York: Creative Age, 1942.

Randolph, Vance. *Ozark Folksongs*. 4 vols. Columbia: State Historical Society of Missouri, 1946–50.

Sandburg, Carl. *The American Songbag*. New York: Harcourt, 1927.

Scarborough, Dorothy. *On the Trail of Negro Folk-Songs*. Cambridge: Harvard University Press, 1925.

Sharp, Cecil J., and Maud Karpeles. *English Folk-Songs from the Southern Appalachians*. 2 vols. in 1. London: Oxford University Press, 1932.

Smith, David Nichol. *The Oxford Book of Eighteenth-Century Verse*. Oxford: Clarendon Press, 1926.

Spaeth, Sigmund. *Read 'em and Weep: The Songs You Forgot to Remember*. Garden City, N.Y.: Doubleday, 1926.

Tillman, June. *Thirty-two Galliard Spirituals*. London: Stainer, 1982.

White, Newman Ivey. *American Negro Folk-Songs*. Cambridge: Harvard University Press, 1928.

Work, John W. *American Negro Songs and Spirituals*. New York: Bonanza, 1940.

Index of Names

In general, names preceded by prefixes are those of Arnold's informants. From the biographies in Appendix A, only the informants' names are indexed.

Index of Song Titles and First Lines

Titles are in italics. Only titles are indexed for songs whose first lines are their titles.